GENETIC
AFTERLIVES

THEORY IN FORMS

A series edited by Nancy Rose Hunt and Achille Mbembe

GENETIC AFTERLIVES

NOAH TAMARKIN

BLACK JEWISH INDIGENEITY

IN SOUTH AFRICA

Duke University Press   *Durham and London*   2020

© 2020 DUKE UNIVERSITY PRESS. All rights reserved
Printed in the United States of America on acid-free paper ∞
Designed by Courtney Leigh Richardson
Typeset in Whitman and Knockout by Westchester Publishing Services
Library of Congress Cataloging-in-Publication Data
Names: Tamarkin, Noah, [dates].
Title: Genetic afterlives : Black Jewish indigeneity in South Africa / Noah Tamarkin.
Other titles: Theory in forms.
Description: Durham : Duke University Press, 2020. | Series: Theory in forms | Includes
    bibliographical references and index.
Identifiers: LCCN 2019054646 (print) | LCCN 2019054647 (ebook) | ISBN 9781478008828
    (hardcover) | ISBN 9781478009689 (paperback) | ISBN 9781478012306 (ebook)
Subjects: LCSH: Lemba (South African people) | Genetics—Religious aspects—Judaism. |
    Jews—Identity. | Race—Religious aspects—Judaism. | Identification (Religion)—Political
    aspects—South Africa. | Ethnology—South Africa.
Classification: LCC DT1768.L45 T36 2020 (print) | LCC DT1768.L45 (ebook) |
    DDC 305.892/4068—dc23
LC record available at https://lccn.loc.gov/2019054646
LC ebook record available at https://lccn.loc.gov/2019054647
Cover art: Lemba man standing on Mapungubwe Hill, 2013. Photograph courtesy of the author.

For my mothers, my fathers, my siblings,
For Mpho, puppy of my heart,
And for Juno, love of my life

CONTENTS

ACKNOWLEDGMENTS

It is overwhelming to try to account for all that has shaped this book and all who have sustained and inspired me in writing it. There would be no book if not for the willingness of the leaders of the Lemba Cultural Association (LCA), Kgoshi Mpaketsane, all of the Lemba people named in the pages that follow, and many others who remain unnamed to welcome my presence and my questions about their histories, their struggles, and their aspirations. One of the problems built into carrying out research over many years is that time passes and people pass with it. I am especially indebted to LCA chaplain Ishe William Masala Mhani (1925–2013), LCA executive board member and later president Ishe Musandiwa Johannes Mungulwa Hadji (1928–2018), LCA general secretary and later president Ishe Khanyakhanya Frederick Charles Raulinga Hamisi (1930–2012), LCA president Ishe Samuel Edwin Moeti (1933–2006), Mogaisi Reuben (Phaahla) Mpaketsane (1939–2012), and Annah Mmakaepea (Morweshadi) Mpaketsane (1939–2016). Among the living, I am profoundly grateful to current president of the LCA Pandelani Mutenda and current LCA general secretary Rudo Mathivha for continuing to teach me over so many years. Each Lemba person who took the time to speak with me contributed to this project. It is not possible to name everyone, but know that I am grateful. I hope you see yourselves reflected here.

This book began as dissertation research in the Anthropology Department at University of California, Santa Cruz. My adviser, Lisa Rofel, pushed me, guided me, and supported me at all stages, from the early days when I did not yet know what I was asking, to the meeting she convened at her apartment with all of her fresh-from-fieldwork dissertating students so she could teach us how to start writing, to reading innumerable drafts over many years, including the penultimate draft of this manuscript. I hope the influence of her incisive critique and clarity of thinking is apparent in these pages. Carolyn Martin Shaw likewise shaped my thinking and this research from the beginning. I am grateful for her skepticism and rigor, which immeasurably improved and clarified my work, and for her friendship over the years. Lisa and Carolyn believed in me and this project from the beginning and will forever be my models of transformative mentorship.

Other faculty, staff, and fellow graduate students across departments at UCSC and elsewhere shaped the earliest iterations of my research and sustained my ability to do it, in many cases into the present. I am especially grateful to Mark Anderson and Eric Worby and my writing-group comrades, Bettina Stoetzer, Zeb Rifaqat, Jason Rodriguez, Liz Thornberry, Sarah Zimmerman, and Rachel Giraudo. For inspiration, critical guidance, and in some instances (when I have been especially lucky), friendship, I also thank Jason Alley, Gil Anidjar, Jon Anjaria, Ulka Anjaria, Patricia Alvarez Astacio, Anjali Arondekar, Sarah Bakker-Kellog, Don Brenneis, Heath Cabot, Melissa Caldwell, Celina Callahan-Kapoor, Scout Calvert, Jeremy Campbell, Nancy Chen, Kristen Cheney, Nellie Chu, James Clifford, Angela Davis, Gina Dent, James Ferguson, Mayanthi Fernando, Carla Freccero, Diane Gifford-Gonzales, Melissa Hackman, Donna Haraway, Susan Harding, Eva Hayward, Colin Hoag, Lochlann Jain, Lindsay Kelley, Dan Linger, Liisa Malkki, Nick Mitchell, Megan Moodie, Olga Najera-Ramirez, Jessy O'Reilly, Hugh Raffles, Micha Rahder, Felicity Schaeffer, Astrid Schrader, Vanita Seth, Danny Solomon, Heather Swanson, Dana Takagi, Kim TallBear, Anna Tsing, Robin Turner, Bregje van Eekelen, Gina Velasco, Kalindi Vora, Logan Walker, Harlan Weaver, Matthew Wolf-Meyer, and Adrienne Zihlman. I'm also forever grateful to the Literary Guillotine.

The Wits Institute for Social and Economic Research (WiSER) at the University of the Witswatersrand became my academic home in South Africa when I was a graduate student research fellow there in 2005–2006, and it has continued to sustain this work through my appointment there as a research associate from 2015 through the present. I am especially grateful to current director Sarah Nuttall, Achille Mbembe, Nolwazi Mkhwanazi, Pamila Gupta, Hlonipha Mokoena, Keith Breckenridge, Catherine Burns, Najibha Deshmukh, Adila Deshmukh, and former director Deborah Posel. Also at WiSER, I am grateful to the other participants in the 2015 Johannesburg Workshop in Theory and Criticism, and especially Anne Allison, Ike Anya, Rachel Ceasar, Thomas Cousins, Jigna Desai, Kirk Fiereck, Claudia Gastrow, Behrooz Ghamari, Kelly Gillespie, Casey Golomski, Ghassan Hage, Julia Hornberger, Ananya Kabir, Dhammameghã Annie Leatt, Julie Livingston, Eileen Moyer, Leigh-Ann Naidoo, Vinh-Kim Nguyen, Michelle Pentecost, Amber Reed, Jessica Ruthven, Gabriele Schwab, Kirk Sides, Kaushik Sunder Rajan, Helene Strauss, Françoise Vergès, Josh Walker, and Tim Wright.

I thank all of the people who housed me in South Africa at different stages of this project, and in particular those I stayed with for extended periods: David and Sophy Mathivha and their children; Matshaya Mathivha; Lucas Thobagkale and his family; Pandelani Mutenda and his family; the late William Masala and his family; Ephraim and Eunice Selamolela; Malebo Hilda, Lephuele Samuel Mpaketsane, and their family; and most of all Phoko John Mpaketsane, Malekgale Monica Mpaketsane, and all who were part of their household while I lived there: the late Faaiza Molatudi, Amina Molatudi, and Lington and Edgar Mpaketsane. John, Monica, their parents, siblings, and siblings' children, their children Bella, Lington, Edgar, and Mothekgi, and their children's families have taken me in as one of their own: not only has this made this book possible, it has made South Africa home. To John and Monica, thank you for ensuring I always have a home in Limpopo, and to Bella and Albert, to Fortune, Hazel, Hope, and Praise, and to Amina, Alex and Kgotso: thank you for ensuring that I also always have a home in Gauteng. Also in Gauteng, Hylton White and Julia Hornberger have modeled warmth and hospitality, and in Cape Town, Kelly Gillespie and Leigh-Ann Naidoo have provided friendship, comfort, inspiration, and a beautiful place to write.

A FLAS fellowship supported my language training at the Summer Cooperative African Languages Institute in 2004. A Fulbright IIE fellowship supported my 2005–2006 research. In South Africa, Magdel le Roux generously met with me in 2004 and put me in touch with Lemba leaders so that I might seek permission to pursue this project; she continued to support my work as it developed, even though it was quite different from her own. Himla Soodyall and Trefor Jenkins generously contributed to my understanding of South African histories of genetic ancestry. Northern Sotho lessons with Sannah Leah Baker at the University of Venda eased communication; Dr. Baker also assisted with some written translations, as did Rirhandzu Sithole, then an anthropology student at Wits (and I thank David Coplan for connecting us). Alex Ntsoane provided exceptional research assistance. He, Phoko John Mpaketsane, Malekgale Monica Mpaketsane, Jedi Ramalapa, Bella Mpaketsane, and Hilda Mpaketsane all made understanding possible when my language skills were not up to the task. I also thank Eli and Eldas Maesela, Tyler Fleming, Robin Turner, Dan Magaziner, Kea Gordan, Jedi Ramalapa, and Celeste and Shane Brebner for their friendship during my dissertation field research. I am profoundly grateful to John and Monica Mpaketsane, Alex Ntsoane, and Celeste and Shane Brebner for their different roles in bringing and keeping me and Mpho together. Dissertation writing fellowships from UCSC's anthropology and feminist studies departments and from Boston College's African and African diaspora studies program supported my dissertation writing: I especially thank Rhonda Frederick at Boston College for her support and humor. A postdoctoral fellowship at the University of Pennsylvania's Penn Humanities Forum supported additional research and writing.

I worked on early drafts of what became this book while I was at Brandeis University as a lecturer in anthropology and at the University of Pennsylvania as a postdoctoral fellow at the Penn Humanities Forum and a lecturer in anthropology. At Brandeis, Janet McIntosh, Elizabeth Ferry, Ellen Schattschneider, Sarah Lamb, and Casey Golomski were especially influential, as were then-master's students Amy Hanes, Stacy Pape, Lindsay Parme, Beth Semel, Samantha Turner, Holly Walters, and Mengqi Wang. In Boston and in the years that followed, I also benefited from the support and friendship of Ringer Park dog crew Andrea Crossan, Miranda Banks, Rhitu Chatterjee, Jay and Jessica Blake, Gary Rand, Paula Coyle, and Jackson Braider, and from friendship, conversation, and in some cases collaboration with Namita Dharia, Lindsay Smith, Amali Ibrahim, Lilith Mahmud, Kian Goh, Nico Cisterna, Darryl Li, Sabrina Peric, Julie Kleinman, Adia Benton, Miriam Shakow, and Lin Idrus. At the University of Pennsylvania, this book took shape in conversation with John Jackson, Deb Thomas, and Kamari Clarke, others in the Race and Empire working group, and the other fellows at the Penn Humanities Forum, especially Rossen Djagalov, Laurent Dissard, Monica Kim, Elidor Mehilli, Rita Barnard, Lauren Ristvet, Jeanne Vaccaro, director James English and peripheries theme director Kevin Platt. I also learned a great deal about genetic ancestry from conversations with Theodore Schurr and Sarah Tishkoff. Jerry Miller, Erica Cho, Chi-Ming Yang, Hoang Tan Nguyen, and Dredge Kang made Philly the place to be, and Juno Parreñas, Jami Mukherjee, Gabe Rosenberg, and Matthew Bender made New Haven the other place to be.

The Ohio State University was the most supportive, generative home as this book became increasingly real. The Space and Sovereignty Working Group, supported for three years by the Humanities Institute, totally transformed this book, more than once. I am especially indebted to Monamie Bhadra, Lisa Bhungalia, Melissa Curley, Cricket Keating, Becky Mansfield, Katherine Marino, Dodie McDow, Nada Moumtaz, Juno Parreñas, Adam Thomas, and Sarah Van Beurden. Through Space and Sovereignty, I was able to have a book manuscript workshop with Kim TallBear as the discussant. I thank Kim and all of the participants in the workshop, especially Lisa Bhungalia, Melissa Curley, Katie Hendy, Gene Holland, David Horn, Lynn Kaye, Hannah Kosstrin, Becky Mansfield, Dodie McDow, Nada Moumtaz, Juno Parreñas, and Ashley Pérez. I am also especially grateful to current and former neighbors Katie Hendy, Kevin

Karpiak, Shannon Winnubst, Jenny Suchland, Johanna Sellman, and Ryan Skinner, who have provided various combinations of substantive feedback, moral support, and friendship. My colleagues in comparative studies have shaped this book more than they likely realize. David Horn and Barry Shank have been especially supportive mentors. My thinking about the potential intersections among anthropology, STS, and religious studies has been immensely enriched by them and by Melissa Curley, Hugh Urban, and Isaac Weiner, as well as conversations across the department about interdisciplinarity. In the department and elsewhere at (and formerly at) OSU, I also thank Amna Akbar, Philip Armstrong, Franco Barchiesi, Nina Berman, Katey Borland, Jian Chen, Jeff Cohen, Mat Coleman, Theresa Delgadillo, Dana Howard, Lynn Itagaki, Pranav Jani, Nancy Jesser, Nick Kawa, Kwaku Korang, Namiko Kunimoto, John Low, Miranda Martinez, Ben McKean, Koritha Mitchell, Dorry Noyes, Joe Ponce, Dan Reff, Dana Renga, Daniel Rivers, Amy Shuman, Mytheli Sreenivas, Maurice Stevens, Mary Thomas, Julia Watson, Sabra Webber, Max Woodworth, Inés Valdez, and Elizabeth Vu. Doctoral students Parisa Ahmadi, Mark Anthony Arcena, Nic Flores, Kevin Pementel, Ariel Rawson, Madeleine Smith, Keren Tanguay, and Ashley Toenjes have also given me much to think about.

Nothing is written in isolation, and the conversations that emerged while I was presenting parts of this book transformed what it became. I am so grateful to Amade M'charek at the University of Amsterdam and Katharina Schramm, then at Freie Universität Berlin, for extending invitations to spend time in residence with them and their working groups in the summer of 2017. They each facilitated major breakthroughs and helped me see what I had started to take for granted. Audiences at talks that I gave at Freie Universität Berlin's Institute of Social and Cultural Anthropology and at the University of Amsterdam's Institute for Social Science Research, especially Sarah Blacker, Hansjoerg Dilger, Thiago Pinto Barbosa, and Simon Mutebi in Berlin and María Fernanda Olarte Sierra, Victor Toom, Lisette Jong, Ildiko Plajas, Roos Hopman, Ryanne Bleumink, Irene van Oorschot, Alana Helberg-Proctor, Emily Yates-Doerr, and Eliza Steinberg in Amsterdam, all made this work better. The same is true for audiences at the University of Washington's Department of Anthropology (especially Rhadhika Govindrajan, Sareeta Amrute, Jenna Grant, and Lynn Thomas), Wits University's Department of Anthropology (especially Julia Hornberger, Hylton White, Kelly Gillespie, Sharad Chari, and Eric Worby), the University of Cape Town's Division of Human Genetics (especially Jacquie Greenberg, Sally Frankental, and Gary Kantor), and Duke University's Department of Anthropology (especially Harris Solomon, Charmaine Royal, Orin Starn, Anne Allison, Ralph Litzinger, Anne-Maria Makhulu, Randy Matory,

Laurie McIntosh, Charlie Piot, and Rebecca Stein). Conversations at Cornell University and the University of Wisconsin crystalized and streamlined my thinking while I was in the midst of the editing process. Discussants on conference papers that later became parts of chapters were also critical to developing my arguments. I especially thank Jonathan Boyarin, Harris Solomon, and Deb Thomas.

I am deeply indebted to organizers and other participants in a number of workshops and symposia over the years. Invitations to be part of two workshops sponsored by the American Society of Human Genetics, the National Institutes of Health, and the Duke Institute for Genome Sciences and Policy in 2013 and 2015 put me in conversation with brilliant scholars who had long been grappling with the implications of the proliferation of genetic ancestry in academic, medical, popular, and commercial spaces. I learned much of what I know about how to think carefully about genetic ancestry from them. I especially thank organizers Mike Bamshad and Charmaine Royal and participants Jessica Bardill, Deborah Bolnick, Duana Fullwiley, Rick Kittles, Sandra Soo-Jin Lee, Sally Lehrman, Jeffrey Long, Yolanda Moses, Alondra Nelson, Pilar Ossorio, Harry Ostrer, Jenny Reardon, Pamela Sankar, Theordore Schurr, Lindsay Smith, Kim TallBear, and Jennifer Wagner.

Katharina Schramm and Lindsey Reynolds's Point Sud workshop, "Political Subjectivity in Times of Transformation," held at the Stellenbosch Institute for Advanced Study in 2016, pushed me in exactly the right ways. I thank Katharina and Lindsey, coordinator Marko Scholze, and fellow participants Joshua Kwesi Aikins, Naluwembe Binaisa, Giorgio Brocco, Encarnación Gutiérrez-Rodríguez, Adam Haupt, Kristine Krause, Christopher Lee, Amade M'charek, Zine Magubane, Lenore Manderson, Zethu Matabeni, Aminata Mbaye, Nolwazi Mkhwanazi, Suren Pillay, Charlie Piot, and Joanna Wheeler. I am also grateful for the opportunities to think through this project at the "Blood as Archive of Dignity and Intimacy" workshop at the Princeton Institute for International and Regional Studies with organizers Jacob Dlamini and Carli Coetzee and participants Victoria Collis-Buthelezi, Laura Murphy, Grace Musila, Kopano Ratele, Stephanie Selvick, and Luise White; at the Brown University Program in Judaic Studies and the University of Pennsylvania Katz Center for Advanced Jewish Studies symposium "Revisiting the Question of Jewish Origins: Myth/Construct/Reality" with organizers Steve Weitzman and Katharina Galor and participants Gil Atzmon, Cynthia Baker, Omer Bartov, Andrea Berlin, Daniel Boyarin, Shai Carmi, Manfred Oeming, Adi Ophir, Eviatar Zerubavel, and Yael Zerubavel; and at the Emory University Tam Institute for Jewish Studies conference "Reframing Jewish Studies" with organizer Eric Goldstein and participants Deborah Dash Moore, Christian Davis, Anna Guttman, Aaron Hughes, Jonathan Judaken, Ari Kelman, Jack Kugelmass, Leslie Morris, Adam Zachary Newton, Craig Perry, Shari Rabin, and Don Seeman. Though my inclusion in two workshops on "Captivity" organized by Kevin O'Neill and Jatin Dua and held at the University of Toronto's Jackman Humanities Institute was based on a different project, Kevin, Jatin, and participants Melissa Burch, Susan Lepselter, Darryl Li, Juno Parreñas, Rhacel Parreñas, Padraic Scanlan, Judith Scheele, Andrew Shryock, Rachel Silvey, and Caleb Smith nevertheless shaped my thinking in the final stages of revising this book.

Some of my previously published work appears in this book in revised, re-configured, and expanded forms. Parts of my article "Religion as Race, Recognition as Democracy," published in the *Annals of the American Academy of Political and Social Science* in 2011, appear in this book in chapters 1 and 3. My article "Genetic Diaspora: Producing Knowledge of Genes and Jews in Rural South Africa," published in *Cultural Anthropology* in 2014, has been revised and expanded into chapter 2 of this book. "African Indigenous Citizenship," a chapter in the *Routledge Handbook of Global Citizenship Studies* (2014) that I cowrote with Rachel Giraudo, informs some of the arguments in chapter 5 of this book. Finally, the ideas presented in my essay "Genetic Ancestry and Decolonizing Possibilities," published in *Catalyst: Theory, Feminism, Technoscience* in 2017, form part of this book's introduction. I thank all of the anonymous peer reviewers of these essays and editors John Jackson and David Kyuman Kim, Anne Allison and Charlie Piot, Engin Isin and Peter Nyers, and Michelle Murphy, Banu Subramaniam, Kalindi Vora, and the rest of the *Catalyst* editorial board.

The peer reviews for this manuscript likewise were transformative. I am enormously grateful to Katharina Schramm for writing one of them, and to the other reviewer who remains anonymous. This book is immeasurably better for your close reading and careful critique. This book also would not exist without Ken Wissoker's encouragement, enthusiasm, patience, and guidance. Thank you for seeing this project through. Thank you also to Elizabeth Ault, Joshua Tranen, Ellen Goldlust, Anne Coulling, and series editors Nancy Rose Hunt and Achille Mbembe. Many people have read drafts of part or all of this manuscript outside of the context of a workshop, writing group, or writing exchange; I deeply appreciate their generosity. In addition to those mentioned elsewhere, I thank Nadia Abu El-Haj, Marla Brettschneider, and Jonathan Marks.

Jim DeGrand at the Ohio State University designed and made the maps that appear in this book, Paul Kotheimer at the Ohio State University's College of Arts and Sciences Technology Services assisted with digitizing and transferring documentary videos in preparation for producing still images for this book, and Jed Tamarkin assisted with improving the quality of one of the drawings.

Although much time has passed, I want to acknowledge the role of early mentors, high school teachers, and college professors in helping me to think about the world in a way that made the research on which this book is based possible. Caroline Leavitt and Jeff Tamarkin patiently supported early explorations in writing and taught me to fall in love with revision. Hope Hartman showed me that it was possible to pursue a life of research and teaching. At Andover High School in Andover, Massachusetts, I thank Tom Meyers for introducing me to anthropology and to the idea of multiple narratives and Craig Simpson and Kathy Cook for sparking an interest in South Africa and the politics of race. At Colorado College, Michael Hoffman introduced me to anthropological genetics, Jonathan Lee introduced me to Fanon, Mudimbe, and the politics of knowledge production in relation to Africa, and Roxi Hamilton and Sarah Hautzinger guided me through feminist and queer theory at a moment when I most needed it. This book would not exist without Sarah's mentorship and support.

My family and friends, many of whom are mentioned above, have sustained me throughout the years of writing and rewriting this book. My father, Kenneth Tamarkin, inspires me with his passion for education and his unfailing optimism. My mother, Susan Solomon, inspires me with her boundless energy. I am grateful to both of them for reading the final draft of this book. My stepmother, Jean Roberts, inspires me with her calm competence, and my stepfather, Marshall Solomon, inspires me with his generosity. My sisters, cantor Tanya Greenblatt and Emily Tamarkin, inspired this work in many ways. Rhacel Parreñas and Celine Shimizu have been exceptional academic role models. Rhacel has read drafts, talked through and helped me identify arguments, listed to practice talks, and expertly advised. I am constantly learning from David Byers. I thank him and Stephen Vider for their friendship. I thank Lin Fraser for insights and support that have spanned the entire existence of this project. Juno Salazar Parreñas has lived with and read through versions of this book for many years now. I treasure the seriousness and directness of her interventions and the joy of her celebrations. Her intellectual companionship, unwavering critical eye, and astounding brilliance have informed every word of this book. I always imagined that one day, our dog, Mpho, would lay his head or his paw on this book's cover as he did on so many drafts. Instead, he lives in our hearts and memories.

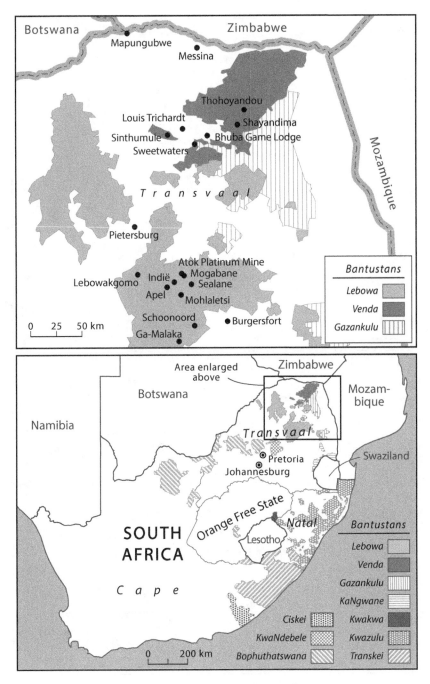

MAP 1 Apartheid South Africa, ca. 1980. Map by Jim DeGrand

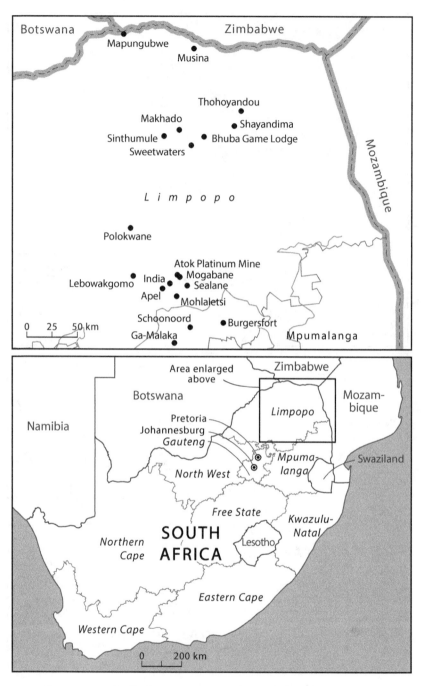

MAP 2 Contemporary South Africa, ca. 2019. Map by Jim DeGrand

received substantial contributions from Semitic males and smaller contributions from Negroid males" (Spurdle and Jenkins 1996, 1131). The BBC series *In the Blood* then publicized the study: the episode, featuring Jenkins alongside Mathivha and other LCA leaders, presented the Lemba as a genetically substantiated lost tribe of Israel whose true origins were in the Middle East, rather than in Africa.[4] Now another researcher, Tudor Parfitt, a Jewish studies professor at the University of London, had initiated a new study that attempted to link Lemba men directly to the Jewish hereditary priesthood of the Cohanim through a recently identified genetic sequence, the "Cohen Modal Haplotype."[5]

These late twentieth-century DNA studies catapulted the Lemba into two international debates: one about the racial and religious parameters of Jewishness, and the other about the claims and implications of genomic science. We might think that DNA can tell us whether the Lemba are really Jews. This book shows instead that DNA provides more questions than answers. It argues that genetic ancestry reinvigorates assumptions about race, religion, relatedness, and belonging—but it can also be an opening through which these assumptions are undermined and reconfigured.

Mathivha had invited Parfitt to be in the audience that day at Sweetwaters to collect saliva samples for the Cohanim study. Parfitt had researched Lemba origins beginning in the mid-1980s, and initially he had argued that the Lemba most likely descended from Arab traders rather than from Jews (Parfitt 1992).[6] But in light of the Spurdle and Jenkins study and recent developments in Jewish genetic ancestry research, he was now reconsidering his conclusions. Parfitt was working toward using genetic evidence to incorporate the Lemba into a collectivity of Jews who at that point, if they knew about the Lemba at all, imagined them and most other African Jews as suspect, invented, or otherwise beyond the boundaries of the Jewish people.[7] But when Professor Mathivha welcomed Hebrews rather than Jews as the overarching category in his opening address, he upended these exclusions. And as he continued his welcome address, he also upended how to think about Lemba genetic ancestry.

Professor Mathivha, other Lemba people, geneticists, Parfitt, and earlier researchers who had asked similar questions about Lemba origins since the late nineteenth century had collectively made possible the nascent fame of the Lemba as genetic Jews. But as Mathivha spoke that day to his gathered people—and to his invited researchers—he sought to reground this fame.

Mathivha invoked blood and Jewish ancestry but also culture and the physical place where members of the LCA that day were gathered. "Here is the cultural center, our home, our inspiration, our refuge, our meeting place with our God, Jehovah," he proclaimed. "The Lembas are members of the large family of the Hebrews. They are Jews with an ancestral home, Zion, where the patriarchs lie buried.[8] The researches which have been done indicate who you are. The result is a confirmation of our oral history. . . . The blood tests which have been done with the Lemba community indicate that the DNA chromosome 'Y' is the same with that which was found amongst the descendants of the ancestor Abraham. . . . I am making a call to the Lemba youth to develop this center as their heritage culturally and otherwise. . . . Should not we officially open it in 1998? . . . The cultural center is the heritage of our people." In this address, Mathivha swiftly moved from the notion that tests of DNA—something found in their blood—showed the Lemba who they are, to the idea that who they are was to be found in their heritage and that their heritage could be made manifest by building a physical structure, a cultural center, on the place where they were then gathered.

Sweetwaters, because of colonial and apartheid laws that restricted black land ownership while claiming black-occupied land for white settlers, had long been owned by the white Henning family. It had once been a village filled with many Lemba people. The story that I heard was that sometime in the second quarter of the twentieth century, white people took the land for a farm and forced everyone to move. But LCA founder and first president M. M. Motenda refused. Instead, he remained in the house that he had built, and the farmer Henning let him stay. He then constructed (with his own hands, the story goes) a one-room school building, which also served as the regular meeting place of the LCA executive committee.[9] In this way, the LCA was born on this site. With each year's annual conference, it became even more established as a Lemba ancestral home and an active facilitator of Lemba culture and connection.

Professor Mathivha explicitly invoked Zion when he pointed out that ancestral homes were places where patriarchs lie buried. But he did so at the top of the hill at Sweetwaters where, a short distance away at the bottom of the hill, Motenda lay buried, along with other past Lemba leaders and their relatives. When Mathivha called on ancestral burials, he was thus claiming for his people both Zion and Sweetwaters, belonging among Jews and belonging in South Africa. Mathivha's speech invoked Lemba Jewishness and therefore a diasporic connection with a center elsewhere. This echoed their growing fame as genetic Jews. But when he identified Sweetwaters as Lemba heritage and future, he also hinted at an emerging African Jewish indigeneity that would begin to flourish among Lemba people over the next decade.

Like Hebrews all over the world, I, too, was not present that day at the 1997 LCA conference. It would be years before I would read about Lemba DNA in a *New York Times* article and begin my own ethnographic research.

The article, "DNA Backs a Tribe's Tradition of Early Descent from Jews," made connections between genetic markers and authoritative truth, demonstrated slippages between race and religion, and relied on colonial tropes about Africa as an unchanging place without history.[10] The *Times* story compelled me to pursue another kind of story, generated in conversation with Lemba people as theorists and intellectuals, that would clarify the stakes of Lemba DNA and that might trouble, rather than reinforce, colonial forms of representation: in short, one that was ethnographic.[11]

I begin with Professor Mathivha's 1997 welcome address rather than with my own interactions with Lemba people in South Africa because his speech marked a pivotal moment in Lemba genetic knowledge production. In this moment, DNA transformed from authoritative knowledge that could tell Lemba people the truth about their origins into evidence that Lemba people could use to challenge others' assertions of who they really were and where they really belonged.[12]

This book analyzes how Lemba people have negotiated their ambivalent relationship to Jewish diaspora, African indigeneity, and South African citizenship, both before and after their association with Jewish genetic ancestry. In doing so, it calls into question where and with whom we locate the meaning and significance of DNA. How might our understanding of the stakes of genetic data change if, instead of primarily seeking to analyze what DNA means for geneticists and their critics, we consider it from the perspective of people who have been part of genetic ancestry studies as research subjects? What stories might unfold if we view published genetic ancestry studies as a starting point rather than an end point? This book tells one such story.

Geneticists' research intentions, data, and analyses are only the starting points of genetic ancestry. As Professor Mathivha's speech suggests and as I have found over nearly fifteen years of working with Lemba people, genetic ancestry continues to matter to research participants after results are published, and how it matters is an ethnographic question with implications for how citizenship and other forms of political belonging are claimed, contested, and experienced.

The central concept of this book, "genetic afterlives," highlights how participants in genetic ancestry research remake the meaning of genetic evidence when they repurpose their data to speak less to researchers' questions and more to their own. I consider their circulations of genetic data as *theorizations*: this, I argue, is a form of genetic knowledge production. Former research subjects like the Lemba, through their interpretations and circulations of their own genetic data, produce new genetic knowledge and new forms of genetic evidence—knowledge and evidence that should be understood as ongoing traces of the genetic studies from which they depart, rather than beyond the boundaries of science.

This book asks us to consider the meaning of genetic ancestry if we look not only to the expertise of scientists who investigate where and how humans have moved in the distant past, but also to their research subjects: the people throughout the world whose blood and saliva scientists seek as a source of answers to questions of deep human history. I argue that it is through former research subjects' genetic knowledge production that we can begin to grasp why DNA so powerfully compels us, and what that might say about contemporary political belonging. In what follows, I aim to more fully account for the work that genetic ancestry does, from ideas that it can bolster about race, ethnicity, gender, nation, and relatedness to how and by whom these ideas might be challenged.

"The Lemba" and the Production
of Genetic Knowledge, Jewish and Otherwise

I use the collective term "the Lemba" above and elsewhere in this book because genetic ancestry always implicates groups rather than individuals alone. This is clear in the growing body of research in anthropology, science and technology studies (STS), and Jewish studies that finds "the Lemba" as such to be a productive example of how DNA and identity intersect.[13] It is also clear in Lemba genetic knowledge production. Only a small number of specific Lemba men were personally and directly former research subjects in the studies that linked them to Jews. But whether or not they were themselves sampled by Jenkins or Parfitt, all Lemba people are potential former research subjects: they become former research subjects as they come to know about, theorize, and act upon Lemba genetic ancestry.

Not all Lemba people are invested in producing genetic knowledge about themselves, just as not all Lemba people have the same relationship to the Lemba Cultural Association, Jewish identity, or even ethnicity as an important way to understand themselves in relation to others. Discovering which people produce genetic knowledge, under what conditions, and for what reasons is therefore just as important as the knowledge itself in illuminating what genetic ancestry means and how it matters.

I was introduced to Lemba genetic knowledge production in July 2004 by Kgoshi Mpaketsane, an unrecognized Lemba traditional leader.[14] On this particular day, Mpaketsane and I were alone in his truck, on a gravel road near his home in a small village in the Limpopo Province's Sekhukhune district. We had met for the first time a few days before, and he had already surprised me by immediately welcoming me as a researcher, as if my presence there was anticipated and my proposed research activities obviously necessary.

I should not have been surprised. As I would soon learn, Kgoshi Mpaketsane had been at the center of decades-long efforts to establish a legally recognized Lemba chieftaincy, and amplifying his knowledge about himself and his people via an international researcher had the potential to bolster his case. Now Mpaketsane surprised me again: he wanted to teach me about who he and I were in relation to one another. As it turned out, it wasn't just his interest in getting his story out via a researcher that facilitated my welcome. Kgoshi Mpaketsane told me that I was a Lemba because I was a Jew. He further explained that the Lemba DNA tests showed that "we are all Jews. It doesn't matter black or white; it's in blood."

I learned three things from him in this moment. First, my interactions with Lemba people were never only as a researcher, but also as a Jew. As he and others made clear, our responsibilities to one another went beyond general hospitality and general research ethics. Second, just as Professor Mathivha did years earlier, Kgoshi Mpaketsane troubled the terms of Jewish inclusivity that could either affirm or call into question that the Lemba are part of the Jews. In Mpaketsane's iteration of this, he was a Jew because he was a Lemba, but *also* I was a Lemba because I was a Jew. Finally, his explanation complicated my thinking about race, Jewishness, and genetics. I had wanted to know why some Jews were accepted as such at their word, while others had to prove themselves, both religiously and, increasingly, biologically: I interpreted the Lemba DNA studies as a form of Jewish racism.[15]

In her own engagement with Lemba genetic ancestry within the larger context of Jewish genetics, Nadia Abu El-Haj offers an important critique of this kind of question. She writes about how the American liberal multicultural Jewish organization Kulanu has partnered with right-wing Israeli groups like Amishav and Shavei Israel to settle "lost" Jews of color in the illegal settlements that have continued to displace Palestinians in recent decades. As Abu El-Haj explains, "Nonwhite Jews become the site for discussions of Jewish racism, which is viewed as an entirely internal Jewish problem. The question of Palestine, the realities of a colonial present, and its very violent forms of racism in a state structured around the distinction between Jew and non-Jew, subject and citizen, and movement and enclosure are displaced" (Abu El-Haj 2012, 214).

The work of organizations like Kulanu, which has long had an interest in "returning" the Lemba to Judaism and perhaps also to Israel, demands an understanding of Lemba genetics in relation to the global racial and territorial politics of Jewishness and Zionism (see chapter 2). Indeed, recent work in Jewish studies positions genetic ancestry, including that of the Lemba, as the cutting edge of these discussions (Baker 2017; Weitzman 2017). But Kgoshi Mpaketsane is not Kulanu, and the recognition he sought was not from Jews, nor was it from the Israeli state. In his reading, having Jewish DNA was powerful not only because it proved Jewish antiracism ("it doesn't matter black or white; it's in blood") but because it also, at least rhetorically, superseded the black-white racial classifications that inexorably shaped the lives of generations of South Africans before, during, and after apartheid ("we are all Jews"). Kgoshi Mpaketsane taught me that I could not understand Lemba genetics without also understanding the national racial and territorial politics of South Africa.

Lemba people live throughout Southern Africa, but for Mpaketsane and the other Lemba people with whom I worked, genetic ancestry was part of a South African national story about colonial, apartheid, and postapartheid power as it was enacted through race, ethnicity, and land. Throughout the second half of the nineteenth century, African, Boer (Dutch and other European settler), and British people struggled for power and authority in the Transvaal, the region of South Africa where most Lemba people live and where most of my research took place. The earliest colonial state in the region, the South African Republic, was established in the 1850s. In other parts of South Africa, such as the Cape Colony, some Africans at least in theory could access limited citizenship rights in the nineteenth and early twentieth centuries. But in the Transvaal, both before and after the establishment of the Union of South Africa in 1910, Africans were denied access to all aspects of political citizenship. Land expropriation, coupled with policies of indirect rule, transformed a complex diversity of people with equally complex historical and contemporary patterns of migration, affiliation, and differentiation into a subject population divided into distinct tribes with static territorial boundaries and colonially designated chiefs.[16]

Apartheid intensified race-based restrictions and ethnic manipulations: its central ideology hinged on racial segregation coupled with ethnic nationalism.[17] Under apartheid, all black South Africans were required to have a tribal affiliation. A series of laws, beginning with the Group Areas Act of 1950 and culminating in the Promotion of Bantu Self-Government Act of 1958, laid the groundwork for the homeland system. The resulting "homelands" expanded on existing native reserves: they were designated self-governing territories, with the goal to declare each of them independent from South Africa. In reality, "homelands," often referred to as "Bantustans" to highlight their illegitimacy, were a means of denying black South Africans citizenship rights while also dividing them from one another based on ethnicity and subjecting them to leaders they did not choose.[18] Pass laws, introduced in 1952, were a central means of enforcing apartheid racial and ethnic mappings. They restricted the free movement of anyone designated nonwhite, and the obligatory passbooks identified each person not only by race but also by ethnic group.

Although "Lemba" was a deeply felt ethnic identity, it had not been one of apartheid South Africa's official ethnic groups. So while apartheid policies violently oppressed all black South Africans, Lemba people additionally experienced them as erasure. Lemba people, depending on where they and their immediate ancestors lived and what language they spoke, were legally classified as "Venda" or "Northern Sotho" and assigned citizenship in the respective Venda or Lebowa Bantustans until apartheid ended in 1994. Against this background of "Lemba" being juridically written out of existence, Lemba people sought recognition from the South African state as a distinct ethnic group beginning in the 1950s. The Lemba Cultural Association had been founded in the mid-1940s, but it consolidated through these struggles for recognition and provided a means for Lemba people in the townships around Johannesburg and Pretoria, in the Venda and Lebowa Bantustans, and across the South African border in Zimbabwe to remain connected to one another.

For the LCA and the Lemba chiefs that they supported, recognition under apartheid became inexorably linked to difference: if they could prove their difference, then perhaps, they hoped, they would be recognized as Lemba. In the 1980s, DNA technology appeared to LCA leaders as a powerful tool of differentiation, one that they enthusiastically added to their growing set of ways to make claims on the apartheid government.

When apartheid ended, racial and ethnic identity was no longer state regulated. Bantustan governments were dissolved, and black South Africans finally became citizens. But postapartheid policies maintained the inherited reified ethnic identities of the past through naming eleven official languages that corresponded to colonial and apartheid understandings of tribal/ethnic groups, and through a support of chieftaincy (now called "traditional leadership") and customary law that some argued impeded democracy by maintaining indirect rule (Buthelezi 2016; Mamdani 1996; Ntsebeza 2005). Through these policies, the erasure that Lemba people endured under apartheid continued, and so did their efforts to become recognized through the established politics of traditional authority, new possibilities for reclaiming expropriated land, and an emerging politics of indigeneity, even as their growing international fame as "genetic Jews" emphasized their origins elsewhere.

Kgoshi Mpaketsane's efforts to be recognized by the South African state as a Lemba traditional leader, as well as those of LCA leaders to achieve Lemba recognition in other ways, are the other reason that the phrase "the Lemba" sometimes appears in this book. These leaders have dedicated their lives to Lemba survival, and in South Africa, this has meant working toward recognition of the Lemba as a distinct ethnic group. Lemba representation always carries the weight of their efforts: this was true for Lemba leaders as they represented their people to me throughout my research, and it is true for me as an ethnographer negotiating multiple forms of knowledge production—including my own. My approach to writing about Lemba people therefore echoes that of Lemba leaders who could never lose sight of these larger stakes, even as they welcomed me into their homes and lives in all of their complexity. From these leaders, I learned that it is obvious and self-evident that "the Lemba" exist as black Jews, and it is equally obvious and self-evident that the term "the Lemba" encompasses a heterogeneous group of people with different politics, religious practices, and access to the power to define "the Lemba" and seek recognition on their behalf.

I conducted fourteen months of ethnographic research in South Africa between 2004 and 2006, followed by shorter research visits over the following decade. My interlocutors were LCA leaders and members and their families and neighbors, other Lemba leaders such as Kgoshi Mpaketsane and their families and neighbors, and various academics who had worked with Lemba people or had other forms of experience or expertise relevant to my questions. I lived and worked with people of all ages, genders, and statuses.[19] But the politics of both recognition and genetic knowledge production favors men, elders, and leaders, particularly when the genetic knowledge in question centers the Y chromosome. Y chromosome studies sample men but pronounce on origins of peoples, thus reaffirming the position of men as representative of both community and tradition. I seek to trouble these biases by highlighting Lemba authorship and internal debates, by contextualizing Lemba organizing efforts, by attending to the politics of gender and generation, and whenever possible by referring not to "the Lemba" but to specific Lemba people and to "Lemba people" as a plural, but never all-encompassing, collective. Most people appear in this text with their real names because they are real historical actors who wish to be regarded as such. Those who did not explicitly wish to be identified, Lemba and otherwise, are anonymized.

Kgoshi Mpaketsane and LCA leaders guided my research to align with their recognition goals, but there are gaps between their projects and mine. Navigating these gaps was a central tension in my research that this book cannot fully resolve. This may not be exactly the book that they were hoping I would produce out of our work together. But my hope and intention are that it will attest to their deep care for their people as they work to assure that their histories are not lost or misunderstood, and that their futures can be realized as Lemba South Africans, with all the rights and recognitions that identity should entail.

In legal claims to land, chieftaincy, and reburial of precolonial remains, DNA became a form of evidence that testified to Lemba ethnic difference against a postapartheid South African state that, like the apartheid state before it, could not recognize them. It became a valuable tool for Lemba people as they chartered new paths to South African belonging in ways that others found contradictory.

There are two approaches, then, to reading Lemba genetic ancestry. The first emphasizes geneticists and their publics as knowledge producers, and genetics as a way to illuminate the racialized and territorialized power dynamics of contemporary Jewish identity.[20] But the second approach shifts the frame: instead of viewing Lemba bodies as raw materials and geneticists as knowledge producers, genetic studies become raw materials for Lemba people as they produce their own genetic knowledge. In doing so, Lemba people redefine genetic Jewishness through the racial, religious, and ethnonational mappings that resonate *for them*.

The Claims of Genetic Ancestry

Genetic ancestry increasingly shapes how we think about ourselves and our pasts on species, population, and individual levels.[21] But it also underwrites and motivates claims that we make—on concepts of race, ethnicity, and belonging, on one another, and on nation-states and various forms of citizenship. Scholars such as Nadia Abu El-Haj (2012), Amade M'charek (2005a), Jenny Reardon (2005), Kim TallBear (2013), and others have shown that genetic ancestry both produces and is produced by research projects that seek to map human diversity on global, continental, and national scales.[22] In doing so, it simultaneously offers universalizing narratives and a renewed investment in racial and ethnic classification. We can see this most prominently in large-scale genome projects, in medical research that uses ancestry as an approximation of a promised future of personalized care, and in a commercial industry that offers millions of consumers, predominantly but not only located in the United States, information about their origins.[23] This book, however, addresses genetic ancestry as something more diffuse, complex, and unpredictable than these well-known examples can account for.

Anthropologists have long held that race is not genetic and that there is more genetic variation within social racial categories than between them. But this anthropological consensus has not been shared among all population geneticists, particularly those involved in large-scale genetic diversity projects (Reardon 2005). Now genetic definitions of race have gained renewed prominence among wide-ranging publics, dovetailing with a resurgence of white supremacy and ethnonationalism.

For example, milk-chugging parties are recorded and posted on the internet by white nationalists in the United States celebrating lactose persistence as a feature of supposed European genetic purity (Harmon 2018a, b). A DNA test is approved in Israel to help immigrants from the former Soviet Union prove that they have Jewish ancestry (Rabinowitz 2020; Sharon 2017; see also McGonigle and Herman 2015). Migrants set to be deported from Canada whose nationalities are contested are given genetic ancestry tests by government officials to determine their deportation destination (Khandaker 2018; Marrocco and Joly 2018; Mochama 2018; see also Abel 2018). In each of these examples, genetic ancestry lends an appearance of scientific validity to essentialist and exclusionary ideas about race and nation.

This book approaches genetic ancestry as a contested political and cultural object. As such, it takes seriously how genetic ancestry is theorized by those who are not geneticists. But this also requires informed critique of genetic ancestry research on geneticists' terms. Most science and technology studies scholars who write about DNA emphasize this kind of informed critique, though they do so for different reasons. Indigenous STS scholar Kim TallBear (2003, 2013) studies scientists ethnographically as a way to reject colonial frameworks that subject indigenous people to scientific scrutiny.[24] For anthropologist Nadia Abu El-Haj (2012), it is epistemological specificity that is at stake: she argues that the theories of history, inheritance, and identity that inform genetic ancestry research are not self-evident and therefore must be excavated in terms of where they come from and what they produce. Others, such as Duana Fullwiley (2007, 2008) and Ramya Rajagopalan and Joan Fujimura (2012), emphasize how genetic ancestry makes race.[25] They show how choices that different geneticists make in sampling, labeling, and computational analysis can produce misleading results that in turn are sometimes taken up by journalists and the general public as evidence for biological racial differences—again, a conclusion that anthropologists have long rejected.[26] Attuned to these and other ways that ideas about genetic ancestry circulate beyond laboratories— what Alondra Nelson (2016) calls "the social life of DNA"—some also extend these analyses, as I do in this book, across multiple social worlds.[27]

Following these scholars, we might distinguish between the claims *of* DNA—what geneticists and others contend it can tell us, and the methodologies that form the basis of their assertions—and claims made *with* DNA as it circulates in social, political, and legal contexts. My focus in this book is on the latter: if the meaning of DNA emerges through social interactions, then the social interactions that happen *after* scientists publish their work must also be considered as part of the meaning of genetic ancestry.[28] But while we can't view the claims *of* genetic ancestry as the culmination of its meaning, neither can we ignore the specificity and nuance of those claims.[29]

Genetic ancestry relies on a core premise that increasingly fine-tuned analyses can accurately reconstruct human migration histories and link contemporary people to ancestral places.[30] These links are usually framed as racial or ethnic origins. Three concepts—population, admixture, and haplotype—are especially important for understanding how geneticists do this, and why we cannot take it at face value.

As used by geneticists, population has no inherent content: it can be any group that researchers find meaningful to compare to another. Populations, then, are never neutral: they are made rather than found. And the populations that geneticists make are inexorably entangled with race. The mid-twentieth-century shift from race science to anthropological genetics replaced "race" with "population" in genetic research.[31] But it continued to describe old categories in new language, even as many scientists' understanding of what they were naming shifted substantially.[32]

Geneticists' use of the concept "admixture" demonstrates how the racial legacies of population work today. Admixture imagines *populations* that are genetically distinct from one another and *individuals* who hail from one or more of those populations. One example is genetic tests that are commercially marketed to individuals, usually white Americans, who suspect or hope that they might have Native American ancestors (TallBear 2013).[33] The results are delivered as "admixture" percentages, such as 80 percent European ancestry and 20 percent Native American ancestry, where "European" DNA and "Native American" DNA are each conceptualized as racially pure, in contrast to the individual whose body contains traces of both. Genetics and society scholars argue that genetic admixture reinvigorates discredited notions of continentally defined biological races that have pure or "unmixed" forms.[34]

"Population" and "admixture" are scaled-up concepts that call to mind whole groups of people and whole genomes, bringing new life to old concepts of race. But the work of differentiation and categorization in genetic ancestry is both smaller and larger than this: it requires linking molecular and global scales to associate people with places. Haplotypes and haplogroups are tools that geneticists use to make these links.

"Haplotype" names small variations that are found on the Y chromosome and in mitochondrial DNA (mtDNA). These are used as proxies for describing paternal and maternal inheritance because, in contrast to all of our other genetic material which recombines in the process of reproduction, they are passed down intact from parent to child.[35] Haplotypes become modal, as in the Cohen Modal Haplotype, through their presence at a greater frequency in any given group when compared to any other group that has been deemed relevant within a particular study.[36]

As a measure of relative frequencies, modal haplotypes thus say more about the classificatory interests of researchers than they do about biologically or historically significant relationships in and of themselves. But once a haplotype is named, it is imbued with classificatory power, which easily slips into claims about biological or historical significance. Joan Fujimura and Ramya Rajagopalan (2011) call this "genetic geography." Expanding this concept, Catherine Nash (2015, 174) points out that to link DNA to place is to argue that all people have a place to which they naturally belong.

These are some of the reasons to be skeptical of the claims of genetic ancestry. There are many others. For example, it inaccurately assumes too much about who moved, who did not, and how often in the distant past (Nash 2015).[37] It often relies on tautological arguments that in turn rely on small numbers of living people as proxies for a given place's past population: geneticists go looking for differences and then assign racial or geographic relevance to these differences based only on their a priori assumptions and the limited contents of their comparative databases (Palmié 2007).[38] Furthermore, it naturalizes and universalizes genealogical, heteronormative methods of figuring relatedness, and it privileges these over other ways of making kin and connections (Clarke and Haraway 2018).[39]

Geneticists usually acknowledge at least some of these limitations, but they also can send mixed messages about how to interpret their work. They promote genetic ancestry by asserting that because it is scientific, it can speak better than other methods to the truth of who people really are—even while they sometimes also claim that they traffic only in probabilities, not in certainties or identities.[40] But these scientific truth claims are inevitably identity claims as well. As Kim TallBear (2013) argues, they disrespect and undermine other knowledge about origins and identity by characterizing that other knowledge as "beliefs" and "myths" that can either be supported or refuted using genetic ancestry's methodologies: when we position DNA as the ultimate authority, we undermine our own histories, agency, and, in some cases, sovereignty.[41]

In this book, I likewise question forms of authority that give geneticists the final word on ancestry and origins. This does not cast doubt upon Lemba Jewishness. On the contrary, it makes room for Lemba identity as well as Lemba epistemic authority—both in terms of the status of their oral history in relation to genetic ancestry, and in terms of their genetic knowledge production in relation to that of geneticists. What is at stake here is when and how genetic evidence as bodily evidence is invoked and to what end. As DNA is increasingly called upon to speak to questions of racialized and exclusionary citizenship and belonging, understanding genetic ancestry as a multivalent political object could not be more important.

Becoming Lemba

It was June 2006 when F. C. Raulinga sat me down in his house, took out his draft of the book that he was writing and his archive of Lemba Cultural Association documents that he had authored in his nearly two decades as general secretary, and began to more formally teach me who the Lemba were and where they came from. He had provided a version of this when we first met in 2004. But now I had been in South Africa continuously for seven months, mostly in Kgoshi Mpaketsane's village in the predominantly Sepedi-speaking region of the Limpopo Province, about two hundred kilometers to the south of Raulinga's home. I had now heard other Lemba people's accounts of their history, and Raulinga felt it was important that I learn his authoritative, elaborated version of things.

He loosely based his narrative on a paper he had written that was, as he explained, "a summary of what we talk during a funeral of a Lemba Jew. . . . We talk about our culture, our history, our religion, our food, . . . the trade of our people, the genealogies, the family, the particular family of the one who is being buried, the praises of that clan, about the Lemba songs." Along with the Lemba Cultural Association annual conferences and the stories told to children by their parents and grandparents as they grew up, funerals were the place where Lemba history and culture came alive, and I attended them frequently throughout my fieldwork. In each of those contexts—the LCA, family stories, and funerals—Lemba elders such as Raulinga communicated in different registers to each other and to Lemba youth what they needed to understand in order to know themselves. Months later, when I attended my first LCA annual conference in September 2006, I would see Samuel Moeti, who took over as LCA president after Professor Mathivha's death in 2003, perform this role. Shortly after that I would see Raulinga do the same at Moeti's funeral. But on this day, Raulinga addressed me directly, as one researcher to another.

More specifically, Raulinga, a knowledgeable researcher without access to publishing his work, addressed me, a novice who would be able to produce a published record based on his and others' guidance. In that respect, we were enacting a dynamic that was familiar in the history of anthropology and that had marked over a century of inquiry into Lemba origins: researchers relied on Lemba expertise to produce accounts that could authoritatively travel.[42]

Cognizant of these dynamics, Raulinga first critiqued others' mistakes: this served to set the record straight, and it was also a warning so that my future published work might not require such corrections. Raulinga explained to me that one author, Hugh Stayt, an ethnologist who had trained at Cambridge in the 1920s, had misidentified one particular clan as Venda when they were really Ndebele.[43] For Raulinga, this mistake called into question the overall quality of Stayt's research. The subtext that Raulinga did not point out, but that I came to understand later, was that Stayt, writing in 1931, concluded that the Lemba were descended from Arab traders on the Swahili coast. Raulinga and most other Lemba South Africans rejected this conclusion as a negation of their knowledge of their historical links to Jews.[44] He also explained that several researchers had said that the Lemba are a lost tribe of Israel: this, he told me, was in direct contradiction to Lemba oral history (see chapter 1). With the warnings about how to avoid potential mistakes now out of the way, Raulinga told me his version of that oral history.

Before they were called Lembas, Raulinga explained, they were known as Senas, after the city Sena (named after Senaa in Judea) that they built in Yemen following the destruction of the temple in Jerusalem in 586 B.C.E. In Yemen's Sena, they were under the leadership of the Buba clan for hundreds of years, until the Hamisi clan took over and founded a new city, Pusela, near the Red Sea coast. When a dam broke, they split into several groups and scattered throughout the African continent: those who became known as the Lemba followed a star, which appeared to the Mhani clan, down the east coast of Africa. They settled, again under Hamisi's leadership, between what are now Kenya and Tanzania in a place that they again named Sena. The Bakari clan led them further south to what is now Mozambique, but following an epidemic they dispersed, moving inland and variously north and south over centuries as circumstances dictated, sometimes in large groups and sometimes small, always as traders and often reuniting in newly established settlements, each associated with a different clan's leadership. In Raulinga's telling, most of these settlements were in what is now Zimbabwe, although they traveled and settled throughout precolonial Southern Africa, and this was centuries before national divisions as we know them were thinkable: at Chiramba they were led by the Seremane clan, at what we know as Great Zimbabwe they were led by Tovakare/Thobakgale, at Shabani they were led by Mhani, at Dumbe they were led by Sadiki, and at Mbelengwa, where they became known as Lembas for the first time, they were led by the Hadji clan.

In Raulinga's Lemba oral history, then, origins were multiple, movements were multidirectional, interaction with others was constant, the past was organized around places of settlement and which clans were leaders in each place, and "Lemba" was a matter of becoming, over time, through these processes and places.

As an alternative analytic to that of "being" or "being from," "becoming" works against narratives that naturalize belonging and its constitutive exclusions. It explicitly rejects the idea of singular origins and instead emphasizes how identities are formed and re-formed over time, in relation to multiple places and events, and in conversation with interested others. In contrast to the claims of genetic ancestry, this aligns with decades of research by historians and anthropologists that has illuminated the contingent, changing, and inventive processes at work in what can appear to a contemporary observer to be primordial, unchanging distinctions among groups of people.[45] It also resonates with regional histories in which key moments of group consciousness emerged out of migrations, social relations, and shifting patterns of leadership.[46]

My use of "becoming" emerges from these literatures and from Raulinga's and other Lemba people's accounts of their histories. It also draws from Stuart Hall's (1990) use of the same term to theorize black diasporic identity and from Donna Haraway's (2008) notion of "becoming with."[47] Hall emphasizes identity, power, and positioning: for him, it is how we talk about the past that makes possible our identities in the present. Haraway moves beyond narrative and also beyond the human: she shows that human and nonhuman actors are co-constituted not only discursively but also materially (Haraway 2008).[48]

As Raulinga's oral history makes clear, becoming Lemba is not only a story about leadership and migration, but also about the agency of place in shaping a people, from the hills that marked migratory histories in the distant past to places like Sweetwaters and Kgoshi Mpaketsane's village that were contested in the present. Origins here are journeys, and it is the movement and the sacred landscapes, both found and made, that shape who Lemba people continually become.

African Semites: Race, Religion, and the Puzzle of Lemba Origins

Genetic ancestry posits some populations as unchanging and therefore sources of baseline data, and others as historically complex migratory puzzles that can be solved by separating out in percentages the admixture of supposedly pure components. If geneticists are puzzle solvers, the Lemba are puzzle makers, in two senses: They have provided biological material to geneticists, thereby offering pieces of the global genetic puzzles that researchers have aimed to solve; and their origins have been regarded as a puzzle for over one hundred years. The Lemba do not fit neatly into racial *or* religious orders of things, not for geneticists, and not for their research predecessors.

Writing in 1908, Swiss missionary ethnologist and naturalist Henri A. Junod had this to say: "The strangest . . . phenomena is the presence of the Balemba in Spelonken and Selati districts: a Bantu tribe scattered amongst the Basuto and Bathonga of those parts, exactly as the Jews amongst European nations. . . . Living and thriving by means of industry, moreover bearing strong Semitic characteristics, is it not enough to awake the interest of the ethnologist and to puzzle him greatly?" (Junod 1908, 276).

Writing in 2000, Tudor Parfitt echoed Junod's puzzlement, as well as his excitement about the possibility of solving it by the methods available to him. Describing the Spurdle and Jenkins study, he writes: "Unknown to me, in the latter stages of my work, a fellow Welshman, Professor Trefor Jenkins . . . had the idea of trying to solve the mystery of the origin of the Lemba by collecting genetic material from the tribe" (Parfitt 2000, 344). Referring to his own collaboration with geneticists, Parfitt explains: "It was clear to me that the tantalizing results produced by Jenkins's research left a number of questions unanswered. To say that the Lemba had 'Semitic' genes did not solve the riddle of their religious origin. . . . We discussed whether genetics could help us determine what religion the Lemba had traditionally practiced" (Parfitt 2000, 345–346).

These genetic inquiries into Lemba origins were just the most recent iteration of similar questions that had been asked for more than a century by those who aimed to define groups of Africans in terms of racial, religious, and tribal categories and to sort these groups out from one another. Yet, the more one knows about African history and histories of racial, religious, tribal, and ethnic formation throughout the world, the stranger it seems that Lemba oral histories, identities, and practices should continue to be so puzzling.

Scholars of Islam in Africa will tell you, for example, that by the eighth century, Muslims from Arabia had crossed the Red Sea to live in and trade from the Ethiopian coast (Levtzion and Pouwels 2000, 5). So why should it be surprising that others, including the ancestors of those who became known as Lemba, might have done the same in earlier centuries? They will also tell you that the people of the Swahili coast became majority Muslim over the course of more than seven hundred years, between the eighth and the fifteenth centuries, and that inland traders traveled to the coast and back throughout much of that time (Levtzion and Pouwels 2000, 6).[49] Why, then, would the community known as Sena not have been part of these diverse trade networks?[50]

These African-Islamic mappings help explain why some researchers over the years have rejected the idea that the Lemba might have Jewish origins in favor of what they regarded as a more likely history of descent from Muslim traders.[51] But it is anachronistic to assume that the clear distinctions that are common today between Jews and Muslims (and between Jews and Christians, for that matter) have such deep historical roots. Religious studies scholar Aaron Hughes (2017) argues that medieval Arabia was home not only to Jews and Muslims but also to people whose range of religious practices should be understood as Judeo-Islam.[52] Recent studies of contemporary Islamic practices in Kenya show that bricolage remains a feature of coastal religious life there (McIntosh 2009). Furthermore, Jews and forms of Judaism are known to have had a presence in North Africa since antiquity (Hull 2009).[53] Given the complexities of migration and religious flexibility that could easily account for Lemba oral histories, why has the quest to solve the puzzle of Lemba origins persisted?

In the nineteenth and early twentieth centuries, Christian missionaries and ethnologists like Junod observed Lemba practices such as endogamy, circumcision, restrictions against eating pig, and slaughter rituals. They concerned themselves with questions about whether the Lemba, given these cultural/religious features, were really native Africans, Muslims, or Jews, and they speculated about Lemba origins outside of Africa. As Hugh Stayt, the ethnologist invoked by Raulinga, put it more than twenty years later, what most interested him about the Lemba was "their non-Bantu qualities and the problem of their origin" (Stayt 1931, 231).

These were racial conundrums. In the nineteenth century, the figure of the Semite encompassed both Muslims and Jews, who as religious, racial, and political Others, constituted the borders of what it meant to be European (Anidjar 2008).[54] But at the same time, the figure of the black African had consolidated a continentally defined racial order that mapped people onto a hierarchical scale of civilization: Semites were now understood as a subgroup of "Caucasoids," and therefore totally distinct from Africans, who were now understood as "Negroids."[55] The Lemba disrupted these turn-of-the-century racial orders because they appeared to have features of each: again, as Stayt put it, their "non-Bantu" qualities pointed to a "problem of their origin."

These missionary and ethnological concerns with racial and religious clas-sifications coincided with and extended projects of colonial administration that sought to govern through racial classification and ethnic mapping.[56] The puzzle of Lemba origins, then, in both its early and late twentieth-century iter-ations, is less a historical question and more an artifact of nineteenth-century race science.[57] Ultimately, it is a story about racialization.

Racialization as an approach to analyses of race recognizes how racial cat-egories are constituted, how they change, and how people come to be associ-ated with and interpolated into specific forms of racial difference.[58] Consider the racial and religious signifier "black Jew." Here "black" modifies "Jew" such that "Jew" without modification excludes black racial identity. Indeed, within the twentieth century, at least some Jews who were viewed at one time as racially Other have become white in South Africa (Krut 1987; Shimoni 2003), in Europe (Bunzl 2007; Arkin 2009), in the United States (Brodkin 2002), and in Israel (Domínguez 1989). Jewish whiteness rendered black Jews both racially mar-ginal to and subsumed within a larger Jewish collective. Labeled "Semitic" first in the nineteenth century when missionaries understood them in these terms and then again in the late twentieth century when the term reemerged to describe their genetic origins, labeled "black" in both apartheid and post-apartheid South Africa, and claimed as Jews in documentaries and newspaper articles and by scholars, the Lemba are enmeshed in multiple racializations, including those that conflate race and religion.

Identifying racial and ethnic origins is at the heart of the contemporary claims of genetic ancestry. But the search for origins reduces history to one point of departure such that it is the only history that matters. For the Lemba, this means that they are positioned as either essentially African or essentially Jewish, depending on where it turns out they are "really" from—an approach that privileges one set of ancestors as more relevant than all others and one historical point as the only significant moment over many possible historical points that they can and do claim.

Lemba people in South Africa were confounding to people because they were racialized in terms of colonial and apartheid law as Native/Bantu/Black, but they also seemed to those who wrote about them as such to be different from other Native/Bantu/Black people in a way that would have removed them from that category if the speculative racializations of Lemba people as Semites/Jews/non-Africans carried more than just rhetorical weight. Indeed, what made it so powerful when people like Professor Mathivha or Kgoshi Mpaketsane spoke about Jews as part of Hebrews or even as part of the Lemba was that their alternate reading worked against the racial hierarchies that had historically made Lemba-Jewish connections within South Africa impossible. Their framings took racial and religious complexity for granted such that they undid the perennial puzzle of Lemba origins by unsettling the racial and religious fixities that underwrote it.[59] Lemba people challenge how we define origins and our expectations that origins, however defined, should shape racial, religious, or political belonging in predictable ways.

Jewish Blood, African Bones:
Rethinking Indigeneity and Diaspora

On September 9, 2006, I attended my first LCA annual conference. Back in 1997, the year of Professor Mathivha's speech with which I began this introduction, the conference theme, "Cultural Centre Our Home," turned inward at the same time that Lemba people were facing unprecedented international attention. The 2006 theme, "Let's Promote Our Culture as Our Heritage," echoed that of 1997, but the slight difference mattered: the main open-air metal structure and poured concrete floor of the cultural center had now been built on the hilltop, and although completing the building remained a goal, all attention in the LCA was now on exciting new national developments around cultural heritage that promised to include Lemba people in postapartheid national belonging in ways that their legal claims to land and chieftaincy so far had not. While ideas of Lemba indigeneity had begun to take shape through these politics, it now began to emerge more explicitly as a potential avenue of identification and transformation.

The Lemba Cultural Association was now part of a joint effort to rebury thirteenth-century bones from the Mapungubwe kingdom near the South African border with Zimbabwe and Botswana. The bones had been excavated beginning in the 1930s and stored ever since at the University of Pretoria. All presentations at the LCA conference that year were about Mapungubwe, both Lemba historical connections there and updates on reburial plans. Finally, in November 2007, LCA and other Lemba representatives joined representatives from several other "claimant communities," as they were called by the postapartheid South African government, at what was now the Mapungubwe World Heritage Site and National Park. There each claimant community performed burial rituals to lay to rest the bones of their ancestors, the now-recognized-as-indigenous inhabitants of the now-memorialized Mapungubwe kingdom. In that act, Lemba representatives claimed African indigeneity for

Lemba people, and they were in turn claimed by the South African state as indigenous Africans.

Long-standing scholarly and public interest in the Lemba hinges on the singularity of origins: were they really Africans or really Jews? The question implied that they either descended from Jews whose origins were in ancient Judea, or that their ancestors were black Africans who had mistakenly (or perhaps instrumentally) taken to heart incorrect missionary theories that they might have Semitic histories. This was the question that genetic research purported to answer. Lemba genetic ancestry, expressed by most as having Jewish blood, and their involvement in the Mapungubwe reburial, through which they claimed their African bones, suggest another iteration of the Jewish/African conundrum: how could Lemba people view their blood as Jewish and their bones as African? Such questions are misleading, because they take on others' logics of purity and stasis that Lemba people, in their multiple articulations of belonging, clearly reject.[60]

In this book, I also reject the logics of origins through which one can truly be only one thing or the other, or a mixture of more than one thing that can be broken into constitutive, original parts. Instead of asking after Lemba origins, I therefore ask how Lemba political subjectivities have articulated with genetic ancestry, and what we might learn from Lemba people about how to think against the grain of mutually exclusive concepts of belonging.[61] Doing so unsettles the ways that race, religion, indigeneity, diaspora, and DNA purport to definitively fix assertions of who people really are, where they are really from, and therefore where they really belong.

James Clifford has argued that diasporas, nation-states, and indigenous claims can be understood as defined against one another as "zones of relational contrast" (Clifford 1997, 254). Indigeneity testifies that those who claim it are original people, not just the first inhabitants of a given place, but substantively constituted through it. Diaspora offers connection and a form of rootedness to those who locate their belonging not only where they are but also in a place where they or their ancestors were before—especially in circumstances where migrations were not freely chosen and return is not possible. Genetic ancestry, with its assertions of continental, racial, and ethnic origins "coded" in "non-coding" haplotypes, promises to sort out one from the other, and to reconstruct the pathways through which all people came to be in the places they call home. Each of these ways of knowing belonging suggests a fixity: one is either indigenous or diasporic, of a place or strangers in a place, and DNA, in this logic, can settle open questions about contested origins once and for all.[62]

Lemba people and their histories and subjectivities call into question the stability of these political and scientific global mappings. Their actions and identifications as both genetic Jews and indigenous Africans complicate what we think we know about indigenous and diasporic belonging and about Jewish and African histories and futures. They also open new questions about the evidentiary claims of genetic data.

Genetic Afterlives

Participants in genetic ancestry studies make sense of and build upon the data that derive from their bodies, often years after findings have been published and researchers have moved on to other questions. If we want to understand the growing importance of DNA as a form of knowledge that is also a form of making political claims, we must attend to *how* genetic ancestry matters and how its meaning can change in different contexts. This is what I mean by "genetic afterlives." These are new sites of genetic knowledge production that can spark a rethinking of what constitutes genetic evidence, who produces it, and for what reasons.[63]

The concept of genetic afterlives builds on a point of convergence between anthropological and STS approaches to scientific knowledge: that facts are produced rather than discovered, and that such production is social and relational.[64] Donna Haraway's (1988) concept of situated knowledges is foundational here. Haraway argues that because one's perspective can only ever be partial, objectivity and indeed the quality of scientific research are strengthened by one's ability to make the particular partiality of their perspective explicit. Furthermore, these necessarily partial perspectives cannot be all-encompassing.[65] Building on these core insights, I suggest that both genetic ancestry studies and related analyses are missing the perspective of the people who are recruited as research subjects: the people whose bodily materials constitute the data that ultimately make genetic ancestry research possible. Including these perspectives offers otherwise unavailable insights into how history, politics, and culture matter in any analysis of the significance of DNA and genetic knowledge.

Alondra Nelson's work exemplifies the kind of shift in focus, from production in laboratories to wider circulations, that I think is necessary to really grasp the contemporary significance of genetic ancestry specifically and of DNA in general. In *The Social Life of DNA* (2016), Nelson shows that DNA circulates not just biologically through reproduction, but also socially and legally. She points to African Americans' use of direct-to-consumer genetic ancestry testing to access genealogical histories that were violently obscured by the slave trade and generations of enslavement in the United States, as well as the use of DNA in efforts to establish legal standing for descendants' lawsuits against institutions that directly profited from their ancestors' enslavement. There is some resonance between these consumers and the former research subjects to whom I attend in this book. For example, both find genetic ancestry compelling as a means of achieving forms of justice, and consumers of personal genetic ancestry testing services such as those Nelson writes about are also in a sense research subjects: in fact, in many cases they authorize use of their DNA in undefined future research when they sign the consent forms that are required in order to purchase their ancestry report.

But there are also some important differences, both between my approach and Nelson's and between the specificity of the people with whom she works and the former research subjects whom I engage here. First, Nelson's approach to circulation does not call into question what constitutes genetic knowledge production: for her, geneticists produce genetic knowledge, and consumers circulate it. We might think of this as a story about scientific knowledge production and its popular circulation. In contrast, the chapters that follow demonstrate that we must ethnographically analyze genetic circulation as knowledge production in its own right. This makes the difference between accepting the fixity of contemporary categories of belonging and destabilizing the ways that concepts like diaspora, indigeneity, race, and religion fix people into (or in some cases, out of) place. Furthermore, the racial geographies and ethnonationalisms that companies both presume and market tend to reverberate in consumer circulations of commercial genetic ancestry. But the former research subjects who are the focus of this book fundamentally challenge such configurations.

I aim to understand genetic evidence from the perspective of people who have been part of genetic ancestry studies as research subjects for three reasons: to take seriously the knowledge practices of people who are more often understood as vulnerable subjects than as political actors, to better situate genetic ancestry in relation to colonial and postcolonial politics of race, ethnicity, and citizenship, and to move away from scientist/nonscientist or expert/nonexpert binaries when thinking about the source, content, and meaning of scientific knowledge.[66]

There are affinities between my use of "afterlives" and the ways that the term has opened productive spaces for others looking to account for and make sense of disparate kinds of lingering effects. Saidiya Hartman, for example, names the ongoing devaluation of black life "the afterlife of slavery," a label she also takes as her own to mark how in living, she is a reminder of the dead and is at once stranger and kin to the descendants of others who were captured in the Atlantic slave trade and those in West Africa who were not (Hartman 2007, 6, 18). Gastón Gordillo, drawing on Walter Benjamin, writes of the "afterlife of destruction" in which rubble is actively reused while also being haunted by histories of past violence—and ruins, in contrast, enact erasure and in doing so become dead (W. Benjamin [1968] 2019; Gordillo 2014). Nancy Rose Hunt, writing about colonial Congo, posits afterlives as an alternative to "aftermath": whereas the latter implies a singular event, the former are multiple (Hunt 2016). Didier Fassin urges ethnographers to claim the public afterlives of their published research—that is, the ways that their work circulates through author interviews, book reviews, and other media—as ethnography in its own right that can illuminate related and new questions (Fassin 2015).[67]

Hartman's, Gordillo's, Hunt's, and Fassin's use of the term marks loss and remembrances, unexpected openings and new circulations: likewise with genetic afterlives. Fassin's formulation offers a productive distinction from what I mean to account for. For Fassin, public circulations are of interest, whereas I differentiate between circulations of genetic research postpublication in general and that which unfolds among research subjects. We might view the former as a public afterlife in relation to geneticists who author these studies, but my interest here is in how research subjects produce genetic ancestry out of their bodies when their samples are taken, and how they reclaim that foundational authorship in their own postpublication circulations of the studies that rely on their participation.

Now regarded as a powerful form of evidence, DNA is increasingly called upon to make and adjudicate competing claims to rights, resources, and belonging. Therefore, what are fundamentally at stake in the meaning of DNA are political subjectivity and questions of citizenship. We can imagine what this might mean for genetics researchers because we can analyze their published work for signs of their unacknowledged assumptions, desires, and commitments. We can also imagine what this might mean for consumers like those whom Alondra Nelson (2016) writes about, who seek kinship reconciliations and reparations for the institution of slavery's theft of life, labor, and liberty over generations, or like those Kim TallBear (2013) discusses, who, upon learning that some percentage of their genome is associated with Native American ancestry, seek tribal belonging in the absence of mutually claimed kinship. But we do not easily imagine what DNA might mean politically for the former research subjects without whom none of the work of genetic ancestry would have been possible.

Lemba genetic studies have served to illustrate insightful arguments such as critiques of the resurgent essentialisms of DNA-based identity (Nash 2004; Parfitt 2003) and the ways that definitions of Jewishness have shifted in relation to American multiculturalism and Israeli nationalism (Abu El-Haj 2012). But these and other invocations of Lemba DNA do not aim to take Lemba agency into account. This makes it possible for readers to assume that Lemba people share geneticists' desires and goals, thus leaving aside an important source of critique of geneticists' global mappings and inadvertently participating in Lemba erasure.

Shifting the focus from geneticists to research subjects, however, is not only a matter of attributing rather than erasing agency. It also enables a broader analysis of forms of political belonging that genetic ancestry opens up and forecloses. These political subjectivities cannot be predicted nor accounted for in even the most thoughtful and thoroughly ethical genetic research designs, because they continue to be moving targets after studies formally conclude.[68] We therefore must locate the meaning and significance of genetic ancestry research in the people who have been part of studies as research subjects. If we take their stories about DNA seriously as genetic knowledge production that is different from but no less significant than the stories about DNA that geneticists tell, then we can better understand how DNA matters socially and politically beyond the now-familiar spaces of laboratories and genetic enterprise.

Genetic studies are world-making projects.[69] Genetic data are not already meaningful, but rather they are made meaningful in relation to both the geopolitical and intellectual contexts in which they are collected, analyzed, and circulated and the conceptual and material tools and technologies that geneticists and research subjects alike use in these processes.[70] My contention is that there are multiple worlds in play in this kind of genetic research that are not necessarily shared among all actors, and if we focus on the knowledge politics of scientists exclusively, it is at the expense of other, often less powerful actors who ultimately must continue to live with genetic ancestry's implications in ways that geneticists are not subjected to.

Genetic afterlives can and should transform our understandings of the possibilities and limitations of DNA as a form of evidence and as a site of social, cultural, and political meaning. To understand contemporary power and politics, we need to understand the emerging political significance of DNA, and to understand the political significance of DNA, we need to attend ethnographically to the people from whom genetic samples derive.

Overview of Chapters

The chapters of this book ethnographically trace a series of genetic afterlives as they articulate with Lemba political belonging in the forms of citizenship (chapters 1 and 3), diaspora (chapter 2), postapartheid traditional leadership and kinship (chapter 4), and indigeneity (chapter 5). Genetic ancestry becomes animated through these forms of political belonging, which I argue must be understood as interrelated rather than separate.

Chapter 1, "Producing Lemba Archives, Becoming Genetic Jews," traces the entangled stories of ethnologists, Lemba informants, and Lemba authors as an ongoing and unequal conversation about the nature of Lemba difference and why that difference should matter. It follows the founding of the Lemba Cultural Association in the mid-twentieth century and unsuccessful efforts by Lemba people to achieve ethnic recognition in apartheid South Africa through labels in passbooks, recognition of chieftaincies, and the hoped-for creation of a Lemba "homeland." The chapter considers genetic ancestry as one among many Lemba archival practices. It examines how genetic ancestry became possible for Lemba people in the 1980s and 1990s, why they decided to participate as research subjects, and with what effects, especially the popularization of the mistaken idea that because the Lemba have genetic links to Jews, they are a lost tribe of Israel. This chapter, then, is the prelife of genetic afterlives: it contextualizes genetic ancestry in relation to other contested knowledges and long-standing projects of belonging.

Chapter 2, "Genetic Diaspora," considers how Lemba people produced genetic knowledge in conversation with published studies; television documentaries that publicized the studies and the Lemba as a lost tribe of Israel; American Jews who, based on this media archive, sought connections to the Lemba as genetic kin; and South African Jews who struggled with how to connect with Lemba people across differences that were at once racial, religious, and historical. Building on concepts of genetic citizenship (Heath, Rapp, and Taussig 2004) and diasporic Zionism (Abu El-Haj 2012), "genetic diaspora" theorizes the contours of diaspora after DNA. Specifically, it provides a means to analyze how genetic knowledge, global politics of Jewishness, and postapartheid politics of race and ethnicity converged in encounters between Lemba people and other Jews. This chapter considers how genetic afterlives facilitate diaspora, but in the process also make possible its undoing.

Chapter 3, "Postapartheid Citizenship and the Limits of Genetic Evidence," analyzes how DNA that was intended to substantiate Lemba-Jewish connections entered into Lemba political and legal struggles for postapartheid state recognition via claims to traditional leadership and land, and how indigeneity began to emerge as a way to describe and achieve these forms of recognitions and rights. It follows Kgoshi Mpaketsane's recognition efforts and explores how genetic afterlives intersected with citizenship as a lived experience in rural South Africa. This chapter shows that genetic ancestry became legible as a means to achieve a form of postapartheid ethnic citizenship through its ability to demonstrate difference. However, it also traces how a series of projects of recognition failed. These failures point to the limits of both DNA and indigeneity as technologies through which to achieve recognition, land rights, and sovereignty in postapartheid South Africa.

Chapter 4, "Ancestry, Ancestors, and Contested Kinship after DNA," reminds us that the "populations" that appear in genetic ancestry studies are made up of people who have both collective and personal stakes in relatedness as it is practiced and experienced. This chapter considers Lemba contestations over genealogy and ancestors, arguing that to fully grasp how DNA mattered for Lemba people, it is necessary to analyze instances where DNA might have mattered, but other ways of figuring relatedness mattered more. Nevertheless, these contestations are filtered through the experience of being collectively subject to genetic ancestry research.

Chapter 5, "Locating Lemba Heritage, Imagining Indigenous Futures," ethnographically examines the events leading up to the Mapungubwe reburial, the reburial process, and subsequent Lemba reflections and visits to the site. It traces the political maneuvering that resulted in a joint claim to the ancient bones in the name of an undifferentiated African indigeneity that ultimately required the decision not to perform genetic analyses on the bones, even while the reburial was done in a way that made future study possible. It theorizes what it means to be indigenous in postapartheid South Africa, what it means to be black Jewish indigenous Africans, and how DNA mediates claims to belonging, difference, and authority.

The epilogue considers the reasons behind a recent Lemba moratorium on future genetic ancestry testing. It argues that such a refusal is itself a form of genetic knowledge production and thus an example of genetic afterlives. Together, the examples of genetic afterlives in this book challenge us to rethink what is at stake in truth claims that link bodies and belonging.

PRODUCING LEMBA ARCHIVES,
BECOMING GENETIC JEWS

William Masala Mhani took emergency leave from his job in the stationery department of the Gencor Mining Company office in Johannesburg, gathered some things from his home in Soweto, and rushed to Venda when he got the news: Lemba Cultural Association (LCA) founder and president M. M. Motenda was in the hospital.[1] It was May 1982. Motenda, born in 1896, was eighty-six years old; Masala, born in 1925, was fifty-six. Mission-educated and a teacher by profession, Motenda had devoted his adult life to bringing and keeping Lemba people together. Masala had already spent ten years in Johannesburg as a cleaner in a white family's home when, in the 1950s, he decided to follow the example of his mother, Tshimbiluni, and his elder brother, France, to become an active member of the LCA. He wrote to Motenda to express his interest, and Motenda connected him with the Soweto branch leadership. The two men grew increasingly close over the years as Motenda mentored Masala from afar. Now with Masala at his hospital bedside, Motenda imparted his final lessons. Handing Masala a small stack of documents that he had written about their people, Motenda told him, "Masala, pray for the Lemba. Don't speak many words. Just say: 'God our father, of Abraham, Isaac, and Jacob, do you leave this nation to die away?'" Masala, telling me this story in 2006 at his home in Sinthumule, went on: "He said only those words: . . . 'Ask the Lord, is he leaving the Lemba people to die?'"[2] Motenda died two days later, less than an hour after Masala left the hospital to catch the bus back to Soweto.

Motenda's passing filled Masala with a renewed sense of purpose to work for his nation, by which he meant the Lemba people, and a bravery and strength that made him feel he could speak his truth about the Lemba to everyone who would listen. But proclaiming the existence of the Lemba could be dangerous: it could have been regarded by the South African state as speaking against apartheid racial and ethnic designations since "Lemba" was not an official category, and it might have been seen by the Venda Bantustan government as a challenge to their ethnically defined rule. The documents that Motenda entrusted to him, Masala explained to me as he guided me through his personal Lemba archive, were therefore to be kept secret lest they endanger the members of the LCA—and by extension other Lemba people—by exposing them as potentially politically subversive in their pushback against apartheid classifications.

Motenda wrote these secret documents in the late 1970s and early 1980s, but they complemented two essays about Lemba history, culture, and identity that he had authored and published years before, one in 1940 and the other in 1958. Unlike the later documents containing secret knowledge intended for future Lemba people so that they would not, after his death, forget who they were and where they came from, Motenda's published work aimed to publicly declare and define the Lemba against an active, real-time process of state erasure. Motenda's secret documents, his published work, and his political organizing through the LCA were interrelated efforts to articulate Lemba ethnic difference in an increasingly repressive context.

Motenda's work in bringing together Lemba people through the LCA and through his published and secret writing, along with Masala's archival practices, points to a long and rich history of Lemba knowledge production about who they are, where they come from, and why it matters—a history that involved considerable resistance to the definitions and assertions of others. Their struggles to define themselves on their own terms would seem to make the LCA's later willingness to participate in genetic ancestry studies unlikely. After all, a genetic test puts the power to define in the hands of scientists and their technologies (TallBear 2013). Yet in 1987, just a few years after Motenda's death, the LCA under the leadership of Professor M. E. R. Mathivha facilitated the first of several blood collections from Lemba men by South African geneticist Trefor Jenkins, so that he and his doctoral students Amanda Spurdle and Himla Soodyall might study Lemba origins via DNA.

If Lemba intellectuals like Motenda, Masala, and Mathivha had long worked against others' definitions of who they are and where they come from, why would they agree to participate in genetic studies that could surrender their own interpretations of their history to scientists and the epistemic power of genetic certainty?[3] How and why did genetic ancestry become possible, desirable, and legible to the Lemba people who authorized and participated in Jenkins's research, what did they hope it might accomplish, and what *did* it accomplish vis-à-vis those hopes?

This chapter shows how Lemba struggles for ethnic recognition from the South African state, beginning in the early twentieth century and intensifying under apartheid, shaped their desires to participate in genetic studies and their expectations about what DNA could or should accomplish for them. Guided by two kinds of archives—publications about the Lemba by Lemba authors and their interlocutors, and Masala's personal collection that he amassed over decades—it traces how Lemba men like Motenda, Masala, and Mathivha worked with and repositioned their liminal status in relation to racial, religious, and national belonging before they considered participating in genetic studies, and how genetic ancestry fit within their existing scholarly and political frameworks as well as with their relationships, both collaborative and contentious, with non-Lemba researchers.

Masala's practice of collecting material and then carefully guiding researchers through it, as he did with me, materialized particular histories that otherwise had left no trace in official archival repositories.[4] The task of Lemba authors was similarly corrective, but rather than materializing from nothing, they aimed to reshape the body of work that documented and debated Lemba origins, identities, and culture.

Lemba intellectual and political histories emerge here as intertwined and inseparable because knowledge production is always politically implicated, and likewise, knowledge claims are critical components of social and political organizing.[5] Considering these intellectual and political histories together makes it possible to read the politics of knowledge production about the Lemba generally and about Lemba genetics specifically in a way that privileges and illuminates Lemba stakes and investments. The point here is not whether Motenda, Masala, Mathivha, and other LCA leaders could or should represent all Lemba people in speaking against the definitions of outsiders. Rather, it is how their entwined political and intellectual work created a Lemba entity capable of doing so in the absence of any formal recognition of Lemba authority.

In this chapter, I examine the contingency of the Lemba as genetic Jews as a way to understand how LCA leaders' intentions in participating in genetic ancestry research have shaped subsequent Lemba genetic afterlives. I argue that Lemba people became genetic knowledge producers from the moment some of them began to consider participating in genetic ancestry studies, which they then did with their own agendas and on their own terms. We cannot fully understand genetic ancestry studies by privileging the perspectives of geneticists, nor should we view such studies as isolated moments of scientific negotiation between geneticists and those whom they hope to enlist in their research. The entangled histories of Lemba knowledge production and politics that made it possible for the Lemba to become genetic Jews demonstrate that genetic ancestry is fundamentally shaped by research subjects who in turn shape the meaning and significance of DNA.

Lemba Culture, Lemba Politics, Ethnic Archives

Before M. M. Motenda founded the Lemba Cultural Association, he published his essay "History of the Western Venda and of the Lemba." This was one of several so-called vernacular histories compiled, translated, and edited by Nicolus J. Van Warmelo in his book *The Copper Miners of Musina* (1940). Van Warmelo was chief government ethnologist of South Africa from 1930 to 1969. His job was to make distinctions among tribal or ethnic groups, to determine how many there were and their relative strength politically and numerically, and to produce texts detailing each group's culture and history. As Sara Pugach observes, "No known people, no matter how small their number, escaped his attention, as he endeavored to 'fix' South Africa's 'tribes' and give them an overarching classification" (Pugach 2004, 831).

Van Warmelo wrote during an era of deep divisions within South African anthropology regarding complicity, first with the colonial project and then with apartheid (R. Gordon and Spiegel 1993; Wright 2016). His work took complicity a step further. His classifications were commissioned by the state and directly informed legal decisions about how many black ethnic groups there were in South Africa and where they were located. Never just an academic exercise, classification for him was an applied science: he had to square the distinctions that he observed and learned about from others with state logics of segregation and, following 1948, with apartheid. His decisions ultimately informed the Bantustan system of separate national development.[6]

By the time Van Warmelo began this classificatory work, broad tribal categories with associated standardized languages had already become popularized, aided by ethnological essays published by Christian missionaries, mission-educated Africans, and anthropologists.[7] In this context, Lemba author Manasseh N. Mphelo published his article "The Balemba of the Northern Transvaal" in the *Native Teacher's Journal* in 1936. As the first Lemba person to publish an account of who they were, Mphelo endeavored to correct others'

mistakes, socially situate informants who had elsewhere been decontextual-
ized, and, through his own role as author and his inclusion of other authors'
direct quotations from Lemba people, amplify Lemba knowledge production.

Mphelo, a lecturer at Adams College in Natal, wrote directly in conversation with the missionary ethnologists who had previously published their assessments of Lemba origins, and more implicitly in relation to contemporary
debates about black and white nationalisms and the expansion of segregationist
laws.[8] He addressed the questions about Lemba racial and religious origins that
had so interested Berlin missionary Reverend Schlömann (1894) and Swiss
missionaries Henri Junod (1908) and Reverend A. A. Jaques (1931) by affirming both Lemba Africanness and their Jewishness. "Like the Jews the Balemba
are wanderers," he wrote; they "are just like the other Bantu of South Africa
in appearance . . . but one can easily distinguish a Mulemba by his straight
nose. . . . The Rev. A. A. Jaques, of the Swiss Mission, describes the writer's
grandfather Maphangwa as having what may be termed a typical Jewish nose"
(Mphelo 1936, 36).[9] He then detailed what he felt should be known about the
Lemba, reframing most of what Schlömann, Junod, and Jaques noted as religious practices as instead aspects of material culture, kinship, and customs. In
the midst of ongoing loss of land and bureaucratization of identity, he worried
about the future—just as Motenda would a few years later. Lamenting that
"thirty or forty years ago they practiced all their customs freely," but now "most
of the young men feel very much ashamed to be known as members of this
tribe, and consequently, when their nationality is inquired into in the Native
Affairs Department offices, they pronounce themselves Bavenda or Bapedi,"
Mphelo encouraged Lemba young people to claim themselves as such, and he
called on all Lemba people to buy land so that they might live on it together
(Mphelo 1936, 44).

The dynamic that developed in the 1940s and 1950s between Van Warmelo
and Motenda, in which they wrote as unequal interlocutors, echoed that of
missionary ethnologists and Mphelo. Van Warmelo wrote about the Lemba
repeatedly throughout his tenure in the Department of Native Affairs, with the
assistance of and in conversation with Lemba people, including Motenda.[10]
Sekibakiba Peter Lekgoathi has argued, following Lyn Schumaker, that Van
Warmelo's publications and the tribal classifications that followed from his research should be viewed as coproductions of cultural knowledge in which his
African informants and coresearchers shaped what he learned according to
their own perspectives and interests (Lekgoathi 2009; Schumaker 2001). Motenda's experiences, however, make it clear that Van Warmelo did not always
accept these perspectives and interests, and that when co-production failed in

this way, it was necessary for those whom it failed to turn to their own writing and political organizing to advance their interests.

From his earliest published work, Van Warmelo found the Lemba unique. In his 1935 *Preliminary Survey of the Bantu Tribes of South Africa*, he divided all of South Africa's tribes into five overarching categories: Nguni, Tonga, Sotho, Venda, and the final catchall category, "Lemba and Others," which consisted of all "those various people who do not belong to the foregoing four great divisions of the South African Bantu" (Van Warmelo 1935, 122).

Aside from the Lemba, the "Others" were relative newcomers to South Africa whose arrival could be definitively traced in relation to colonial displacement: Van Warmelo considered them migrants to be managed more than natives to be divided and ruled. But the Lemba, he explained, had been there as long as those in his four great divisions. He wrote, "They are beyond doubt Semites (Arabs?) who have gradually drifted thus far to the South" (Van Warmelo 1935, 122). His certainty stemmed from physical, cultural, and linguistic evidence. The physical evidence was that their noses were "plainly non-Negro," so much so as to be "positively startling." The cultural evidence was that they practiced circumcision, endogamy, and kosher killing, lived by trading and manufacturing clay pots and metalwork, and observed moon rituals. Finally, the linguistic evidence was varied but contradictory: they used a word for non-Lemba people, *vhaSenzi*, that was also used disparagingly by east coast Swahili people; they were known as *Mushavhi*, from the Tonga *sava*, meaning "buy"; and some Lemba people at times used a language, tshiLemba, that was a form of Karanga, yet notably "they have no quite distinct language of their own, but use the language of the people who are, or were, their hosts" (Van Warmelo 1935, 122).

Out of this varied evidence, most of which had already been discussed in missionary ethnologists' publications, Van Warmelo made two new conclusions that would have reverberating consequences for Lemba people. First, he suggested a Lemba connection to Great Zimbabwe and Mapungubwe: "In view of the remarkable position these unmistakable Semites occupy amongst the Bantu, and their suspicious proximity to the ruins of Zimbabwe and Mapungubwe, there is a great temptation to see a connection between the Lemba and the builders of these ruins" (Van Warmelo 1935, 122). To be clear, earlier and widely known Lemba oral histories placed them at these sites. But Van Warmelo expressed the links in racial terms that had been forged through nineteenth-century colonial dispossession and that continued to be invoked to justify and expand it throughout the twentieth century. Second, he wrote that in Rhodesia, the Lemba were estimated to number about fifteen hundred males, but that in South Africa, there were only a few hundred; furthermore, they did not have their own chief, and so they therefore "form no tribe" (Van Warmelo 1935, 122).

In Motenda's 1940 essay, he agreed with Van Warmelo's assertion of Lemba distinctness, but where Van Warmelo noted cultural features as if they evidenced essential difference, Motenda explained the same as historically emergent. Van Warmelo, for example, saw endogamy as evidence of Semitic origins. But Motenda explained the phenomenon as a recent innovation tied to the defeat of a Lemba chieftaincy in what is now Zimbabwe that had led to their migration south.[11] Van Warmelo echoed missionary ethnologists' increasingly racialized assessments of Lemba/Semitic resemblance as if it betrayed racial origin. But when Motenda noted that "the Vhalemba in respect of their faces and noses are well known to have been very handsome people, their noses were exactly like those of Europeans" (Motenda 1940, 63), it is not origins that he emphasized, but rather resemblance and the aesthetics of hierarchical racialization in a colonial context.[12]

For Van Warmelo, the Lemba were clearly culturally distinct from the Venda but lacked the language, the numbers, and the chieftaincies to form a tribe. In contrast, Motenda's history documented Lemba chieftaincies, demonstrated that language was a shifting and emergent phenomenon, and complicated the premise of Van Warmelo's work of tribal classification by presenting the Lemba as simultaneously separate from and intertwined with the peoples who, with Lemba support, went on to become the Venda. He explains that it was the Lemba chief Nkalahonye who, traveling with only a few people, arrived at Mbelengwa in what is now Zimbabwe, subjected all others, and there became known as Mulemba—but upon defeat by Mulozwi, the great-grandfather of Thoho-ya-Ndou, "they became one tribe and afterward emigrated together and came to Venda" (Motenda 1940, 52).[13] Here Motenda acknowledges that the Lemba adopted the language of others rather than keeping their own, but he points out that those who are now known as the Venda are actually the people of Ramabulana, son of Tshikaranga-speaking, Rhodesia-dwelling Thoho-ya-Ndou. Together with the Lemba, they defeated the people of Raphulu and then adopted their Venda language when they took over their land. "In course of time," he writes, "the Tshikaranga language disappeared, and only Tshivenda survived. Today we are all Venda" (Motenda 1940, 54). In Motenda's view, it was possible to be both separate from and intertwined with the Venda because these were matters of changing political fortunes, solidarities, and travels rather than permanent cultural features, essences, and origins.

If for Motenda, Lemba origins were multiple and Lemba difference was a matter of historical innovation and perspective, for Van Warmelo, Lemba difference evidenced distinct origins that confounded classification. In his 1937 contribution to Isaac Shapiro's *The Bantu-Speaking Tribes of South Africa*, Van Warmelo explains,

> The grouping largely coincides with geographical distribution, and also . . . the groups are almost a picture of the language-groups of South Africa. With primitive folk it cannot be otherwise. Roads, travels, and communications being virtually non-existent, or at best feebly developed, a geographical unit inevitably becomes the seat of a particular dialect and form of culture, provided it be left undisturbed. It is the migrations, and the enclaves of not yet assimilated conquerors or conquered which these leave in their wake, that therefore make the exceptions and provide the surprises. (Van Warmelo 1937, 44)

The Lemba were one of these surprising exceptions.

As with his 1935 classification, Van Warmelo included the Lemba in 1937 as the final distinct group, and when his essay was republished in 1946 and 1950, it failed to take up Motenda's 1940 interventions. Instead, he reiterated his 1935 estimate of fifteen hundred Lemba males in Rhodesia and a few hundred in South Africa, and he emphasized that although "they are strongly suspected of being Semitic in origin," "about the history of the Lemba nothing definite is known," and "in the Union they have no chief of their own but live scattered about amongst the Venda, to whose Chiefs they are subject" (Van Warmelo 1946, 65; 1950, 65). Van Warmelo was thus directly responsible for the fact that the Lemba were not a legally recognized ethnic group in South Africa but rather were subsumed under the ethnic labels "Venda" and "Pedi" when new apartheid policies dictated that all black South Africans must belong to one of the official black South African ethnicities.[14] The Lemba simply failed to meet the language-culture-chieftaincy model of apartheid ethnicity.

Motenda responded in 1958 with an article that disparaged Van Warmelo's ignorance, reframed scientific discovery such that instead of a site of new knowledge it was an indication of a prior lack thereof, and called on the government to fix Van Warmelo's mistakes:

> It is interesting to learn that there is always something NEW out of South Africa, which draws the admirable attention of the NEW generation of the Europeans in the modern days as scientific. . . . It is a well-known fact that ignorance makes a thing that existed before to be a new thing

or new discovery. . . . The Lemba problem appears to be insoluble to the European section because of their curious habits and behaviours which vary from those of other Bantu sections. The Lemba people seem not to know where they came from, although they are strongly suspected to be Semitic or Black Jews of Africa. . . . The original home of the Lemba is "SENA" near Blantyre in Nyasaland [Malawi]. They call themselves: Vha-SENA or Ba-SENA. (Motenda 1958, 61–62)[15]

With that, Motenda settled the question of Lemba origins. But still to be tackled was the question of legal classification: both of Motenda's articles were government publications, but neither carried the weight of scientific authority that Van Warmelo's classifications did.

In the 1950s, state incursions into people's identities and autonomy gave the still-new LCA a sharp sense of urgency and purpose. The Group Areas Act of 1950 tied black South Africans to a territory, defined by language and tribe. But as Van Warmelo had asserted in 1935, with no language of their own, there could be no Lemba tribe. The Bantu Authorities Act of 1951 thoroughly bureaucratized chieftaincy in South Africa by granting new duties and power to chiefs and by increasing their numbers. But because they had no status as a tribe, Lemba chiefs remained unrecognized. The Pass Laws of 1952 required all black South Africans to write their tribe/ethnic group in their passbooks, but "Lemba" was not a possible entry.[16] Each of these laws further marginalized Lemba people: Van Warmelo had long noted their small numbers and their status as scattered among and subject to Venda chiefs, but now this meant that as a distinct group, the Lemba were legally erased.

These apartheid laws changed the political landscape in which Lemba people could come together. They made it much harder to organize, especially when that involved crossing borders into Rhodesia and traveling from designated black rural areas in the northern parts of the country into white urban centers like Johannesburg further south. They also made it more necessary to do so.

In its first decade, the LCA took on three projects. First, they enlisted as many Lemba people as possible in Venda and Pedi areas of South Africa and in Rhodesia to join the organization so they could demonstrate that they were one people, divided only by others' borders. They also lent support to Lemba chiefs so that they might become officially recognized. Last, they launched a two-pronged campaign about passbooks: they petitioned the government to allow Lemba people to identify themselves as such, and they urged people to violate the law by writing in "Lemba" as their tribe. These projects were a direct response to apartheid policies that mined Van Warmelo's classifications to produce official lists of South Africa's tribal groups and to link each to a tribal territory.

The first LCA constitution was written in 1952 as these new apartheid laws were reshaping the South African state and the LCA was developing its strategies of opposition. It put forward a mission statement that was intended to facilitate Lemba survival under increasingly threatening conditions and which listed three objectives:

1 To foster and maintain the culture of the Balemba tribe
2 To encourage and facilitate the educational and commercial pursuits among members of the tribe as well as general progress of the people
3 To assist and render reliefs among members of the tribe, educationally, legally, and otherwise, on all cases recommended by the Executive Committee and approved by the Lemba Cultural Association.

Additionally, the LCA required a joining fee and an annual membership fee, which were to be used for the traveling expenses of an LCA emergency committee consisting of members of the northern branch, based at Sweetwaters, and the southern branch, based in Soweto.

That the main purpose of collecting money from members in the 1950s was to support an "emergency committee" is instructive. The first mission statement of the LCA emerged as a multifaceted plan for Lemba survival—cultural and otherwise—under increasingly oppressive apartheid policies. Cultural survival was the first priority, closely followed by the goal of helping Lemba people succeed in education and business. The provision to pay legal fees and the existence of an emergency fund speak to the increasing police repression that they faced under apartheid, and the now-dangerous actions of asserting Lemba tribal existence.

So it was that when Motenda wrote his 1958 essay, the stakes were less about settling the question of Lemba origins—for him, a simple question with a known answer that was, at any rate, beside the point—and more about Lemba survival in an increasingly ethnically defined political terrain. And more than anything, since Van Warmelo had already attested to Lemba difference, this came down to numbers. Motenda, claiming his authority as "an absolutely pure Lemba by birth" and "Chairman of the Lemba Cultural Association" wrote,

The numbers of Lemba mentioned in both countries are too far below the true figures of Lembas that could be roughly estimated correctly. I can unhesitatingly say that roughly about half of the population of Zoutpansberg are Lembas . . . The Bantu officials issuing reference books objected too, stating that they do not know who are Lembas. Therefore, some were registered as Vendas, Pedi, Karanga, and Sotho, etc., merely because they spoke those languages which they adopted in their environment. Lembas are profoundly grieved at such hindrances and frustrations by ordinary people but not by Government Authority. I humbly appeal on behalf of Lembas to the Government Authorities that this mistake should be rectified in order to find approximately correct numbers of Lemba men. We are taken today as a minority, yet it is not true. (Motenda 1958, 61)[17]

This went beyond Mphelo's 1936 account of Balemba men registering themselves as Bavenda or Bapedi out of shame: no longer a personal decision, this was a state imperative to choose among a specific, limited set of ethnic options.

At the same time, government policy and its implementation were very much in flux. Knowing this, Motenda wrote to members of the LCA, instructing them to gather other Lemba people and together demand to be identified in their reference books as Lemba. Among those who received this letter was France Masala Mhani, elder brother of William Masala Mhani: it was France's experience with Motenda and the pass laws that so impressed William and motivated him to seek out Motenda and become a member of the LCA.

Masala told me the story in October 2006: when France got the letter, he was afraid. Because he was a headman, he showed it to the chief, who shared his fear and suggested the two of them take it to the native commissioner. Upon seeing the letter, the commissioner ordered the police to bring in Motenda. Then, in front of the police, the chief, and Motenda, the commissioner demanded that France explain the letter and what it instructed him to do. Upset by France's lack of solidarity, Motenda yelled at him, "You are not a Lemba? Tell me you are not a Lemba!" Finally, the commissioner asked France directly, "Are you a Lemba?" Even with the police present, he answered, "Yes." Motenda's fervor and France's eventual bravery won the day: the commissioner took France's pass, wrote "Lemba" on it, and said, "Here. You are a Lemba. Take it." This small victory further motivated Motenda and captivated William Masala.

Chaplain Masala's Fight for His Nation

Inspired by his elder brother and Motenda, William Masala devoted the rest of his life to the LCA: politically, spiritually, and intellectually (figure 1.1). He was an active member of the LCA's Soweto branch from the 1960s until he retired

FIGURE 1.1 LCA chaplain William Masala Mhani around the time of his retirement in the late 1980s.

in 1987 and returned to his family's home in Sinthumule, which had been part of the Venda Bantustan since it was created as a separate self-governing territory in 1973. In the 1970s, as government scrutiny of anything potentially subversive intensified, Masala helped establish the Lemba Organization to cordon off any activities that could be interpreted as political rather than cultural, in order to protect the LCA, its members, and Lemba people in general.[18] In 1984, two years after Motenda died, Masala became the official LCA chaplain. His interest in scripture converged with his commitment to the survival of the Lemba people: he combed his collection of Bibles and biblical dictionaries for correlations between places and events listed there and those mentioned in Lemba oral history, and he collaborated with other researchers who had their own questions about, fascinations with, and interest in Lemba culture and origins. All of these activities left material traces, and Chaplain Masala archived them in his home.

Chaplain Masala's archive and his multifaceted presentation of Lemba history occupied most of our time together in the weeks that I stayed with him in 2006. Unlike other hosts, who wanted to show me their fields, cows, schools, or businesses, Masala primarily wanted me to see and learn about his archive. It consisted of VHS tapes of Lemba documentaries in which he had appeared; documents such as LCA conference programs from the 1980s and 1990s, loosely gathered in files; a meticulously organized scrapbook titled "Lemba Tribal Authority"; correspondence between LCA leaders and Jewish organizations; poems and illustrations; and several bookshelves full of books, including nearly a dozen Bibles and biblical dictionaries.

Each day Masala and I would sit in his study and pore over the materials that he wanted to share with me about his life, his identity as a Lemba person, and his history with the LCA. His narrative regularly jumped between decades and across genres as he tried to convey a sense of his own history and the history of those he passionately considered to be his people. Through each mode of telling, Masala shared something of himself with me. Now an elder, he simultaneously looked back on what he had accomplished in earlier years on behalf of the Lemba, considered what remained unfinished in LCA efforts to achieve Lemba recognition in postapartheid South Africa, and enlisted me in a potential future where the Lemba were recognized and his role in making that happen was remembered. He relished being heard in multiple registers, and his satisfaction challenged me to understand his history and the larger history of the LCA as a complicated layering of identity, affect, and constrained responses to exceedingly difficult circumstances.

Through several of these registers, Masala returned again and again to the events of 1982, the year that President Motenda died. Masala took to heart Motenda's deathbed instructions that he should speak up for the Lemba to keep them from dying away. He told me he was not afraid then, even though "at that time, they catch you or they kill, the government, because they don't want somebody who does something they didn't like, pressing that my nation must be there." He continued: "So from there I said, I must hit. What can I do? I must put in the newspaper. It will spread. They will read everywhere. Even if they caught me, they kill me, that newspaper will speak."

But first, he tested his strategy with his boss. He had worked at Gencor Mining Company since 1959, first as a cleaner before he was promoted to the stationery department. On that day in 1982, he went all the way to the top, to the "big boss." The boss's secretary laughed at him, expecting he would be turned away, because low-level employees were never granted entry into the boss's office. But the boss agreed to see him. Masala placed two drawings in front of his boss and told him that the government did not want to see the Lemba come together and develop like the other nations, and that they were being buried alive and would soon die away if their existence continued to be denied, as it had been for years.

The first drawing depicted a group of abandoned and pleading faceless men, as well as one woman holding a baby, standing and sitting on the ground under a tree (figure 1.2). The group was labeled "Lemba" and the caption read: "Where do we stand?" In the tree were disembodied heads drawn with African features, each labeled with a banner declaring their ethnicity: "Xhosa" read one, then "Venda," "Zulu," "Tswana," "Swazis," "Shangaans," and "Basotho." Halfway up a ladder resting on the tree was another African head with a banner reading "Ndebele."

This picture was Masala's apartheid map, drawn circa 1979, as the Venda Bantustan shifted from its initial status as "self-governing" to that of "independent." Those who would bear fruit and flourish had been singled out by the government as nations that would develop—separately and slowly—in their own homelands. Needless to say, "fruitful and flourishing" was not how most black South Africans viewed the homeland system. But as Masala's image depicted, his belief in the homelands as essential for Lemba prosperity was not about the relative oppression or thriving of individuals, but rather about the recognition and thriving of an ethnic identity. The Ndebele head, which also had an African face and was halfway up a ladder on its way to join the others, reflected the ambiguous status of the Ndebele at that time.[19] It demonstrated Masala's belief that there was a path to a different future, and it illustrated for his intended audiences exactly how that future would be achieved. To prosper like the others, the Lemba would transform from a faceless group of individuals to a single face that could portray who they really were: Lemba.

The second image showed a man who, Masala told me, represented Venda (figure 1.3). With a pleased expression on his face, the man pushed down on the concrete slab covering the dirt over a lowered casket, while below, multiple heads and hands emerged from the darkness of the grave, grasping the earth and pushing up against the concrete. The caption read: "Lembas are buried alive!"

The first image depicted Masala's sense of where and how the Lemba belonged in relation to the apartheid state and other black ethnic groups, and the second image illustrated his feelings about the treatment and fate of the Lemba within the Venda Bantustan.[20] He feared that the now "independent" Venda Bantustan might render the Lemba altogether a thing of the past, gone because they were dead, dead because they were buried. It was therefore up to the South African state to give them their collective face and ethnic banner that would ensure their prosperity. Masala shared his story and his images so that

FIGURE 1.2 "Where do we stand?" by LCA chaplain William Masala Mhani, 1979.

LEMBA'S are BURIED ALIVE !

the Lemba would have their ethnic face visible and known instead of being buried alive. He told me that after listening to him, his boss was convinced that the Lemba were different and should therefore be recognized as such. In their meeting, Masala told me, the boss encouraged him to continue to work for his people and to pursue their development as a nation.

But then he showed the images to Dr. Margaret Nabarro. A Jewish ethnomusicologist living in Johannesburg, she had first encountered Lemba people in the 1950s in Mozambique's Inhambane province, where she was researching Portuguese Marrano music (Buijs 1998, 676).[21] In the 1960s, she connected with Lemba people in South Africa through her work with the South African Broadcasting Corporation, where a number of Lemba people worked at that time (Buijs 1998, 675). As she started to research Lemba music and compare it to what she knew from her previous studies on Marrano and Yemeni Jewish music, she became convinced that the Lemba were Jews, as they said, and that others' theories of Lemba origins were incorrect. She began attending the LCA conference annually as an invited guest, occasionally sharing her research as well as more general information about comparative Jewish music and culture. Over the years, she grew close to Masala and he trusted her, so when she told him that it was dangerous to talk to the newspapers at all and even more dangerous to give them the images, he took her concerns seriously. Masala explained that Nabarro was convinced that publishing the images would trigger his arrest or worse: "She saw the power I had, and she thought they will kill me because it was the heavy time for apartheid."

In the end, Masala decided to meet with a journalist from the *Rand Daily Mail*, but he did not bring the images with him. The resulting article, published in September, began, "South Africa's 250,000 'black Jews,' the Lemba, are claiming descent from the Jews of biblical times in an effort to strengthen their case for their own tribal authority" (Moolman 1982). The instrumentalism apparent in the opening line was the journalist's interpretation of the fact that Masala talked about three different issues: biblical proof that the Lemba are Jews, the need for a Lemba tribal authority, and the large numbers of Lemba people unrepresented in South Africa because there was no such authority. For Masala, each of these was true and important, independent of the others. In his view, if anything was instrumental, it was not the claims about Jewishness but rather those about numbers. Indeed, he told me that the number itself was subversive and potentially dangerous—the Lemba were known for being few and therefore insignificant to the state as a collective entity.

Next the article pointed out that the Lembas were one of five separate tribes in Venda but the only one without their own tribal authority, and that they had appealed for one directly to Venda chief minister Mphephu. Had Masala's second image accompanied this article, the gleeful man burying the Lembas alive would have seemed obviously to be Mphephu, so perhaps Nabarro's concern was warranted. Had the first image been included, it would have appeared that the Lemba wanted not just a tribal authority as they claimed but also a "homeland," which by then could only have been carved out of land designated for whites or removed from the already established Bantustans. Either option would have been politically impossible and much more subversive than a simple request for recognition of tribal authority within Venda.

Politically, the LCA's goal of tribal recognition was subversive in some respects, but in others, it aligned with the apartheid emphasis on fundamental cultural difference that required segregation and separate development. This was clear in a 1978 article in the Afrikaans newspaper *Hoofstad* that reported on an LCA rally in Soweto, attended by 150 people. M. J. Mungulwa—then the branch president—told the crowd, "Our folk will always strive to follow its own culture and to live it to the fullest in our own manner. . . . Just as no plant has hope to grow healthy if it doesn't receive its own sunshine so too no nation can continue existing if it cannot manage its own unique culture in its own way and maintain it separately" (Verslaggeefster 1978). According to the article, Mungulwa was answered at the rally by C. J. Jooste, the director of the South African Bureau for Racial Affairs, the apartheid government division responsible for implementing separate development policies. Jooste responded enthusiastically to the LCA's apparent endorsement of apartheid, although his response must have been somewhat discouraging for the LCA leadership, who hoped for his immediate help in establishing their own tribal authorities and/or their own homeland. Jooste told them the most important thing was to maintain and preserve their own language, and that they should form a trust fund to pay for their own development.

Like the LCA's 1970s and 1980s ethnic politics, which could be understood as either dangerously subversive or aligned with apartheid, the association's racial politics were ambiguous and open to interpretation. In the 1982 article, Masala was quoted as saying, "We are the descendants of white men who became black-skinned through intermarriage" (Moolman 1982). One could read this as an alignment with, belief in, or desire for whiteness: in other words, a claim to privilege in a racialized political landscape. Indeed, it echoed racist endorsements of the Lemba, imagined as once-white Jews, as the real builders of Great Zimbabwe (see, for example, Gayre of Gayre 1967, discussed in chapter 5). But there was another implication of claiming an ancestral white past and a contemporary blackness: it called into question the foundational apartheid ideology that white and black should be inherently separate.[22]

The 1982 *Rand Daily Mail* article ended by advertising the upcoming LCA annual conference. This apparently got people's attention: many Lemba people attended, but so did twelve special-branch security police. It seems that even without the images, the newspaper story was enough to put Masala and the LCA at risk. Masala told me how afraid others were of the security police, but once again, he was proud of his own lack of fear. He made his conference address as planned, while the police watched and listened. To his way of thinking, the article was already in print, he had said what he needed to say, and all they could do was kill him or arrest him. They did neither, and in that sense, the conference was uneventful. Still, the presence of the security police confirmed for Masala that Nabarro had been right to warn him against publishing his images.

When Masala showed me the 1982 newspaper article and the unpublished images that he had hoped might accompany it, he also showed me a third drawing that he had made, inspired by his gratitude to Nabarro for helping to

CAN THESE BONES LIVE AGAIN ?

EZEKIEL 37 : 11-14

By the Chaplain of the Lemba Cultural Organization

W.M MASALA MHANI.

Dr. Margaret Nabarro
is pulling them out of the grave.

FIGURE 1.4 "Can these bones live again?" by LCA chaplain William Masala Mhani, n.d.

save his life and the collective life of the Lemba (figure 1.4). This one depicts Nabarro standing over an open grave and lifting out a bag filled with bones. The caption reads, "Dr. Margaret Nabarro is pulling them out of the grave," and a heading quotes the Bible: "Can these bones live again? Ezekiel 37:11–14." The image reflects not only Masala's belief that Nabarro saved him from the security police but also the role that she had begun to play as a researcher and advocate of the Lemba and their Jewishness. Her research brought her into contact with colleagues in Israel, and together they were convinced of the historical accuracy of Lemba oral tradition about their origins. Though she did not attend the 1982 conference, she sent a speech to be read in her absence, which conveyed the similarities that she had found among Lemba, Yemeni, and Ethiopian Jewish traditions.

Taken together, the political stakes and contexts of these two burial images condense the fears that by the 1980s animated the LCA as well as the method that assuaged them. The fears were twofold: that the Lemba as an ethnic group would die away because it was not recognized by the apartheid state and was suppressed by the Venda Bantustan, and that speaking out against Lemba non-recognition and suppression could result in death or detainment. Nabarro's interest, friendship, and research lent the safety of a white advocate, the legitimacy of a researcher's support of Lemba knowledge about themselves, and a new momentum for the LCA to come together through Jewish difference: they were now being taken seriously as Jews by someone who not only had relevant expertise but who was a white, Jewish South African.[23]

Nabarro put the LCA leadership in touch with the chief rabbi in Johannesburg, who also believed their oral history and attended a subsequent LCA conference to tell the Lemba about Judaism as he knew it. She and her husband, Dr. Frank Nabarro, a physicist at the University of the Witwatersrand, also discussed the Lemba with scholars and friends in Israel and in South Africa, including Wits Professor Trefor Jenkins, who then designed and conducted the first Lemba DNA tests in the late 1980s.

Although the LCA's organizing efforts were geared toward becoming recognized as an ethnic group by the apartheid state and, at the very least, as a distinct tribe requiring a separate tribal authority from others in Venda, their successes came instead from scholars and Jews (and Jewish scholars) who began to take them seriously—not just as an ethnic group, distinct from the Venda (despite being Venda speakers), but as ancient Jews who could and should be accepted as Jews, by Jews, because of their commonalities. This was the historical and intellectual context that Professor M. E. R. Mathivha entered into when he became LCA president after Motenda's death. This was what was at stake for Lemba people as genetic ancestry studies appeared as a possible option.

Professor Mathivha's Call for
Scientific Research: Producing Lemba DNA

By the mid-1980s, when Professor Mathivha became LCA president, Lemba leaders had grown increasingly frustrated at the lack of response to their efforts to obtain legal recognition for Lemba chiefs and to consolidate land so that they would not be forced to live under the rule of the Venda and Lebowa homelands. In 1987—the year that, in consultation with the rest of the LCA executive board, he approved the genetic study proposed by Wits geneticist Trefor Jenkins—Professor Mathivha presented a paper at a conference called "Minorities: Self-Determination and Integration." The paper, "The Lemba Characteristics," which was subsequently published (Mathivha 1987), begins as a simple act of naming and claiming existence but immediately segues into a call for objective research: "This paper aims at drawing attention to academics, researchers, anthropologists, congress delegates and all interested people to the fact that the Lembas exist as a tribe and that there is need to study this tribe extensively and objectively" (1). After briefly describing elements of Lemba culture and religion, Mathivha ends his essay with a call for objective research, explicitly identifying it as a corrective for those who misrepresent the Lemba: "Many writers today who are objective are beginning to come nearer the truth about the origin and characteristics of the Lemba as a distinct group. They are beginning to discover some false or unscientific statements that the Lemba are a handful and that they do not and never had their own political organization. It is essential to undertake more research to establish facts without any doubt" (6). By invoking objectivity, truth, and science, this paper laid the groundwork to embrace Lemba DNA as definitive evidence of Lemba difference.

In 2013, more than twenty-five years after Professor Mathivha published his call for scientific research on Lemba origins, his daughter Dr. Rudo Mathivha (then general secretary of the LCA) explained to me why the studies were done and how they mattered for Lemba people. She told me that the initial Jenkins study was approved as a way to "back up" Lemba oral history, and that they were happy with the results (the conclusion of that study was that they have a Semitic link, in part evidenced by their higher statistical affinities with "caucasoid" samples than would be expected for black South Africans). This is why they agreed to a second study, which produced the Cohen Modal Haplotype (CMH) results: they were encouraged that their confidence in science to support their oral history was well placed, and they were interested in the possibility of a study design that could go beyond demonstrating a general Semitic link, the specificity of which had been debated for over a century. She also noted that the CMH study showed that Lemba people had the marker in a higher percentage than any other group of Jews that had been tested, which indicated that the Lemba were the original Jews. For Rudo as for her father, Lemba oral history remained the bedrock of Lemba identity, but the genetic studies built additional scaffolding that shifted the conversation from cataloguing Lemba characteristics to pointing to the body as the evidence of difference.

Co-Constituting Lemba DNA

In November 1987, when Professor Mathivha published his call for scientific research to prove that the Lembas exist, Dr. Trefor Jenkins had just completed his first DNA collection trip to that year's LCA conference at Sweetwaters. Just as Mathivha's interest in the possibility of Lemba DNA emerged from his experience of apartheid, so did Jenkins's interest in conducting this research. By 1987, Jenkins was known not only as a pioneer in the study of genetic polymorphisms and genetic diseases but also as an ethicist opposed to apartheid. He was one of six doctors who successfully petitioned the South African Supreme Court to force the South African Medical Board to conduct a new inquiry into the ethical conduct of the doctors who failed to treat Steve Biko, the founder of the black consciousness movement, after he was beaten by security police in 1977; the same doctors had also falsified records leading up to and after Biko's death.[24]

When I interviewed Jenkins in 2013, he told me that the Lemba study served two purposes: it gave him a chance to be in the field, to collect samples from (and thus interact with) black South Africans at a time when such interracial contact was regulated and therefore difficult, and it allowed him and his students to use new technologies of DNA analysis to contribute to long-standing Lemba efforts to substantiate their oral history. For him, this was an exercise in antiracism, both interpersonally in facilitating black-white interaction, and in terms of lending scientific authority to an unrecognized ethnic group's oral history. So when his colleague Dr. Frank Nabarro—prompted by his wife and her research—mentioned the Lemba to Jenkins over a meal at a Wits University faculty dining club and suggested that a genetic study might settle the doubts about who the Lemba are, Jenkins saw another opportunity to merge his personal ethics with his professional expertise.

It is important to analyze Jenkins's understanding of his work. First, in thinking through the cultural politics of DNA in South Africa, it matters that his research can fit squarely into an economy of extraction of black bodies by white scientists, while he saw it instead as a form of anti-apartheid action of interracial exchange. Second, his enthusiasm for substantiating Lemba self-knowledge with genetics has an interesting parallel with another of his side projects, which began in the 1960s.

In apartheid South Africa, race was a legal category that limited, among other things, where one could live, what livelihood one could pursue, and who could constitute a legal family. Classification boards used a combination of physical and social criteria to determine the legal race of anyone they deemed to be not clearly white (see especially Bowker and Star 1999; Posel 2001). There was an appeals process, and a number of people who wanted to change their classification sought out Jenkins for potential genetic help in supporting their cases. Although his genetic evidence was always thrown out in court, Jenkins nevertheless granted the request of those who asked to be tested. In an interview with Peter Harper, he explained, "We were in a situation where we could help people negotiate some legal hurdle. . . . In all cases, I would write, 'Given the genotypes these data are compatible with Mr. so and so being classified as white, in the South African context'" (Harper 2007, 18). This statement echoes the closing sentence of Jenkins's Lemba study published in 1996, which reads: "The Y-specific genetic findings presented here are consistent with Lemba oral history" (Spurdle and Jenkins 1996, 1132).

Amanda Spurdle and Himla Soodyall were the graduate students who worked with the Lemba samples, Spurdle with Y chromosomes and Soodyall with mtDNA. Soodyall never published her Lemba results explicitly; rather, her findings that Lemba mtDNA did not differ significantly from their black African neighbors were folded into her other published work (Soodyall, Morar, and Jenkins 2002). Spurdle published her Y chromosome Lemba research in 1996, with Jenkins as coauthor. When I interviewed Spurdle in 2013, she echoed Jenkins's enthusiasm about this study but in a way that also critiqued what was then the status quo of genetic research with black South African research subjects. The study, she explained, was significant to her for two reasons. First, unlike others whose blood samples made their lab's work possible, the Lemba explicitly wanted to be studied; she cites this as "the most satisfying study I ever did because I proved what people wanted to know!" Second, whereas most of their previous work seemed to reinforce the idea of distinct racial categories, with cluster charts showing "that all the blacks were on one side and the whites were on another side and the coloureds were halfway in between," the samples of Lemba people who, as a group, were legally classified as black were "in between" as well.

So it was that Lemba DNA came into existence. Here, Lemba and geneticist motivations for co-constituting Lemba DNA were aligned enough to make its existence possible: both desired to substantiate Lemba oral history, and both desired to improve the situation of Lemba people in apartheid South Africa. This study, which by 1997 had put the Lemba on the global Jewish map, took nearly ten years to be published after the samples were collected in 1987 at the LCA conference at Sweetwaters. So while Lemba DNA emerged from apartheid ethnic and racial politics, by the time results were published and television documentaries were produced, apartheid was over. Nevertheless, Lemba DNA as a political-scientific object continued to matter because Lemba ethnic difference continued to matter: it was, for Professor Mathivha, what had mattered the most all along.

Mathivha, Spurdle, Jenkins, Soodyall, and all of the Lemba people who gave their blood to prove the existence of their nation co-constituted Lemba DNA: for the geneticists, Lemba DNA made possible a modified concept of South Africa's apartheid racial order, while for Lemba people, it made possible scientific proof that they exist as a distinct ethnic group. Trefor Jenkins retired in 1997. Amanda Spurdle left genetic ancestry research and South Africa to become a cancer genetics specialist in Australia. Himla Soodyall has emerged as one of the most prominent genetic ancestry researchers in Africa and as a strong advocate of the use of DNA as an archive. In a 2002 essay, "The Human Genome as Archive: Some Illustrations from the South," she and her coauthors argue for "the value of the genome archive in refining and/or testing theories based on historical, anthropological, archaeological, and cultural data" (Soodyall, Morar, and Jenkins 2002, 191). This Lemba study is a central example for their position that social scientists should cultivate an interest in genetic data as a potential archive that can validate their theories, and that geneticists must draw on these other forms of data so that they know what to look for in their archival searches. Meanwhile, Professor Mathivha, Chaplain Masala, and other Lemba leaders incorporated the genetic findings that supported Lemba difference into their existing archives and their ongoing efforts at ethnic recognition.

Lost Tribe? Redefining Lemba Origins after DNA

What do Lemba genetic ancestry and DNA mean when viewed not from the perspective of Jenkins, Spurdle, and Soodyall, nor from that of the coauthors of the Cohen Modal Haplotype study that followed, but rather through the lens

FIGURE 1.5 LCA Chaplain William Masala Mhani as seen in the 2000 Nova special *Lost Tribes of Israel.*

of these Lemba scholarly and political histories and through the narrations of LCA leaders several years after the studies' publication?

When I was introduced to the idea of Lemba ethnic difference in the early 2000s and to members of the Lemba Cultural Association between 2004 and 2006, this difference was presented to me as thoroughly bioethnic. I spent days and sometimes weeks at a time staying in the homes of different LCA leaders. My first day at Chaplain Masala's house began and ended with him placing me in front of his living room television so we could watch documentaries that had been produced about Lemba DNA: a NOVA special called *Lost Tribes of Israel,* produced in 2000 to coincide with the publication of the Cohen Modal Haplotype study, and an episode of a six-part 1997 BBC documentary, *In the Blood* (figures 1.5 and 1.6).[25] For Masala, these documentaries were the ideal point of entry to his extensive archive of Lemba political organizing, because they established simultaneously that Lemba people were distinct and different enough to appear as such on television, and that their difference was supported by science. The Lemba difference, which Masala imagined would make it possible for me to understand Lemba political histories and current LCA and related politics, was biological: embodied, objective, and scientific.

Yet, there was a problem: Masala knew that the Lemba were not a lost tribe of Israel. This was yet another misunderstanding, now popularized by others, that had taken on a life of its own. For example, when I entered a Lemba home

FIGURE 1.6 In this scene from the 2000 Nova special *Lost Tribes of Israel*, Jewish studies professor Tudor Parfitt collects a cheek swab for DNA analysis from LCA president M. E. R. Mathivha.

one day in 2004, my host greeted me with a copy of Magdel le Roux's 2003 book, which represented the latest research on Lemba origins and culture and was titled *The Lemba: A Lost Tribe of Israel in Southern Africa?* "Are we lost?" the man asked rhetorically. To everyone's amusement, he answered his own question with the punchline: "We are not lost! We know exactly where we are!" His joke spoke to the ongoing tension between Lemba assertions about their history and its continual appearance as an unresolved scholarly question about origins, always in need of new methods to produce better answers.

Le Roux's framing of the question of Lemba origins around the idea of lost tribes of Israel has its roots in early 1985, when South African news stories about Operation Moses, the airlift of Ethiopian Jews to Israel, characterized them in this way (*Johannesburg Star* 1985; *Rand Daily Mail* 1985).[26] The first news story linking the Lemba with the tribes of Israel was the very one that Masala initiated in 1982: the headline read, "Tribe of Israel Claim" (Moolman 1982). This was more a play on words, reflecting that the Lemba were advocating for their own tribal authority and also claiming ancestral biblical links, than an assertion that the Lemba were part of any mythologies about the lost tribes of Israel. But by 1986, news writers put the two ideas together and described the Lemba for the first time as a lost tribe of Israel; one article, titled "Are the Lembas of Makanye a Lost Tribe?," framed the issue almost exactly as le Roux did seventeen years later (Bachar 1986; *Drum* 1986).[27] Then Tudor Parfitt, who had already written a book about Operation Moses (1985), published *The Thirteenth Gate: Travels among the Lost Tribes of Israel* (1987). His first book to include the Lemba, it presented them as one among many groups of Africans and Asians whom he characterized as potential lost tribes.

Chaplain Masala's guided viewings of documentaries that celebrated genetic ancestry research in general as much as they did the Lemba as genetic Jews in particular were in a way Professor Mathivha's vision realized. Through the documentaries, Masala presented Lemba difference as genetic difference and genetic difference as a point of entry to Lemba politics. At stake was the need to demonstrate the existence of the Lemba on their own terms, as a political entity in apartheid South Africa. This was clear in Masala's archive, in Mathivha's 1987 paper, and in Motenda's writing three decades earlier. Lemba social and political goals shaped their willingness to engage with researchers, but Lemba authors were then repeatedly compelled to argue against existing misinterpretations of what they and others had shared, both of which were factors that informed Lemba interests in genetic ancestry research.

And so it was that the last thing Masala said to me came in the form of a question. It was August 2013, and he was lying in a bed in a shared room in a small hospital in Makhado, having suffered a stroke two days earlier. I had arrived in South Africa only days before, intending to visit him and others to share copies of my first published article. I had expected to visit him in his home in Sinthumule, where he could add the article to his extensive library of Bibles, biblical encyclopedias, scholarship by and about the Lemba, and original LCA documents stored in file cabinets and in bound scrapbooks in his study. Instead, I became one of a steady stream of visitors by the bedside where he would spend his final days. With my article in his hands and with the hope that I had understood what he had tried to teach me seven years earlier, he asked: "Did you manage to separate the northern and the southern kingdom?" His question was a culmination of a lifetime of research into the specific details of Lemba history, conducted alongside and in conversation with other researchers, Lemba and otherwise, whose obsession with origins above all else demanded Lemba engagement.

Chaplain Masala thus worked to the very end of his long life to research and communicate the history of the Lemba people and to advocate for his vision of this history among the researchers—including me—who had long relied on his and other Lemba people's scholarly, cultural, and historical expertise in their published accounts.

With his final question, Masala was asking if I had perpetuated the narrative that the Lemba were a lost tribe of Israel, part of the northern kingdom destroyed and dispersed by the Babylonians, or if I had more accurately reflected what he had taught me, that the Lemba people instead traced their ancestry to the linked cultural worlds that made up the southern kingdom of Judah and the Yemen-based trade relations that connected Judah and other Arabian kingdoms with those to the west and south on the African continent.

But what did it matter if the Lemba were a lost tribe of Israel, as they were increasingly viewed after the genetic studies, or if they were black Jews, Lemba, or Bashavi, all terms that most Lemba people told me they preferred to "lost tribe"? The discrepancy made a difference rhetorically. Were they the descendants of lost refugees who had become unwillingly separated and forgotten by their people, their knowledge of their history, religion, and culture fading over time, and requiring instruction from others to bring back what they had lost? Or were they descendants of cosmopolitan traders who flourished through their cross-cultural knowledge and connections, using their experience and networks to migrate to more promising southern futures? The former description comes closer to how lost tribes are imagined by those who search for them, while the latter resonates more with how Lemba people most often frame the migration histories that brought them to southern Africa. The discrepancy between "lost tribe" and other preferred terms also made a difference historically and cartographically: descent from the so-called lost tribes would place Lemba origins firmly in the Levant, while their oral history of descent from Yemeni traders provided openings for different Lemba people, depending on their own orientations to race, religion, and history, to locate their ancestors as part of Levantine, African, or Indian Ocean worlds.

Perhaps most important, Chaplain Masala's concern about the distinction between northern and southern kingdoms echoed long-standing Lemba struggles to define themselves against others whose definitions of them constituted varying degrees of epistemic and political erasure.

GENETIC DIASPORA

I met Hilda Mpaketsane in December 2005 at a wedding in a small village in the Greater Sekhukhune district of the Limpopo Province of South Africa. Hilda lived nearby, worked as a cleaner for the local municipality, and was a cousin of the bride, at whose elderly parents' house we were celebrating. It was after dark but still hot out; the ceremony and meal were finished, and music played from speakers set up outside while some danced and others sat in groups drinking cold drinks and beer, both store-bought and home brewed by the bride's mother. Hilda walked up and joined a conversation that I was having in English and Sepedi with a group of women about what it means to them to be Lemba people.

One woman explained to me that she is proud to be Lemba because they are culturally unique and because they are business people. Another said she was told by her parents from when she was very young that the Lemba are part of the Jews. Hilda agreed that they had always known their distinctive history and culture, but she elaborated that it was only recently that they heard that they were the black Jews and that this would connect them to other Jews in the world: "We discovered [it] after the arrival of [Tudor] Parfitt. He was doing the research; he took the saliva. You go to the laboratory. After that he came back and told us, 'You are the Jews, the black Jews in Africa.'" I responded that I am a Jew and asked if that meant there was a relationship between us. She explained, "The research made that relationship—because we didn't discuss that we were the Jews. After [the research] we discovered that we are the Jews."

She was referring to the Cohen Modal Haplotype study: Parfitt had collected saliva samples for it in 1996, the same year that the *American Journal of Human Genetics* published the Spurdle and Jenkins study that first brought the Lemba international media attention (Spurdle and Jenkins 1996; M. Thomas et al. 2000). In the eighteen years between the beginning of these Lemba DNA studies in 1987 and my conversation with Hilda in 2005, much—but not everything—had changed.

In South Africa, and especially in the rural areas where my research took place that had been "homelands" under apartheid, political landscapes had transformed, but economic precarity remained the norm for many, including most of the women with whom I spoke at the wedding. In molecular biology, the mapping projects of genomics had partially given way to postgenomic epigenetic inquiry, rendering these types of studies more peripheral than cutting edge (Abu El-Haj 2007). Internationally and especially in the United States, the study of genetic ancestry had transformed into a robust industry, marketing the idea of scientific certainty to individuals seeking personal connections to their unknown pasts. Among many Ashkenazi Jews, a post-Holocaust aversion to any biological association with Jewishness had given way to an embrace of Jewish genetics.[1] And unlike Hilda's assessment that the genetic research *created* a relationship between Jews and the Lemba, television documentaries produced by the BBC, NOVA, and the History Channel had encouraged an approach to Lemba people as a newly *discovered* lost tribe of Israel. Prompted by this representation, American Jews had traveled to South Africa beginning in the late 1990s to connect with Lemba people on the basis of the presumed commonalities of a shared Jewishness.

By the time I met Hilda, she and many others strongly identified with their knowledge that they were the Lemba people, black Jews who were genetically certified as such. But Lemba concepts of Jewish genetics and diasporic connection do not simply mirror discourses established elsewhere, and Hilda's repetition of Parfitt's message to the Lemba that they are Jews does not necessarily replicate his meaning. Consider, for example, the perspective of another Lemba woman who was part of our conversation. She told me that because I am a Jew, "it means you are a Lemba." How does her framing, reversing which group might be incorporated into the other, challenge ideas of diaspora, DNA, and agency that create an image of the Lemba as a lost tribe of Israel? Brought together by the idea of genetic connection, how do Lemba people and their Jewish interlocutors navigate their different understandings of the biological and cultural commonalities they hope to have with one another? How do divergent genomic knowledges articulate with the politics of belonging and the pursuit of citizenship in South Africa and transnationally? In short, what are the contours of diaspora after DNA?

I frame Hilda's and others' assertions about their identities in terms of knowledge production rather than history or categories such as "genetic Jews" because it was knowledge—both its source and its implications—that was at stake. Following Hilda's insistence that the genetic research made a relationship between Lemba people and Jews, in this chapter I contend that genetic data have enabled a novel way of imagining and enacting diaspora. I use the concept "genetic diaspora" to theorize how new connections, marked by inequality, are tenuously forged through national, racial, and religious differences that are imagined to be the same. Genetic diaspora constitutes an assemblage through which knowledge and belonging are contested.[2] It continually reemerges through new connections that some, but not all, participants experience as the rekindling of old ones.

The television documentaries that publicized the Lemba DNA studies and the subsequent actions sparked by their American and British audiences can be understood as an afterlife of genetic research in the sense that Didier Fassin (2015) uses the "afterlife of ethnography," although here it refers to how others represent and interpret the work of geneticists rather than that of anthropologists. But the genetic afterlives produced by Lemba people like the women with whom I spoke at the wedding are different. These result from Lemba people's own knowledge production, based on their role as the subjects of genetic studies. This chapter considers what happens when these two very different kinds of afterlives intersect. For Lemba people, this intersection is the point where their genetic knowledge articulates with others' concepts of Jewish diaspora.

Recent research has examined the production of genetic diversity, the epistemologies of genetic history, the politics of selling personal genomic ancestry, and the subjectivities of American seekers of such information.[3] Through this work we have learned that geneticists and consumers can hold varied assumptions and come to different conclusions about what genetic ancestry tells us about biology, culture, identity, and history. But what can get lost in a focus on geneticists' questions or the consumer genetic ancestry industry is that genetic ancestry draws on DNA samples collected from people all over the world (Nash 2015; Sommer 2010). These people, too, are part of the ongoing production of genetic knowledge. This chapter therefore offers an alternative reading of the social and political significance of genetic ancestry: it considers encounters between American ancestry seekers and those they imagine as their genetic kin, and it privileges the subjectivities, genetic knowledge practices, and political stakes of the people on the African side of such encounters. Here Lemba people produced genetic afterlives as entangled conversations with others who were themselves making sense of how Lemba DNA might fit within or transform their own Jewish identities and experiences of diaspora.

In the previous chapter, I showed how Lemba intellectual and political history created the conditions of possibility for genetic inquiry into their origins, and how Lemba Cultural Association leaders' goals in pursuing Lemba genetic ancestry only partially overlapped with the goals of the researchers who completed the studies. This chapter considers how Lemba people with varied relationships to the LCA and other forms of Lemba leadership produced genetic knowledge after the Lemba genetic ancestry studies were published, and specifically, how they did so in conversation with a media archive that publicized the research results, with American Jews who subsequently sought connection to the Lemba as genetic kin, and with South African Jews who grappled with what their connections to Lemba people might be.[4] In what follows, I consider the Lemba DNA studies and their subsequent media archive alongside a series of Lemba encounters with South African and American Jews, including me—because in the eyes of many Lemba people, I was present as both a researcher and a Jew. I demonstrate that those implicated in genetic studies transform DNA into a resource that authorizes their own histories and politics of race, religion, and recognition. I argue that DNA and diaspora converge to create new sites of political belonging, ones marked by precarious connections that balance on the production of knowledge and its refusal.

Mapping Lemba DNA, Recapturing Genetic Jews

American Jews and Lemba South Africans have become imagined as two parts of one whole through a series of mediations: the genetic data mediate the possibilities of representation; the Lemba media archive mediates the projected desires of Lemba leaders, filmed researchers, and television hosts; and different Lemba and Jewish interpretations of genetics mediate their desires for and relationships to Jewish diasporic connection. Deborah Heath, Rayna Rapp, and Karen-Sue Taussig (2004) introduced the idea of "genetic citizenship" to describe the blurring of state and civil society and of public and private spheres, evident in the lobbying efforts of parents of children with rare and debilitating genetic diseases.[5] Their idea of genetic citizenship as a new kind of public within a nation-state enables me, by contrast, to examine a public—what I am calling "genetic diaspora"—that is organized through genetics but falls outside of any concrete recourse to states and the claims of citizenship.

For the Lemba men who authorized Trefor Jenkins's and Tudor Parfitt's Lemba genetics studies, South African citizenship was indeed at stake in Lemba DNA. But genetic diaspora instead organizes a public in which hypothetical Israeli citizenship, both undesired and unrealizable by Lemba people, is the issue. Nadia Abu El-Haj calls this phenomenon "diasporic Zionism" (Abu El-Haj 2012, 217; see also Abu El-Haj 2011). Diasporic Zionism names the power of the Israeli state as a point of reference for American Jewish questions about who is a Jew. For Abu El-Haj, American Jewish debates about whether the Lemba should have to undergo Orthodox conversion to be granted citizenship in Israel as Jews, or whether the genetic evidence should be considered "proof" enough, is a central example of diasporic Zionism. The American Jewish use of genetic data to imagine potential Israeli citizenship not for themselves, but for a group of black South Africans whom they mistakenly imagine desire it, underscores a need to revisit the ideological work of diaspora. Genetic diaspora accounts for diasporic Zionism while also leaving as an open question what diaspora means for Lemba people, even as they are claimed for others' diasporic mappings.

The DNA studies newly thrust the Lemba into a transnational spotlight, but the studies' premises were more reiterative than novel. The work built directly on earlier interconnected forms of knowledge production and emerged from already established relationships between researchers and Lemba leaders. Missionaries, ethnologists, Lemba authors and informants, and geneticists and their coauthors had pursued inquiries into Lemba origins for different reasons and with different effects. But all studies about Lemba origins, including those involving DNA, relied on the words and bodies of Lemba informants, and Lemba authors repeatedly asserted their expertise: knowledge production about the Lemba was always multidirectional and interconnected. It was possible for Jenkins in the first case and Parfitt in the second to collect Lemba biological samples because Lemba leaders, who had for decades sought ethnic recognition from the South African state, felt that genetic data could potentially corroborate what they already knew, in a way that might help their cause.

My reading of these studies builds on work in race and genomics that highlights the production and political implications of research involving genetic ancestry. I aim to illustrate that Lemba DNA is not one fixed thing but rather is continually co-constituted, emerging as labeled samples in laboratories and reported findings in published studies and documentaries, and through encounters among Lemba people and between Lemba people and Jews from elsewhere.[6]

Following Duana Fullwiley (2008), I am particularly interested in geneticists' choices about which populations to include in their comparative analyses and how to name them. Fullwiley argues that the racial categories used in genetic research design are not given or fixed; rather, they reflect which social categories are meaningful to researchers (727). These categories will therefore change depending on researchers' objectives; analyzing them suggests the politics of knowledge production at work within a given study. In other words, the comparison categories used in genetic studies must be examined as matters of cultural politics rather than matters of fact.

Categories can be subverted, and Lemba and American Jewish interlocutors alike critically read them against their own knowledge archives. But categories also form consequential points of reference: the categories used in Lemba genetic ancestry research shaped and at times constrained its subsequent circulations and readings. Analyzing these categories therefore serves as a way to make sense of not only the epistemological underpinnings but also the multiple circulations and political effects of genetic ancestry research.[7]

In the Lemba studies, different ideas of race and political belonging converged, positioning the Lemba in two distinct analytic frames. The first compared Lemba genetic samples to "Caucasoid," "Negroid," and "Khoisan" samples and found that a greater percentage of Lemba Y chromosomes had "Caucasoid" than "Negroid" origins (Spurdle and Jenkins 1996). The second study found that Lemba samples were significantly similar to those labeled "Ashkenazic Israelites" and "Sephardic Israelites"; they differed significantly from, among others, samples labeled "Yemeni" and "Palestinian Arab" (M. Thomas et al. 2000).

The Lemba were thus drawn into two distinct racial-political imaginaries that exceeded their own desired test outcomes. In the first study, the categories that researchers used map onto apartheid categories of racially defined citizenship, but they disrupted the idea of known, fixed, and developmentally significant racial difference that formed apartheid's ideological core. The second study, in contrast, implied a measurable difference between Jews and Palestinians, an idea of consequence in Zionist projects (Abu El-Haj 2012). Lemba DNA emerged through these studies as three distinct racial-political objects that nevertheless became unevenly conflated for Lemba people, researchers, and visiting Jews.

The studies' different conclusions, both markedly cautious, were not only conflated in the media archive, they were also transformed—sometimes by coauthors of the studies themselves—into "proof" that the Lemba are a lost tribe of Israel. Consider a 2008 documentary featuring the Lemba produced by the History Channel. Tudor Parfitt narrates:

The Lemba were convinced that they were a lost tribe of Israel. The problem was that no one believed them. They appeared to be completely African. But I discovered a number of mysterious legends and customs that were very un-African. Men from other tribes were not allowed to marry into the Lemba, they refused to eat pigs. . . . They practiced the ritual slaughter of animals with a special knife, and they circumcised their male children at an early age. I had become convinced that the Lemba claim that they were of Jewish origin could be true, . . . but final proof only came when the science of genetics was applied to Lemba oral history. (Kemp 2008)

Parfitt conflates the Lemba DNA of oral history (they were "convinced that they were a lost tribe of Israel"), South African racial categories ("they appeared to be completely African"), and Jewish genetic essentialism (genetics provided final proof that they were of Jewish origin). Furthermore, Parfitt's cited "legends and customs" are the very same noted by missionaries and others as proof that the Lemba might be Jews. The assertion that these practices are un-African tethers culture to place while also erasing African practices of endogamy, food taboos, ritual slaughter, and circumcision.

Here and in other documentaries, two images exist in tension: on one hand, the Lemba are shown as already practicing Jews, and on the other, they are shown as genetic Jews whose knowledge about Judaism is of the past rather than of the present. Through the "lost tribes" discourse, these documentaries traffic in familiar tropes about Africa as spatially and temporally isolated (Fabian 1983). The Lemba are presented as long-forgotten and now-reconnected members of a Jewish diaspora that is at once ancient and contemporary and that has normative histories and traditions that can—indeed, must—be learned in order to facilitate a Jewish "return."

From 1999 to 2002, the American Jewish organization Kulanu attempted to bring about exactly such a return: informed by media reports about the Lemba as a lost tribe of Israel, they sponsored so-called recapture seminars to bring the Lemba "back" to Judaism. Kulanu's choice of name for their activities with the Lemba implied a double meaning: that the Lemba might recapture their Judaism, presumably lost over the years, and that they might be recaptured *for* Judaism, in a spiritual sense as well as a biopolitical one. But the events did not proceed as planned.

Several of the seminars were led by Leo Abrami, an Arizona-based, reform-ordained, "postdenominational" rabbi who had survived Vichy France as a child by disguising himself as Catholic (Abrami 2010). He framed his work as "a mission to the Lemba tribe," part of his larger lifelong mission to return secular Jews, or ones otherwise adrift, to Jewish religious practice.

Rabbi Abrami initially expressed enthusiasm about Lemba recapture, but he suspended his involvement after Lemba leaders included their own Christian prayer services at a weekend session during which Abrami had planned to teach Judaism to Lemba youth. He had imagined that Lemba Christianity was an artifact of colonialism that persisted only because of isolation from Jews, and he was dismayed when confronted with widespread Lemba resistance to giving up their religion.

For Abrami, the Lemba remained lost Jews because they would not commit to learning and practicing Judaism as a religion necessarily distinct from Christianity (Abrami 2010). For their part, Lemba leaders at first enthusiastically welcomed Abrami and others as *emissaries*, there to exchange knowledge and form new connections. But in retrospect, some viewed the seminars as *missionary* encounters instead: they resented the implication that current Lemba practices were not Jewish enough, and most especially the suggestion that if they wanted to be recognized as Jews, they would need to convert to Judaism.

Genetic diaspora, as it emerged through Kulanu's recapture seminars, was full of hope and frustration all around. Lemba DNA prompted seminar teachers to believe that they were saving lost Jews; but while it prompted Lemba leaders to consider Jewish visitors as potential brothers, it also renewed their conviction that their own knowledge about their history surpassed the expertise and understanding of others, missionaries and scientists alike.

Race, Biology, and Culture: Lemba Jewishness Reframed

Initially, three men carefully managed my research with the LCA; I was hosted exclusively by Ephraim Selamolela, who facilitated meetings for me with Samuel Moeti, F. C. Raulinga, and himself. Selamolela presented himself as the third-most expert in Lemba history and culture, after Moeti, who ranked first, and Raulinga, who was second. Moeti at the time served as the LCA's leader and the executive mayor of his municipality. Raulinga had long been the LCA secretary; he was also a member of the state language board and had translated biblical texts into Tshivenda on behalf of the Catholic Church. Selamolela was a successful businessman with the means, the time, and the desire to be a gracious host to me as he had to others in the past. These three men by then had a long history of working with researchers, journalists, and visiting Jews. From them, I learned how LCA leaders had represented themselves to visitors and what lessons from visitors they had found most resonant. The instruction they gave me about Lemba history, genetics, and Jewish connection provided a window into the context and content that had informed the production of knowledge about the Lemba during the previous decade.

Every day for two weeks, I accompanied Selamolela as he drove his truck between his home in a village not far from Makhado and the Bhuba Game Lodge, where the recapture seminars had taken place. The lodge was an event venue and farm that Selamolela built in the 1990s as a resort for American Jews whom he hoped would continue to visit South Africa. "Bhuba" was Selamolela's clan name; his use of it to name his resort was an important part of his marketing strategy that played on presumed American Jewish knowledge about the details of the second genetic study, published in 2000. That study pivoted on the presence within Lemba Y chromosome samples of the Cohen Modal Haplotype (CMH), named for its presence among Cohanim, or Jewish priests. The significant finding was that the CMH was present in seven of the thirteen samples that had been collected from Buba clan members, a rate similar to the 50 percent of self-identified Cohanim found to have the CMH in an earlier study (M. Thomas et al. 2000).

Selamolela's vision for the lodge is an example of the kind of identity-based self-promotion for tourist consumption examined by John and Jean Comaroff (2009) in *Ethnicity, Inc.* Yet the resort was strikingly empty of visiting Jews. Its emptiness raises an important question with a broader significance among economically marginalized groups throughout Africa and elsewhere who have turned to cultural tourism as a means of income generation: What happens when this kind of product is on offer, but nobody is buying? In this case, Selamolela recouped his losses by marketing his lodge to locals as a wedding venue, and much of the surrounding land was a working farm; he also continued to hope for future visiting Jews.

Years later in 2016, I learned of another such venture, this one sponsored by the LCA. I was back in the village where I had met Hilda Mpaketsane ten years earlier, this time for a funeral. I noticed a T-shirt worn by an older woman who was part of the group preparing food for the postfuneral meal. On one side, the shirt said "LCA," with the association's insignia of an elephant encircled by a Star of David; on the other side were the words "Lemba Cultural Village." The next day, I saw a young man—who, at the age of five, had become my adoptive brother when I moved in with his family—pull on a shirt with the same design. I asked him, "Where is the Lemba Cultural Village?" He said, laughing, "No, it is nowhere. There is no village." It seemed that here, too, this form of tourism remained an aspiration, though it served a different role.[8] Instead of aiming to reach visiting Jews, it advertised the LCA to Lemba people who were not already active members.

Selamolela, Moeti, and Raulinga greeted me as a fellow Jew, informed me of plans to build a synagogue, and instructed me at length about Lemba history and culture. The tone of instruction reflected my youth and their status as elders but also my role as researcher and their roles as star informants who had previously appeared on television: Raulinga in particular asked all of his own questions, which he then proceeded to answer. He included references to the Torah and to Hitler, as well as explanations of kosher laws, Lemba endogamy, and Lemba migration into Africa after the destruction of the temple in Jerusalem in 586 B.C.E. Through this instruction, I was assumed to be already enacting a Jewish connection with these three Lemba men, and I was also prompted to extend that sense of connection outward in both directions so that it was not just between myself and the three of them, but between all Jews and all of the Lemba.

This was genetic diaspora in its Lemba institutional emergence: as Raulinga explained to me, people do not become Lembas by circumcision, language, religion, or their place of residence. Rather, people become Lembas by blood, which for him slipped easily into DNA. He explained, "DNA will show you who you are. That is blood. At least 50 percent of the Lemba genes are of Jewish blood. . . . We had the test. We are one. The Jews have said openly color is not the issue; it is the blood." His message was clear: we shared the same blood and the same DNA, and therefore, regardless of ritual, linguistic, religious, geographic, or phenotypic differences, we were one. The ground of our common Jewish identity was DNA, understood as shared blood, while everything else was variable.[9]

The extent to which I was implicated in ideas of a physical, essential Jewish connection perplexed me. This was partially because my own personal trajectory, as a transgender person and a feminist, had led me to embrace ideas of antiessentialism and indeterminacy. It was also because I knew that the Y chromosome tests that were the basis of our supposed genetic commonality could not include me personally, nor most women, Jewish, Lemba, or otherwise; I worried that this devalued and obscured women's histories.[10]

At the recapture seminars, Rabbi Abrami had raised different concerns about Y chromosomes. He noted that modern Jews determine descent from the mother, but Lemba Jewish DNA was derived from men only. His position was that because Lemba Y chromosome genetic proof of Jewish ancestry necessarily could vouch for only male descent, it could not, in and of itself, confer Jewish status to contemporary Lemba people, who therefore should be persuaded to undergo formal conversion. For LCA leaders, this was not only insulting, but ahistorical. As Rudo Mathivha, daughter of past LCA president Professor M. E. R. Mathivha, who was herself LCA general secretary beginning in 2013, put it, "In my community it's a patrilineal descent. If you go back to the Torah it was patrilineal until the rabbis and the sages and whatever decided to make it matrilineal." This, she told me, is how she responds to white South Africans who invariably question her when she attends Johannesburg synagogues, and she had the same frustration with Abrami, other visiting Jews, and especially researchers who would look at these kinds of differences as a reason to call Lemba Jewishness into question.

Susan Kahn's (2000) work on assisted conception in Israel offers a case in point that descent-based definitions of Jewishness are historically contingent and changeable. Kahn explains that the emergence of assisted reproduction in Israel has resulted in new Halakhic distinctions between blood and birth as the source of matrilineal Jewishness. In contrast to Rabbi Abrami's genetic essentialism that called into question Lemba Jewishness because their Jewish genetic markers were not matrilineally inherited, the new Halakhic distinction in Israel asserted that Jewishness is conferred at birth when one is born to a Jewish mother, regardless of the Jewish or non-Jewish status of the egg donor. In other words, like the research subjects of genetic ancestry studies based on the Y chromosome, so too would Jews born through this form of assisted reproduction lack genetic evidence of maternally inherited Jewishness.[11]

The significance of descent-based Jewishness in Israel and among Lemba South Africans differed. As an ethnonationalist state, the priority in Israel is to maintain a Jewish demographic majority regardless of a perceived scarcity of gametes generated by Jewish people. But for LCA leaders like Raulinga and Mathivha, the first concern was asserting the autonomy of their own definitions of Jewish peoplehood over those that developed elsewhere for reasons that had nothing to do with them. Their definitions drew not on Halakha, filtered through Israeli anxieties, but on a Toraitic (rather than a rabbinic) understanding of descent, augmented by a blood essentialism that could encompass all Lemba people, even though it followed specifically from the DNA of Lemba men.[12]

In addition to questions of gender, I wondered: If our supposed point of connection dated back twenty-five hundred or three thousand years, as the Cohen Modal Haplotype hypothesized, why not five thousand years, or ten thousand? For me, diasporic time as it was enacted through genetic data fell off the grid of intelligibility. But just as Rudo Mathivha reframed the gender of genetic Jewishness, other LCA leaders reframed the timescale of genetic diaspora in a way that also reassessed the origins, content, and authenticity of the concept of Jewish diaspora that informed the genetic studies and documentaries.

Moeti, for example, told me that all the original Jews had been black, and that intermarriage had turned European Jews white. M. J. Mungulwa, then an executive board member and later LCA president from 2012 until his death in 2018, explained to me that the Lemba are "original Jewish, not nowadays for the changing things for the reform and the Christianity and the orthodox. . . . We're African Jewish, because all Jews are from Africa, even the white. . . . We're not the same as the white Jew because we don't change; we stick on the law!" In this framing, the Lemba sustained Jewish ancestral pasts, and Reform Judaism, Orthodox Judaism, and Christianity were equally divergent; it was not the old that needed to be brought up to date, but the new that needed to reconnect with what had been lost over time.

Ephraim Selamolela inverted Mungulwa's ideas of race and Jews. He was deeply invested in Judaism and in Israel, and for him, our supposed genetic connections were also racial. He told me that Jews were white, and because we shared the same blood, he was also white, despite his dark skin. He enjoyed immensely having greater economic success than the white Afrikaners from whom he could demand service when we went to town to buy groceries or plants for the farm, and on several occasions he took my hand as he told these white workers, "Look, he is my son; he is my white son." In this way, he conflated whiteness, Jewishness, wealth, and power.

In our time together, Selamolela made a point of eating only at Nando's and not at KFC because the chicken at Nando's was halal, which he explained was just the same as kosher. Over meals, he told me about his childhood under apartheid as a laborer on white-owned farms, and that everything he had he had built himself through becoming a businessman. Like many other Lemba people who told me that being Lemba meant being successful in business—although many of these same people worked as miners, cleaners, teachers, or nurses or lived entirely on government pensions—Selamolela felt that his Jewish ancestry was directly responsible for his business acumen. He linked this explicitly to DNA: he explained that he was successful because he was part of the Bhuba clan, which meant he had "the best gene" (the Cohen Modal Haplotype).

Selamolela's pride in possessing "the best gene" is, in two ways, an unexpected outcome of the DNA tests in which he participated. Nadia Abu El-Haj argues that in the view of its practitioners, genetic history reinterprets the relationship between biology and culture: instead of culture being biologically determined, biology inadvertently retains historical evidence (Abu El-Haj 2012). But Selamolela inverted the studies' underlying logics of biology and culture by attributing his business success to genetic predisposition associated with his Jewishness: not a matter of culture or choice but rather an incontrovertible fact. He also took personal pride in his result from a test that aimed to determine population frequencies rather than individual genetic profiles. His understanding of the test's purpose and the implication of the results demonstrates that the reception and interpretation of genetic data by specific audiences can significantly alter their meaning.

The biological and cultural commonalities that these Lemba leaders expected to have with me included a blood connection that demonstrated either our common black African ancestry or our common Jewish whiteness. Despite this divergence, I was widely assumed to share whichever Jewish cultural attributes or practices each Lemba person held personally important, whether business success, Torah and prayer, or not eating pork. In our interactions, I felt claimed through genetic diaspora by LCA leaders and others as a former African who had over time become racially and religiously less authentic, although I was still connected to them by blood, which in turn defined me as part of a Lemba nation in South Africa, especially to the extent that I could learn about and know Lemba culture.

This point about me learning Lemba culture, as opposed to the idea that they should learn Jewish religion, was the unintended result of the recapture seminars. These encounters had prompted a serious rethinking and a formal decision about the relationship between being a Lemba and being Jewish. By 2005, most LCA members referred to the partially built "synagogue" as the "cultural center," and the LCA had issued an executive decision separating out religion from what it meant to be a Lemba, concepts that documentaries and visiting Jews had conflated. The decision was entered into the LCA minutes as follows: "It was agreed that Lembas are a Nation and not a religion. The Lembas may belong to different religions, but are unified by their culture."[13]

This decision hinged on the need to reaffirm Lemba ideas about religion, culture, and nation through the LCA, so as to not alienate the very people whose consolidation was the reason for the organization's existence. The LCA stance of one culture, many religions inverted the logics of one religion, many cultures that motivated Lemba inclusion among Jews invested in genetic ideas of Jewish diaspora. As they brought me into *their* production of genomic knowledge, they also inverted the flow of knowledge production: no longer the recipients of others' expertise, they expected me to circulate their own.

Political theorist and Jewish studies scholar Marla Brettschneider argues that approaches to Lemba Jewishness that emphasize a need for education to learn how to be Jews are colonial and racist impositions that presuppose what Jewishness and Judaism are according to a normative rabbinic definition that excludes African Jews. For Brettschneider, Jewish diversity needs to be rethought, not just in relation to race and culture, but also in relation to the status of nonrabbinic Jewish practice. Ultimately, she believes, the point is to rethink Jewishness and Judaism in Africa in a way that centers the black majority of African Jews, and that takes their religious and cultural innovations seriously and on their own terms instead of as a litmus test to prove or disprove their Jewish authenticity (Brettschneider 2015).

Overlapping with Kulanu's recapture seminars, and as the LCA was beginning to see the necessity of officially redefining Jewishness as nation and culture and explicitly not as religion, one American Jewish researcher, Deborah Grenn-Scott, embarked on such a project. Inspired by an episode of *60 Minutes* that explained the Lemba CMH genetic study and featured Rudo Mathivha's commentary (figure 2.1), she designed her research as a feminist investigation of comparative Judaism among Lemba women and Jewish women in the United States who variously identified as Reform, Conservative, Orthodox, secular, cultural, and goddess Jews. Genetic ancestry was the basis of the Lemba-Jewish connection that Grenn-Scott hoped to find. But for her, DNA was a starting point for learning about Jewish *religious* diversity alongside Jewish racial, cultural, and historical diversity. She ultimately interviewed fifty-five Lemba women aged fifty to over ninety, mostly in group interviews, with Rudo Mathivha as a coresearcher and interpreter.

I position Grenn-Scott similarly to how I position myself in this chapter: as a researcher with distinct questions and arguments, but also as a Jew whose encounters with Lemba people must be read ethnographically as an example of genetic diaspora.[14] Her encounters provide an important counterpoint to my own. Whereas my interest in genetic afterlives pushed me to engage with those most invested in Lemba DNA and to learn from Lemba people what *they* felt was the basis of our potential connection, her interest in pushing the boundaries of feminist and antiracist Judaism and her investment in not being a missionary pushed her to foreground a Jewish religious pluralism and to seek out a wider range of Lemba women for group discussions and interviews about their own ritual and religious practices.

Although she was inspired by the Lemba DNA tests to think of them as fellow Jews, Grenn-Scott disregarded the publicized conclusions that emphasized

FIGURE 2.1 Dr. Rudo Mathivha as seen in a 2000 segment of 60 *Minutes* that featured Lemba genetic links to Jews.

a three-thousand-year-old origin of the Cohen Modal Haplotype and therefore an origin in ancient Israel. Instead, she expanded questions into evolutionary time and the African origins of all humans (Grenn-Scott 2002, 1–4). Upon arrival in South Africa, she interviewed LCA president Professor Mathivha. Among other things, he told her that the Lemba had originated in Africa before returning there after migrating to Judea (6). For him this was a historical statement about the specific Lemba past and not a statement about the African origins of all people. But it reinforced Grenn-Scott's reframing of the timescale of Lemba-Jewish ancestral connection: "I thought much about the line that might have been traced out of Africa to Mesopotamia and Palestine and back to Africa, and wondered where the biblical Abraham and Moses fit into this picture" (115). For Grenn-Scott, thinking about Jews in human evolutionary time rather than biblical or Zionist time coincided with a deep questioning of the boundaries not just of *Jewishness* but of *Judaism*. She asks, "What is Judaism? What is it *not?*" (160).

In her interviews with Lemba women, Lemba DNA and human evolutionary time dissolved all religion, ritual, and spiritual practice into an African Judaism, even when the women did not connect to the African ideas and practices that captivated Grenn-Scott. When she asked one group if they had stories about or spiritual connections with the python, some explained that the snake is a bad omen, while others offered that its fat can be used to heal burns. But one of the women pushed back, asking why she was posing the question and why she attached significance to the python. Grenn-Scott explained that the snake is thought of as God in Yoruba culture, that she had read about a

Venda python mythology, and that she saw the snake as a female sacred symbol linked to menstruation. She was sharply rebuked. Rudo Mathivha, as her coresearcher, translated one woman's objection: "She says it's rubbish!" As the women laughed, Mathivha translated further: "She said that [people who] believe that the snake is a sign of renewal and rebirth and has supernatural powers do not know God and that's why they believe that" (Grenn-Scott 2002, 240–241). The Lemba women's rejection of Grenn-Scott's Africa-centered Jewish universality was at once an affirmation of the specificity of their own spirituality and a pointed reminder that pan-African identification was but one way for African people to understand themselves.

Grenn-Scott was looking for African roots for Judaism in a universal sense of Africa as the root of humanity. But for her Lemba interlocutors, Africa was neither universal nor undifferentiated. Still, Grenn-Scott understood as Jewish by definition Lemba practices that resembled other African traditions, and she had a growing conviction that the answers to her spiritual questions could be found in Africa. She was especially moved by the LCA conference at Sweetwaters, which she attended in 2000. By then, a foundation and a metal open-air structure had been built, and it was the lack of walls that she found most powerful. The beautiful views and the open air evoked for her what it might have been like in the ancient temple in Jerusalem, and she believed she was witnessing "an African Judaism, a powerful combination of diverse religious and cultural elements" (Grenn-Scott 2002, 208). But while Sweetwaters and the LCA conference are indeed central to Lemba becoming in South Africa, their significance cannot be reduced to an idea of religion or the sacred. Though an African-centered Jewishness resonated for many Lemba people, Africa—like DNA—was multivalent. For Grenn-Scott, Africa was both universal origin and juxtaposition to the forms of Judaism with which she was most familiar. For Professor Mathivha, it was *historical* origin and point of reference in connecting Lemba people to Jews around the world, even while he was keenly aware of the tensions present for Lemba people in embracing an overarching Africanness while also seeking specific ethnic differentiation from other black South Africans. And for the women who pushed back against the idea that Venda or Yoruba python mythology might resonate with them as part of their Jewish religious or cultural repertoire, it was God and not Africa that could best be understood as universal.

Genetic diaspora for Grenn-Scott was a profound self-transformation inspired by her experiences of Lemba practice. Her starting point had been that she and Lemba women had Jewish genetics and religion in common, but over time she became less invested in the idea that their religious commonalities needed to be understood as "Jewish" per se to be spiritually significant. Eventually, her research question shifted away from one in which multiple Judaisms challenged a singular one to "how do we *all* connect with God?" (Grenn-Scott 2002, 338). At the same time, she remained committed to the idea that the Lemba should fundamentally be understood as Jews. She rejected a *religious* essentialism in which there are correct and incorrect ways to practice Judaism in favor of an expansiveness that, in the end, relied on a *biological* essentialism through which Lemba people had the same authority to shape Jewish practice as did other Jews. As she puts it, "If Jewish women are doing it, it becomes a Jewish ritual" (308).

And for the Lemba women? In spite of their skepticism about some of what Grenn-Scott noted as spiritually significant, they did share with her their own practices and rituals, and one group even asked her to join them in prayer at the close of their time together. Their encounters reinforced for these women that visiting Jews would regard religion as the basis of their commonality. But Grenn-Scott's feminism, openness, and affinity for the idea of Africa as the root of Judaism and her pre-Judaic spiritual inheritance also introduced the possibility that Judaism could be definable on their own terms, and with them at the center.

Not Diasporic Enough to Be a Jew in South Africa

I finally met Rudo Mathivha in April 2006, at a Passover seder at the Johannesburg home of a white Jewish South African couple, a historian and her husband, a medical doctor. The historian, whom I had met at the University of the Witwatersrand, had invited me as a way of providing welcome to a Jew away from home. Her husband had invited Mathivha, his colleague at Chris Hani Baragwanath Academic Hospital, where she was chief specialist of critical care medicine. Dr. Mathivha was the only Lemba person there and the only black participant in the seder. She and I were seated beside each other and across from another historian.

Ostensibly a religious occasion, a Passover seder can be many other things as well: it is often a central site of Jewish cultural and political commonality as well as disagreement.[15] A seder lends itself to an intimate and interactive format in which differences in what are considered "traditional" practices and foods can be animatedly discussed and debated. On this occasion, we compared knowledge of eastern European Jewish traditions that would have been shared among the recent common ancestors of my hosts and me one to three generations back with our own experiences of recent South African and

American adaptations, and with Mediterranean and Middle Eastern variations that we knew about or had experienced.

Throughout, Mathivha stayed silent. Eventually, the historian sitting across from us asked her directly about Lemba Passover traditions. She explained that Lemba people do not have a tradition of Passover, which led to more questions about other holidays and other practices. The discomfort in the room was palpable. The white South African Jews eagerly anticipated a point of traditional commonality, different in variation, but nevertheless recognizably the same. As Mathivha's answers to each question failed to deliver the commonality they hoped for, the questions shifted to more open-ended ones about what traditions and practices the Lemba *did* have.

These questions were directed to both of us—to her as the native informant and to me as the researcher—and they began to feel more like demands to explain why the Lemba should be included as Jews than had the earlier questions, which had incorrectly anticipated that such inclusion would be obvious in Mathivha's answers. In the end, we both pointed out the Lemba traits that had been noted as potentially Jewish by writers since the nineteenth century, the same traits that Parfitt would later call attention to as un-African in his 2008 documentary: circumcision, ritual slaughter of animals, and endogamy.

For the progressive white South African Jews at this Passover seder, the biological essentialism of genetic links could only be suspect because it evoked apartheid racial ideologies, so they sought other forms of connection in common traditions, practices, and culture. But when they did not find it, they were left with a reinforced binary in which Jewish and African were opposed categories, the former diasporic and the latter indigenous. The seder continued, but it seemed to me that people were left thinking that while Mathivha herself might have become a Jew, larger Lemba claims were dubious. Ironically, it was the fame of the Lemba as genetic Jews that created a situation in which other Jews expected to find commonality, and that resulted in new doubts about the legitimacy of Lemba Jewishness. This was quite different, however, from Rabbi Abrami's recapture seminar disappointments. Where he hoped to convert, the South African Jews at the seder hoped only to connect. Similarly, however, his efforts at conversion and theirs at connection demanded from Lemba people that their Jewishness be recognizable on terms that were not their own.

Lemba leaders have grown accustomed to answering questions from Jews hoping for connection and from others who doubt that the Lemba really are Jews. Two months after the Passover seder I was at an LCA meeting where Raulinga, in his capacity as secretary, read a letter asking permission to interview LCA members for a new documentary. The letter included a list of questions that the filmmakers, in this case black South Africans with non-Lemba ties to the predominantly Venda-speaking region of the Limpopo Province, intended to pose: "What is a definition of a Jew? How do the Lembas fit in that description? Where do Jewish people originate? When did they have their first contact with the African continent? What culture and observances did the ancient Jews share with the ancient Africans? How does modern Judaism differ from traditional African religion? Have you been able to establish a kibbutz?"

Lemba people get such questions from all directions: from American and Israeli Jews who have a specific idea of what kinds of Jewish experience, belief, or observance Lemba people must demonstrate before they are willing to accept them as fellow Jews, from white South African Jews who cannot imagine that black South Africans might be kin in this way, and from black South Africans who are suspicious of Lemba ethnic identity. Some Venda people, for example, see the Lemba as an occupational subgroup of the Venda and think that Lemba assertions about being Jews are false. Some even feel that such claims are politically reactionary because of the ways that they articulated with apartheid logics of cultural difference, or because of assumptions that by declaring themselves to be Jews, Lemba people are really claiming to be white.

The accusatory tone of the questions in the letter did not register with everyone at the meeting, but it did with some. One man perceived that they were designed to elicit answers that would pointedly demonstrate that the Lemba were not so very Jewish after all, and he resented the persistence of demands that the Lemba prove they were really Jews. Knowing that the LCA had authorized several documentaries in the past, he was concerned that those at the meeting might vote to grant the requested permission, so he stood to address them and said, "You know what? We're being *exploited*. . . . Don't you think, people, that your story has been told? Aren't you tired of that?"

The issue was tabled, but soon he stood again, interrupting the next agenda item. He pointed to me and declared forcefully, "An Ashkenazi Jew expects himself to be like him. He won't even give you a chance. . . . In the end, they end up telling you that no, Judaism is like *this*. It's not the way *you* understand Judaism. *Our* Judaism is the *right* Judaism. The creator is *our* creator. The one you believe in is *not* the right one. . . . That's why I say our story has been told."

His objections to the research questions slipped into his frustrations about the barriers he had faced as a Jewish-identified Lemba man, and specifically the accusations he had endured from white Jews like me that his Jewish identity was measurable only on their terms. The exclusion that he evoked echoed the one that was politely but definitively enacted at the Passover seder.

Lucas Thobakgale, a Lemba Cultural Association elder who for much of his life has been an active recruiter into the organization, also grew frustrated at these kinds of exclusions. While attending a conference in San Francisco put together by Be'chol Lashon, a Jewish multicultural organization similar to Kulanu, he stood during a session and asked the mostly American organizers and attendees if they spoke Hebrew; most did not. This proved to him that despite their presumptions, they had no more claim to defining Jewishness than he did. On another occasion, at a meeting between Johannesburg's chief rabbi and a small group of LCA delegates, Thobakgale asked him,

> When you grew up as a youngster in your home, you had Lemba men working in the kitchen or the garden. . . . Did you ever invite them to your ceremonies . . . or were they there just as workers serving the visitors tea? . . . There was a very big accident in the history of life, especially in the South African context when your great-grandparents migrated into South Africa, [and] they were classified as white. It was a privileged position, isn't it? . . . You can't escape your privilege to accommodate someone who is not within your circle, who is being excluded. . . . Maybe if they had been classified as nonwhite the state of us would have been different.

It was precisely in these moments of attempted connection across racial difference that the obstacles to a South African Jewish diaspora inclusive of Lemba experience and knowledge were acutely evident.

In his book *Global Diasporas*, Robin Cohen ([1997] 2008) explains that people demonstrate their membership in a diasporic community "by an acceptance of an inescapable link with their past migration history and a sense of co-ethnicity with others of a similar background," and the Jews are his paradigmatic case (ix). But diasporic belonging for Lemba people is more complicated than simply demonstrating their membership, and it is precisely the issues of migration history and coethnicity that prompt others' exclusions. Lemba migration history follows a different trajectory than that of others who see themselves as Jews, resulting in a lack of common history and traditions. And despite what the genetic tests might imply about the essentialism of Jewish ethnicity, white Jews and black Jews in South Africa did not have a similar background because of the dominance of racial categories in shaping their histories and lives.

When it came down to it, the practices that Rudo Mathivha and I had mentioned as the basis of Lemba Jewish links—circumcision, ritual slaughter of animals, and endogamy—are not the primary points of identification for Ashkenazi Jews, and they are also not exclusive to Jews. These same traits had also been used to interpret Lemba identity as African, as Muslim, or as both of these in combination. In 1908, missionary ethnologist Henri A. Junod puzzled over these very same traits, which he considered to be "Semitic," and how they had taken hold among the Lemba, whom he considered to be "natives." He concluded that the Lemba were an African tribe who had "been submitted to Semitic influences . . . in the contact with Moslems of unknown regions" (Junod 1908, 282). Junod's reasoning set up a dichotomy that echoes still in the critiques of those who doubt Lemba Jewish histories: since they could have been Muslims and they seemed to be Africans, then they could not really be Jews.

The Exchange of Knowledge and Its Refusal

The recapture seminars had ended in 2002. Ultimately LCA leaders had rejected what they viewed as coercive efforts by others to define for the Lemba how to be Jewish, rather than those others learning new meanings of Jewishness from Lemba people. Unable to accept the LCA's approach to Judaism, Kulanu moved on to work with other Lemba people in Zimbabwe who were more amenable to formal conversion and to sending young people to Israel to train as rabbis and Jewish educators.[16] But occasional American Jewish visitors continued to attempt to connect with Lemba people in South Africa on the basis of assumed religious commonality. One such visitor was Roby Simons, who had grown up as a member of the American Conservative Movement and many years later became Modern Orthodox. Roby had heard about the Lemba DNA tests, as well as about other Jewish genetic studies, and he thought that they proved his own and the Lembas' irrefutable and essential Jewishness, and therefore their diasporic connection.

In 2005, Roby and I were both in South Africa conducting research funded by Fulbright. He had heard about my project and asked to visit one of my field sites. I was reluctant, but when I mentioned the possibility, people expressed interest.

At the time, I was following the chieftaincy struggles of Kgoshi Mpaketsane: the South African state had long refused to acknowledge his status as a traditional leader, and he had just submitted his claim to a newly convened commission for traditional leadership disputes (see chapter 3). Kgoshi Mpaketsane was one of the 136 Lemba men who had offered a DNA sample to researchers in 1996, and his recent submission included several published accounts of the Lemba as genetic Jews, including the first DNA study (Spurdle and Jenkins 1996). He included the article with the rest of his claim because he believed that proof of Lemba biological difference would support his contention that they were culturally distinct from their neighbors, and therefore necessarily subject to their own traditional leader. Since the only legally recognized traditional leader was not Lemba, he reasoned that acknowledgment of Lemba difference would compel the South African government to support his position.

During his visit, Roby asked many people about Lemba Jewish practices and beliefs, and in turn he shared his own. When it became clear that most people were members of the Zion Christ Church, Roby pointed out that Jews do not believe in Jesus—but unlike Rabbi Abrami, he did not dwell on it. Instead, he instructed, both verbally and by example. His two-day visit involved frequent conspicuous prayer. Roby traveled with his prayer book, yarmulke, tallis, and tefillin.[17] He prayed outside, chanting softly in Hebrew and swaying back and forth while the chickens, goats, and dogs ran around him and people stared and wondered. Many asked me about it later, because they knew I was a Jew like him (white, American, and presumably religious); they hoped I might be able to explain his prayer, wondered if I prayed similarly, and considered his presentation against their own religious practices.

Roby's visit culminated with his encounter with Kgoshi Mpaketsane. Roby wanted to hand-deliver the leather-bound Torah that he had brought as a gift and to demonstrate directly to Kgoshi Mpaketsane, as the resident Lemba authority, how to properly pray as a Jew. When he discussed kosher laws, Kgoshi Mpaketsane interjected that they already knew about the subject and that he had written about it in his application to the government for recognition. When Roby explained that at the time of a boy's bar mitzvah, when he is thirteen, "for a while he's a chief, he's the leader," Kgoshi Mpaketsane seemed a bit put out, since his entire adult life had been dedicated to securing that status for himself. But he let it pass. And when Roby put on his tallis and yarmulke, wrapped his tefillin, and started to pray, Kgoshi Mpaketsane chuckled uncomfortably (figure 2.2).

For Roby, the Lembas' genetic Jewishness was a point of departure, leading into Judaism. Identifying with the Lemba, he imagined that they might choose to become observant, much as he had in his own adult life. But Kgoshi Mpaketsane and most other Lemba South Africans considered Jewishness something they *had*, not something they had to prove, choose, or learn: DNA had simply reinforced their certainty. Many people in the village and elsewhere, including Kgoshi Mpaketsane, had told me that they were *Bajuta amaso* (black Jews). But their politics of identity and ethnicity were not primarily directed at recognition of Jewishness, and their Jewishness was not principally understood as a

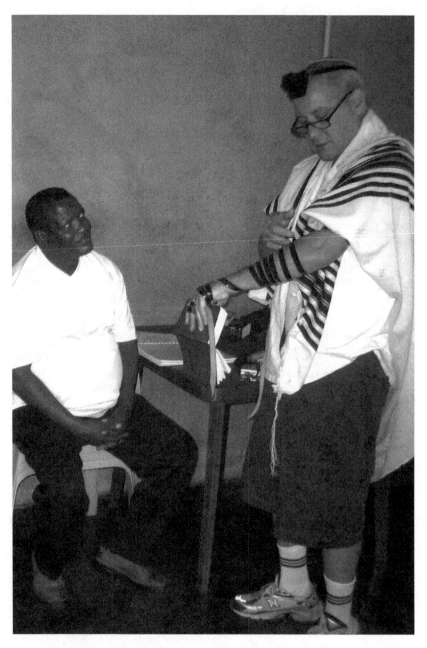

FIGURE 2.2 Roby Simons illustrates Jewish prayer for Kgoshi Mpaketsane while the latter looks on. Photograph by author.

religion. Although Roby's religious instruction failed to resonate with Kgoshi Mpaketsane, the American left the encounter feeling connected, and Kgoshi Mpaketsane left feeling properly recognized because of the gift, though disconnected from Roby's idea of Jewishness.

Their meeting illustrates how much must be overlooked in terms of religious practice, political goals, and identity for American Jews and Lemba South Africans to experience connection as two parts of one Jewish whole. Furthermore, since this was something Roby experienced but Kgoshi Mpaketsane did not, it demonstrates that one person's experience of disconnection could go completely unrecognized in another's experience of profound connection from the same encounter.[18] The sense of connection that did occur hinged on both men affirming their own and each other's positions as leaders—Roby as prayer leader, and Kgoshi Mpaketsane as traditional leader. Roby's leadership was affirmed through Kgoshi Mpaketsane's polite, though ultimately detached, attention, and Kgoshi Mpaketsane's leadership was affirmed through Roby's Jewish presence in his home and its potential to uphold his cultural difference. Ultimately, their connection proved to be contingent on a precarious balance between the exchange of knowledge and its refusal. Each offered the other his knowledge of who they together are as a people, and in turn each disregarded what did not resonate.

Locating Jewish Diaspora in Israel and Africa

The Lemba "Lost Tribes of Israel" episode of the History Channel's show *Digging for the Truth* is framed by two overarching and interwoven concepts of diaspora, one old and the other more recent: the storyline begins with the biblical narrative of the dispersal of the ten northern tribes of Israel in the eighth century B.C.E., and its climax is an explanation of the Lemba Cohen Modal Haplotype genetic test. In the episode, these two concepts of diaspora converge: the test results are ultimately the proof that demonstrates the ancient dispersal; this convergence brings the Lemba into a larger category of "the Jewish diaspora." Indeed, when the show's host, Joshua Bernstein, asks historian Hillel Halkin if the lost tribes of Israel were the first Jewish diaspora, he answers simply, "Yes."

This larger category, the Jewish diaspora, emerges in the episode as a normative descriptor for an entity that began in biblical times, that accounts for and links together all Jews in the world, and that pivots on identification with the contemporary nation-state of Israel. For example, in one of the first scenes of the episode, Bernstein, an American Jew, searches for and finds the graves of his grandparents and great-grandparents in the Mount of Olives cemetery in Jerusalem. As he places stones on their graves, he says, "This means something to me. There's a connection for me that speaks to what the significance of heritage is. And for the Lemba, I understand why they might be interested in claiming some sort of historical identity with Jerusalem." The slippage here between Jewish diaspora and an identification with Jerusalem comes across as a self-evident connection. Bernstein's physical presence in a Jerusalem graveyard that holds the remains of his own recent ancestors seamlessly merges the political-historical reality of Jerusalem as part of the Israeli nation-state with meanings of Jerusalem that are mythical and symbolic, effectively presuming a universal Jewish significance of the former while eclipsing the possibility of a sole identification with the latter or a lack of identification with Jerusalem altogether.

As the host of *Digging for the Truth*, Bernstein must compellingly insert himself into all of the episodes. But because he highlights his own Jewish identity as well as his interactions with Lemba people at the 2004 LCA annual conference, I view the episode both as an example of genetic diaspora in action that can be read ethnographically and as a dominant text in communicating to American Jews what the content of their connection to the Lemba should be.

The LCA conference is the most widely attended gathering of Lemba people. In fact, the rationale for the existence of the Lemba Cultural Association, made literal at their annual conference, is that Lemba people are scattered and must be gathered together. In this sense, the LCA is a diasporic organization—but what it organizes is a Lemba diaspora in Southern Africa, not a Jewish diaspora all over the world.

While many Lemba people appear in the episode as conference speakers, performers, or audience members, only two actually speak on camera. Samuel Moeti, in his capacity as acting president of the Lemba Cultural Association, is interviewed by Bernstein as they walk around the conference grounds, and M. J. Mungulwa, longtime LCA leader and future LCA president, is filmed while addressing the gathered audience during the conference's formal presentation. Moeti tells Bernstein, "The Lembas are the original Hebrews, and they were scattered as you know, and they crossed into Africa. So they were scattered all over. So in South Africa, in many parts of South Africa, you'll find the Lembas who are actually Hebrews. . . . We always believed that the Jewish people who live all over the world are our brothers, because we come from the same root" (figure 2.3). Moeti's explanation of the tie between the Lemba and the idea of Jewish diaspora privileges the notion that the Lemba people are

FIGURE 2.3 In this still from the History Channel's *Digging for the Truth* episode "Lost Tribes of Israel," host Joshua Bernstein speaks with LCA president Samuel Moeti.

"the original Hebrews," that in the past they were scattered, and that there is a lateral connection between them and "the Jewish people who live all over the world," which is based on a past point of common origin.

Mungulwa speaks only briefly and seems to reiterate Moeti's ideas of diaspora; however, there is a twist. In the final scene of the episode, he says to the crowd, microphone in hand, "Brothers and sisters, we are here. We are not lost; we are scattered. We are original Hebrews." The shot is framed so that he appears to be addressing not only the crowd but the camera, and therefore the television audience (figure 2.4). In keeping with the rest of the episode's narrative, American Jewish viewers in particular can imagine themselves as the "brothers and sisters" to whom he is speaking, and they can take his insistence that the Lemba are not lost, and that they are the original Hebrews, as confirmation that these Jews have now been found, although their Judaism is of the past rather than the present. Yet in the context of the conference, Mungulwa's brothers and sisters are not Jewish people who live all over the world but rather the Lemba people gathered before him. His insistence on presence and his rejection of the discourse of lost tribes ("we are not lost; we are scattered") reframes the ideas of diaspora that dominate the narrative of the episode's producers and editors and that have prompted Jews to seek out the Lemba. This reframing, however, is not necessarily legible to all audiences.

FIGURE 2.4 M. J. Mungulwa addresses his audience at Sweetwaters and the television audience in this still from the History Channel's *Digging for the Truth* episode "Lost Tribes of Israel."

The Precarity of Connection and the Productiveness of Disconnection

The diaspora literature suggests that its power as a category of belonging is its articulation of cultural, racial, and/or religious commonality over distance, often in the face of more proximate experiences of exclusion and discrimination. Though always actively forged through difference, diaspora also invokes common history, culture, or identity: in the encounters that I have described, these do not exist.[19] It is precisely under such conditions of absence that DNA becomes significant as a diasporic technology, and that diaspora reemerges as a necessary site of analysis.

Diaspora is made, not given, and as such is always being remade; furthermore, it is remade within and across global hierarchies.[20] African diaspora and Jewish diaspora, each the focus of genetic ancestry studies, provide a productive comparison: they are both entangled in the same global hierarchies through which Americans are the seekers and Africans the objects of projected desires.[21] Like the Jewish connections that I have explored here, the articulation between African diaspora and genetic ancestry can be theorized through genetic diaspora: both phenomena hinge on a desire to find one's past in Africa's present, reiterating a trope of African belatedness and isolation that is a primary object of postcolonial critique.[22]

But it is the differences rather than the similarities that most interest me here. Genetic ancestry has emerged as a technology through which Jewish diasporic belonging is explicitly expanded, bringing entire populations into its newly imagined parameters. By contrast, in African American ancestry testing, people seek ethnic differentiation through DNA and then find meaning in learning about their specific, newly found, possible ethnic group (Nelson 2008b, 2016; Palmié 2007). This difference turns diaspora on its head: research about diaspora that considers it a critical alternative to exclusive or coercive practices of belonging within nation-states, and as a critical analytic to denaturalize the nation-state form, assumes that diaspora is desired and chosen as an alternative site of identification (D. Boyarin and Boyarin 1993; Clifford 1997; Gilroy 1993; Ho 2006; D. A. Thomas 2009). But "diaspora" was not a concept that Lemba people, including LCA leaders, used to explain their connections to each other or to Jews from elsewhere.

For the Lemba people I knew, their new Jewish connections were not ends in themselves but rather means toward two ends not shared by their Jewish interlocutors: Lemba ethnic recognition in South Africa and Lemba communication of their own knowledge production about genes and Jews. But DNA enables the Lemba to be claimed by the idea of diaspora, which demands both their difference *and* their assimilation. This is, to borrow Michael Montoya's term, a kind of "bioethnic conscription" through which the Lemba are brought into a story about Jewish diaspora via media dissemination of scientific data (Montoya 2007). But crucially, it is a conscription that Lemba people speak through and against, using the connections it conjures to further their own politics of recognition and to disseminate their own truths about their histories.

Lauren Berlant argues that "the case" organizes particular publics by serving as an example or an exception that proves a normative rule (Berlant 2007a, b). In the DNA-certified lost tribe of Israel discourse, the Lemba are the exception to Jewish identity that proves a normative rule that Jewishness is fundamentally genealogical, which in turn is fundamentally biological. They are the exception because of race, religion, and geopolitical location: normative Jews are not black, they are not Christians, and they do not have histories in South Africa that predate European colonialism. But the Lemba are Jews nonetheless because of their DNA. Thus genetic connectedness becomes the new normative rule. This runs counter to critical readings of Jewish identity such as those of Jonathan Boyarin and Daniel Boyarin, who point out that "Jewishness disrupts the very categories of identity because it is not national, not genealogical, not religious, but all of these in dialectical tension with one another" (D. Boyarin and Boyarin 1993, 721). The public that is organized around the case of the Lemba and the (new) normative Jewishness that privileges genealogy is the public of a Jewish genetic diaspora. Genetic diaspora is a version of Jewish diaspora that naturalizes and therefore depoliticizes Zionism—a contentious politics of Jewish nationalism—by mapping Jewish genetic origins onto the contemporary Jewish nation-state. This makes genetic diaspora different from the Boyarins' theory of Jewish diaspora in which diaspora is precisely *counter* to Zionist ideologies. In their account, Zionism is an antidiasporic discourse in that it positions a Jewish nation-state as the only place of Jewish survival. Their theory of Jewish diaspora, in contrast to Zionism, is a model of Jewish survival that explicitly rejects the logics of nation-states and ethnic nationalisms (D. Boyarin and Boyarin 1993; J. Boyarin and Boyarin 2002).

Other, earlier Lemba archives had their own networks of circulation and publics to organize, but this post-DNA media archive organizes a Zionist public with a diffuse center that includes Britain and the United States as sites of media production and Israel as the primary point of reference. The Lemba as a case depoliticizes this highly charged configuration; in doing so, Lemba people fall away entirely, as do South African histories and politics. Berlant asks, "What does it matter who one is?" Noting the way that the case "confirms the authority of the decider," she wonders about its potential to disrupt—its potential, then, to exactly *not* make the case it is supposed to make, to disrupt the public it is employed to consolidate (Berlant 2007a). What does it matter who the Lemba are? Can excavating and documenting some of the ways in which they confound lost tribe and other origin narratives disrupt the public of genetic diaspora that their misrepresentation helps consolidate?

Genetic diaspora points to a space beyond diasporic Zionism and also beyond genetic citizenship—a space where the rights that are at stake and the rights that are imagined to be at stake slip past each other completely, in two separate conversations that are imagined to be the same. While I was in South Africa conducting ethnographic research, only two other American Jews visited the Lemba people I knew. This suggests that genetic diaspora is a failed project of connection. But despite the almost complete absence of visiting Jews, Lemba production of genomic knowledge thrives among themselves, and meanwhile, the image of Jewish connection continues to be promoted to American Jews in television documentaries, on the internet, and through Kulanu-sponsored speaking tours that emphasize a Lemba Jewishness that is both genetic and religious. Ephraim Selamolela's hopeful business vision of a thriving "Bhuba Game Lodge" and the ongoing international promotion of the idea of the Lemba as Jews demand an understanding of genetic diaspora as instead a *partially* failed, and yet also always potentially emergent, project of connection.

The convergence of diaspora and genomics examined here is a complex site of aspiration for social and political belonging. Actors such as Jewish teachers and researchers from the United States and Lemba leaders and their constituents each attempt to communicate their divergent, situated knowledge of what they understand to be a collective, transsituational self and in doing so reconstitute relationships between biology and culture while also reconfiguring the possibilities and the politics of precarious connection. The ongoing interplay between failure and potential emergence that I have illustrated illuminates a wide range of attempts at connection, genetic and otherwise, in which identification and difference entwine. We can thus think of genetic diaspora as one example of the precarity of connection on unequal ground.

For an ever-growing number of Lemba South Africans, it was the disconnections of genetic diaspora as much as its connections that mattered. Whether I was being asked or being told about our Jewish ties, I was invariably being challenged to reexamine my own knowledge about Jews to account for Lemba histories. Ultimately, disconnections like those between my existing knowledge and theirs provided possibilities through which new knowledge about genes and Jews could be produced and circulated. Diaspora emerges here as a site through which knowledge is contested, and DNA as an opportunity to rewrite the meaning of race, religion, and culture.

Months after I met Hilda Mpaketsane at the wedding and after I had stayed at her home with her family, we had the following conversation:

HM: You say you are a Jew. What tribe are you from?

NT: I don't know which tribe, just that I am a Jew.

HM: Is that like black . . . or like being Pedi?

NT: It is complicated because it is more than one thing. . . .
What is Lemba? Is it like Pedi?

HM: Not exactly. You see, we did not come from this place,
and now we are scattered.

Hilda then recounted how Lemba people came to be where they were: they followed a star, and each time the star rested, they stayed and settled there.

For Lemba South Africans, having Jewish blood confirms their oral history of migration. But it *also* confirms their distinctness as an indigenous African people who belong to the continent of Africa and to the South African state, no less than other black South Africans. So while the genetic tests have aimed to determine the Jewishness of the Lemba, I found that for Lemba South Africans, it is actually the *Africanness* of Jewish history, culture, and identity that is more compelling.

POSTAPARTHEID CITIZENSHIP
AND THE LIMITS OF GENETIC EVIDENCE

Kgoshi Mpaketsane and I sat across from each other in the front room of his two-room house, the door open to allow the hot December air to circulate. It was 2005, and I was in my second month of living in the village. I lived in the four-bedroom house of Phoko John Mpaketsane, the son of Kgoshi Mpaketsane's father's younger half-brother, and his wife, Malekgale Monica Mpaketsane, along with them, two of their children, and Monica's nieces. It was part of my daily routine to take the five-minute walk from John and Monica's house, located in the center of the village near the primary school and next to the only tuck shop, to the home of Kgoshi Mpaketsane and his wife, at the edge of the village where it bordered the mountains. On that day, the green plastic table between us was strewn with photocopies of Kgoshi Mpaketsane's applications to government commissions and programs. The table had been purchased with five-rand donations pooled together from his supporters to facilitate the taking of notes, by both him and his royal council, at the chieftaincy meetings that he convened at least once a month.[1] These meetings took place in the Mpaketsane royal kraal, the dirt yard that extended downhill from where Kgoshi Mpaketsane's house lay nestled against the side of the mountain to his six-foot-high sliding metal gate about twenty yards below.

The transition away from apartheid rule in the mid-1990s had included a massive amount of new legislation designed to implement democratic principles while simultaneously honoring and advancing the place of African tradition in government policy.[2] In practice, these two goals were often at odds with each other, especially in relation to the status of traditional leadership, communal land rights, and customary law: critics argued that these were fundamentally undemocratic institutions, but supporters claimed that they were a necessary part of decolonization because they evoked the authenticity of a precolonial past.[3] Decades later, much of this has yet to be resolved, and the task of bridging the gaps between democratic principles, legislative imperatives, and transformative implementation has fallen on commissions of inquiry.

The government commissions and programs to which Kgoshi Mpaketsane applied were part of these postapartheid efforts toward transformative justice: he petitioned every commission that might grant him some aspect of the broad recognition that he sought. These applications, if successful, had the potential to legally recognize his chieftaincy, to give him and his Lemba followers communal land rights to the village that they lived in alongside their non-Lemba neighbors, and to grant him a permit to prospect for platinum there.

Kgoshi Mpaketsane's applications were the point where village politics, national belonging, and genetic ancestry converged. By walking me through their contents, he explained to me the larger stakes that both shaped and amplified long-standing local power struggles, and he taught me why he participated in genetic ancestry research and how he transformed its meaning. As we flipped through pages of applications, denial notifications, and reapplications, Kgoshi Mpaketsane emphasized their most pertinent contents. He explained that Lemba people established the village before the white people named it "Indië," and before the arrival of the Ndebele people, by which he meant his non-Lemba neighbors, many of whom had the family name Maesela.[4] His proof was that only Lemba people knew the original, real name of the village: they called it Mohlotlwane, after a river in Zimbabwe that had been significant to Lemba people in the past. Referencing the two genetic studies, published in 1996 and 2000, that had aimed to demonstrate Lemba links to Jews, he further explained, "No one can argue with me because this is evidence we have on the Y chromosome."

This chapter asks why Kgoshi Mpaketsane thought DNA would be helpful in meeting his recognition goals and how he made use of it. The link that Kgoshi Mpaketsane forged between genetic studies that located the Lemba outside of Africa and a place name that located them within it begs these questions: How did Lemba people as political actors translate a genetic ancestry study highlighting their belonging elsewhere into proprietary claims to traditional authority, land, and platinum mining that would territorialize their identities in South African places? What work did genetic ancestry do in this context, and with what implications for the idea of genetic Jewishness that the published studies had popularized?

The previous chapter considered how Lemba people transformed genetic ancestry in relation to ideas of diasporic belonging. The genetic transformations that are the subject of this chapter look instead at postapartheid legal arenas and related local struggles that had been ongoing for decades. Citizenship emerges here through legislative and judicial processes, but also as a locally contested experience in a context in which the distinction between citizen and subject was being actively entrenched rather than dismantled.[5] In what follows, I trace the intersections between genetic afterlives—the new knowledge about his DNA that Kgoshi Mpaketsane produced when he invoked Lemba genetic ancestry toward his own goals—and citizenship as a lived experience that is shaped by both past exclusions and present possibilities. I do this for two reasons: to show that the meaning of genetic ancestry in Kgoshi Mpaketsane's hands departed from its meaning for geneticists, and to examine what his selective deployment of genetic evidence might tell us about postapartheid citizenship and belonging.

Kgoshi Mpaketsane's emphasis on the transformative potential of genetic ancestry suggests that in his hands, Lemba DNA became something that geneticists could not have anticipated: it became a technology of indigenous recognition, which in turn was a means of fully realizing what Kgoshi Mpaketsane otherwise experienced as circumscribed citizenship in postapartheid South Africa. This was not, however, a disavowal of Jewish genetics. Rather, Kgoshi Mpaketsane's genetic afterlives intertwined Jewish and African pasts toward his vision of indigenous, democratic South African futures.

Historicizing Recognition, Producing Ethnic Subjects

Kgoshi Mpaketsane's village was small enough to walk between any two points in less than twenty minutes, and it was home to only a few hundred year-round residents, an overwhelming number of whom were elderly, children, or unemployed adults—though many more who worked and maintained houses elsewhere considered the village "home" and would return for weddings, funerals, and holidays (figure 3.1). Most of these present and absent villagers were related through either common ancestors or common descendants. Yet the conflicts there required each person to choose one of two sides, Mpaketsane or Maesela, which were introduced to me as representing distinct groups of people, with different histories and cultures. No one publicly referred to the village as "Mohlotlwane"; rather, it was known to locals there and in neighbor-

FIGURE 3.1 India village as seen from the mountain that borders it, c. 2006. The area closest to the edge of the mountain is known within the village as Ga-Mpaketsane. Kgoshi Mpaketsane's house is visible in the lower left corner. Photograph by author.

ing villages either as "India" or as "Ga-Maesela." Calling the place one name or the other often signaled which side the speaker supported. In what follows, I refer to this village as India to reflect the preferences of Lemba people who live there.

Both Kgoshi Mpaketsane and Kgoshikgadi Maesela sought communal land rights over their village to the exclusion of the other's claims.[6] The disputes between Mpaketsane and Maesela both reflected and produced a boundary between two groups of people who had to work hard to emphasize their differences while they also lived together, worked together, and even parented children together. As Kgoshi Mpaketsane's invocation of DNA and place-names attests, these local struggles utilized new forms of evidence as culture and tradition took on renewed significance in postapartheid South Africa. But their roots lay in longer histories of land alienation, political subjugation, and the bureaucratization of chieftaincy.[7]

The issues at play between and among Mpaketsane and Maesela people were replicated in countless other disputes throughout the province and nationally. Colonial and apartheid chieftaincy manipulations bore much of the responsibility for these disagreements, but interfamily chieftaincy contestation was not a colonial invention. Rather, and in contrast to how postapartheid commissions imagined disputes, precolonial chieftaincy had been flexibly inherited, with room for ambiguity and debate in rules of succession (Delius 1984; Oomen 2005). So, too, with land rights. While precolonial struggles over territory had often led to migration and reestablishment elsewhere, settler colonialism had long rendered "elsewhere" inaccessible and ownership the condition of secure access.[8]

Land alienation had begun in this region of South Africa in the mid-nineteenth century with the arrival of Boer settlers, and it became definitively linked to chieftaincy under British indirect rule in the 1880s, after their defeat of the independent Pedi kingdom under Sekhukhune I in 1879. Land speculation and appropriation emerged even before Sekhukhune I's 1879 defeat, despite the presence of established villages on most of these same lands. Mohlotlwane became part of the farm Indië when the British colonial government authorized and profited from its sale to a land speculator; soon after, this village, along with all others that had been part of the territory of Sekhukhune I, was subsumed into a newly delineated "native location."[9] The new South African Union's 1913 Native Land Act further linked land, chieftaincy, and tribal difference. It outlawed nearly all black land ownership, except that within native locations land could be collectively purchased to be held by the native commissioner "in trust" for tribally defined groups.[10] Starting in the early 1920s, Sekhukhune II—still considered by many in the region to be the Pedi *kgoshikgolo*, or king, but under South African law now just one of several location chiefs—instituted a plan to buy back Pedi land using extra taxes that he levied on migrant workers in his jurisdiction (Delius 1996).

The decision to buy land on behalf of "the Bapedi tribe," and to allow it as a *collective* purchase in which the actual holder of the deed was the South African government, cemented the shift in both government policy and popular perception from what had before been acknowledged as an independent Pedi kingdom, defined by political alliance, to the Bapedi tribe, now defined by ethnicity. In 1933, Indië farm was purchased as part of Sekhukhune II's buy-back plan, and like other such properties, it was held "in trust" by the Department of Native Affairs on behalf of "the Bapedi tribe." By this time, at least one marriage had taken place between the Lemba and Maesela communities, and Maesela and Lemba households were more interspersed than segregated. But this demographic reconfiguration of India into one interrelated community coincided with the increased emphasis on tribal identity as the means toward accessing now-circumscribed sovereignty.

During the 1950s and 1960s, apartheid laws increased the number of recognized chiefs and their political power and further cemented the link between ethnic difference and tribal authority. This was the context in which Kgoshi Mpaketsane's late father, Kgoshi George Mothakge Mpaketsane, with the support of the Lemba Cultural Association, unsuccessfully sought legal recognition as a chief, and in which Kgoshikgadi Maesela's late husband, Kgoshi Maesela, had legal chieftaincy status conferred upon him.

Lemba people here faced a double erasure: apartheid notions of ethnicity that linked them to language and territory had rendered their ethnic difference illegible at the same time that legal recognition of small-scale chieftaincy resulted in their new status as subjects of their neighbors, without political power. Recognized chiefs like Kgoshi Maesela now received a government salary, and it was their responsibility to monitor and stamp the passbooks of everyone within their jurisdiction when they traveled to urban or white areas to work. In protest of his political erasure, Kgoshi George Mothakge Mpaketsane also performed these tasks, and when his son, the Kgoshi Mpaketsane whom I knew, took over the position upon his father's death in 1989, he did the same.

In a sense, then, the apartheid government refused to recognize the Mpaketsane chieftaincy, and the Mpaketsane chiefs for two generations in turn refused to recognize that refusal. When Kgoshi Mpaketsane inherited the chieftaincy, he also inherited the conviction that Lemba difference should justify Lemba recognition, and that Lemba recognition would be signaled by recognition of Lemba chieftaincy. And because Kgoshikgadi Maesela was the only legally recognized traditional leader in the village, Kgoshi Mpaketsane's struggles were never only against the state, but also necessarily against Maesela and her supporters.

Postapartheid Justice and the Promise of Genetic Evidence

On December 9, 1996, Kgoshi Mpaketsane appeared alone and without legal representation before six members of the Northern Province's Commission of Inquiry into Traditional Leadership Disputes and Claims, and by all accounts, it was not a very good experience.[11] The commission, popularly named after its head, Professor Victor Ralushai, was an experiment: it was the first post-apartheid effort to tackle the question of chieftaincy, which had been renamed "traditional leadership." This renaming was a way to reclaim the legitimacy of the precolonial past from the illegitimacy of chieftaincy under apartheid, when it was a primary means of control and oppression of black South Africans in rural areas. The Ralushai Commission aimed to determine who had been improperly deposed or appointed, and who should have been recognized but was not, because of the degree of their cooperation with or opposition to Bantu Authorities laws and the apartheid state. Convened in February 1996, the commission adjudicated hundreds of submissions based on oral testimony given at hearings beginning that April, supplemented in some cases by applicants' written submissions and commissioners' consultation of ethnological sources (Oomen 2005; Ralushai 1998).

At his hearing, Kgoshi Mpaketsane represented himself as chief of the Balepa, which is the Sepedi name for the Lemba. He emphasized two things: Balepa migratory histories and the longevity and legitimacy of his chieftaincy. His account of Balepa migration followed the contours of Lemba oral history beginning in Yemen and ending in the 1880s with the founding of his village. He explained that his family's chieftaincy—including his own—had been recognized by the Pedi paramountcy for generations and that it had been established among their own people even before their 1884 move to their present home. But the commissioners were skeptical.

Their doubt derived in part from their sense that Kgoshi Mpaketsane's genealogies were difficult to follow and impossible to verify. But it had more to do with their framing than with his evidence. Their final report judged not only Kgoshi Mpakesane's chieftaincy claim but also the existence of the Lemba as black Jews. They wrote,

> The application is based on the existence of the Balepa tribe, sometimes known as the Black Jews of South Africa. The Balepa believe that they originated in the Middle East centuries before the birth of Christ and Mohammed. . . . This Commission finds that the Mphaketsana [Mpaketsane] did not clearly tell the Commission whether they claim their chieftainship on the fact of their strange and non-African [religious] and cultural practices, or on the fact that they were rulers when they arrive[d] at Sekhukhuneland. Mphaketsana sketched the route of the Balepa from Yemen down to Mozambique, Zimbabwe and South Africa and claimed to be black Jews, but never mentioned the Fallahins of Ethiopia, who

were discovered and recognized as the lost tribe and thus true black Jews. (Ralushai 1998, 317–320)

In his testimony, Kgoshi Mpaketsane had aimed to demonstrate the longevity of his family's chieftaincy, but what the commissioners heard was that he claimed "strange and non-African" "beliefs" that did not align with the histories of those they regarded to be "true black Jews." They dismissed his claim.

Although the decision was not in the end explicitly based on the commissioners' disbelief that the Balepa existed and were black Jews, their skepticism on that point carried over into how they judged the rest of Kgoshi Mpaketsane's testimony. Their official rejection hinged on their certainty that those whom Kgoshi Mpaketsane represented as his people were not actually his and that the recognition he sought fell outside of the Ralushai Commission's purview. They wrote, "The Commission recommends that the status quo be maintained, as the 800 families mentioned are not all Lepa people. They are in fact Sekhukhune people occupying land which was tribally purchased. Chief Sekhukhune holds the title deed and not Mphaketsana. The Commissions problem is that Mphaketsana's application is for promotion to chieftainship or for recognition. Both cases fall outside the scope of this Commission's mandate (Ralushai 1998, 320)." Their recommendation supported the status quo, not just with regard to Kgoshi Mpaketsane's lack of recognition, but also in terms of the links among land, chieftaincy, and tribal identity that had found their fullest expression under apartheid Bantu Authorities laws.

To better understand the commission's decision, I interviewed Professor Ralushai himself on July 31, 2006, at a casino hotel near his home in Thohoyandou.[12] He told me that he agreed with the consensus that Lemba chieftaincy does not exist, that this belief informed his sense that Kgoshi Mpaketsane's application was only an instrumentalist power grab in a newly contested space, and that he knew the claim could not be legitimate because he had grown up and lived his whole life alongside Lemba people in Venda, so he knew firsthand that Lemba people did not have chiefs. While reinstating deposed chiefs from established royal lineages fit with the commission's goals, creating entirely new chieftaincies did not, and even if it had, creating a chieftaincy for Kgoshi Mpaketsane would have been particularly impossible when the head of the commission was convinced that there was no traditional, cultural basis for his claims.

Ralushai's certitude that his personal experiences with some Lemba people could be used to assess the legitimacy of chieftaincy among all Lemba people ensured that as long as he remained in charge, Lemba chieftaincy would remain only an aspiration. Ralushai had even worked to block his colleague Professor M. E. R. Mathivha, then president of the Lemba Cultural Association, from influencing the decision because he felt that Mathivha's pro-Lemba politics led him to endorse what Ralushai regarded as the newly invented idea of Lemba chieftaincy. Professor Mathivha was also a member of the Ralushai Commission: he was assigned to hear applications in another part of the province, and Ralushai had denied his request to be present during Kgoshi Mpaketsane's hearing. Ralushai was so persuaded by his own experiences in which there were no Lemba chiefs that he did not trust Mathivha's insistence that outside of Venda, there had been Lemba chiefs for generations.

The Ralushai Commission was Kgoshi Mpaketsane's first opportunity to work toward the transformations that he sought, but it was not his last. Three weeks after his hearing, he submitted his application to the Land Claims Commission. The Ralushai Commission had been established by order of a provincial proclamation (2 of 1996) that emerged in the absence of national policy on the status and regulation of postapartheid chieftaincy. The Land Claims Commission, by contrast, was national in scope; it reflected the material and symbolic urgency of undoing the territorial infrastructures of apartheid.[13]

Although the Ralushai Commission had not yet compiled its findings, and Kgoshi Mpaketsane did not know whether his claim would be successful, he was aware that his hearing had not gone well, and in his subsequent land claims submission he responded not only to the questions asked on the form but also to the Ralushai group's skepticism. He included the same full migration history, including a starting point in Judea, but omitted any explicit identification of the Lemba as black Jews. Instead, he invoked competing chieftaincies, and his evidence was based on land use.[14]

In the space provided for "any other information you would like to bring to the Commission's attention," he criticized the Ralushai Commission and emphasized apartheid injustice as the root of his community's land insecurity: "I wish . . . the Commission would call Maesela and question him about the land in our presence.[15] Maesela refused to attend the Ralushai Commission in the Northern Province on the 9-12-96. That Commission could take into account this matter. More so it is a burning issue where Mpaketsane has lost right in land. That Commission could eradicate all apartheid systems prevailing within our new dispensation."[16] By explicitly linking his land claim to his chieftaincy claim, and by framing both as burning issues that, if resolved, could help truly transform South Africa, Kgoshi Mpaketsane aimed to graft his vision of postapartheid justice onto that of the commissioners, whose own visions were controversial because their emphasis on communal land claims in rural areas favored chiefs at the expense of ordinary people (Mamdani 1996; Ntsebeza 2005).[17]

Although he had downplayed ethnic difference in his application form, Kgoshi Mpaketsane's supplementary evidence, which was a two-page document titled "Kgoshi Mpaketsane (History)," necessarily invoked ethnic particularity in the process of demonstrating migration and leadership specificity toward a communal claim. The document began, "Kgoshi Mpaketsane is one of the old chiefs of the Basena who migrated from Judea many centuries ago. . . . Ramadi (Rametsi) together with other Lembas crossed the Limpopo river into the present Transvaal and settled at Musina in 50 B.C. From Musina the Mhani settled at Tshifulanani under 'Gunununu' Mhani. . . . The son of Gunununu Mhani left Phusela with Malaka and settled in the East but West of Phalaborwa. He was called Mbengezana (Mpaketsane)."[18] It ended with a community call to action:

> We the "Lembas" want our Kgoshi to be registered and the land to be given back to the owners. A commission must be sent to investigate this matter. Firstly to approach King Sekhukhune III, Rhyne Thulare to remind him about the first nation to settle at Indië. The nation or the tribe that named the mountains and the rivers of Indië. The nation or the tribe that knows that farm from the bottom up to the top. The nation that knows the forts and the farm in and out. The tribe that has chosen fertile ploughing fields, next to their homes. The tribe and the nation that knows the farm from above to below.[19]

This statement grounded Kgoshi Mpaketsane's legitimacy in the fact that he had followers who believed him to be their traditional leader, in the claim that the Lemba were a nation/tribe, and in the assertion that knowledge of the landscape was evidence of ownership—all elements of emerging postapartheid concepts of indigeneity.

Kgoshi Mpaketsane's "History" document crystallized a basic evidentiary logic that laid the foundation for subsequent claims, actions, and activities. The narrative that appeared to the Ralushai commissioners as paradoxical, because Kgoshi Mpaketsane was in their reading simultaneously claiming non-Africanness and legitimate African leadership, comes across in the land claim as a logical narrative of migration history that was similar in form to how other local rulers recounted their own: they came from somewhere else, consolidated their authority by relocating under a new ruler or by subordinating others, and in doing so established their territory. Like so many others, including the Sekhukhune royal family, Mpaketsane made no claim to primordial land-people origins. Rather, like others, he claimed origins in a distant place that was home in a distant time, with a right to a present place that was based on the consolidation and recognition of power.

In the land claim, evidence of Lemba difference emphasized both Lemba origins in Judea and local ties to the land. In this context, the migration history served to position the Lemba as a legitimate nation, like the Pedi, their allies: this framing downplayed the question of whether they were really African but could not avoid it altogether. Kgoshi Mpaketsane was careful to note that although Sekhukhune gave them their land, he did not create their chieftaincy. Rather, it had already existed, and the land gift was further evidence that Sekhukhune recognized that. All of this spoke to the logic of communal land ownership, which necessitated that Kgoshi Mpaketsane demonstrate that he was the leader of a distinct community. But his means to do so also necessarily emphasized a non-African Lemba origin—the very thing that the Ralushai Commission had latched onto as evidence against him.

Just weeks before Kgoshi Mpaketsane submitted his land claim in December 1996, Amanda Spurdle and Trefor Jenkins's Lemba DNA study appeared in the *American Journal of Human Genetics*, and just weeks after he submitted the claim, Tudor Parfitt arrived in Limpopo to collect DNA samples for the Cohanim study. Jenkins's DNA collection had been mediated through the Lemba Cultural Association, as was Parfitt's first collection trip in January 1997. Parfitt's second trip, in October 1997, brought him to Sekhukhuneland (Parfitt 2000, 346). For Kgoshi Mpaketsane, this seemed to promise exactly the evidence he was looking for to overcome the skepticism about the existence of the Balepa as a distinct nation with a separate, legitimate, traditional leader and a need for communal land rights. A total of 136 paternally unrelated Lemba men gave Parfitt DNA samples; the results were published in February 2000. Meanwhile, Kgoshi Mpaketsane waited. There had been no word on the status of the land claim. The Ralushai Commission had completed their rulings and written their report, but they did not release it to the public. Kgoshi Mpaketsane knew that his claim had been rejected, but he did not know precisely why. As he waited, he did everything that he could to work toward his recognition goals.

Making DNA Useful: Indigeneity on Trial?

On a cool winter day in July 2004 at the Greater Sekhukhune district court in Schoonoord about an hour's drive from his home, Kgoshi Mpaketsane took the stand, prepared to defend himself from the two separate but related charges that had been brought against him. The first was that he had cut down several trees in order to plow some land not far from his house—an action deemed to be illegal not only because the trees were protected as an indigenous species but also because he was allegedly not the owner of the land where the trees grew. The second charge was that he had convened a circumcision ceremony as part of a boy's initiation school, even though his application to do so had been denied. The cluster of issues that this court case brought together—legitimate traditional leadership, circumcision rights, land use rights and land ownership, and questions about who and what were protected by whom and for whom—signaled the national legal context in which the future of rural South Africa was being played out and the terms through which rural post-apartheid citizenship could be contested.

Both charges arose from postapartheid legislation that aimed to balance a need to serve a generic public good with the imperative to affirm rights that were defined as cultural and traditional. The 1998 National Forest Act (84 of 1998) had designated forests and woodlands as protected areas, and it had also provided additional protections for a list of indigenous species of trees to be determined by forestry officials and subject to public hearings. While communities could potentially obtain rights to use forest and woodland products, cutting down protected trees was punishable with a fine and possible imprisonment of up to three years, regardless of one's status as a landowner or member of a rights-bearing community. Circumcision was a provincial legal matter rather than a national one, but laws regulating it stemmed from national debates. In 1996, following a national public health controversy spurred by the deaths of hundreds of young boys in the Eastern Cape from circumcision-related accidents and infections that critics blamed on unqualified individuals who, they claimed, were only out to make money, the Limpopo legislature outlawed anyone except a recognized traditional leader or a doctor from performing circumcisions.[20]

From Kgoshi Mpaketsane's point of view, his identity, authority, and authenticity were on trial, played out through his relationship to the bodies of his people and the land on which they lived. Both charges stemmed from the fact that he acted as if he had the legal standing of a recognized traditional leader, which he still lacked despite having been regarded as a chief by his own people for fifteen years. Although he faced fines on both counts, Kgoshi Mpaketsane did not deny the allegations. Instead, he used the court appearance to make a case as to why he was in fact the legitimate owner of the land, why he was entitled to facilitate circumcisions, and why the government should acknowledge him as a traditional leader.

For Kgoshi Mpaketsane, it was the action of cutting down the trees that demonstrated his ownership of the land, and the application to convene a circumcision ceremony that demonstrated both his authority to complete the ritual and that Lemba difference was significant enough to warrant their own ceremony, separate from their neighbors. In court that day, he aimed to demonstrate that he did not stand alone, with only his own actions as evidence: rather, he had multiple histories and forms of authority on his side.

Kgoshi Mpaketsane illustrated his relationship to the land by putting the Pedi kgoshikgolo K. K. Sekhukhune on the stand. As the current ruler of the lineage whose authority represented precolonial power, Sekhukhune commanded the entire courtroom's attention, from those who were there to support Kgoshi Mpaketsane to those awaiting their own trials.[21] Sekhukhune testified that Mpaketsane people were separate and distinct from Maesela people, and that they had settled the land first, in the nineteenth century.

Kgoshi Mpaketsane illustrated his relationship to the bodies of his people in two ways: historical precedent of past circumcision rituals and genetic evidence of Lemba distinctness. He noted that before circumcision schools required permits, he had held them for seven years, beginning in 1989 when he took over the chieftaincy after his father's death. And he invoked Lemba DNA by submitting into evidence Magdel le Roux's 2003 book. Although le Roux remains agnostic throughout her text about whether the Lemba should be understood as a lost tribe of Israel, she presents the two Lemba DNA studies as corroborating evidence (le Roux 2003, 224). Furthermore, the book itself authorized the collective status of the Lemba as a distinct ethnic group, different enough to have entire volumes devoted to speculating about their origins, and within its first few pages, Kgoshi Mpaketsane appeared in a photograph captioned "Chief Mpaketsane of Sekhukhuneland, addressing his people during a LCA conference at India Village" (5). The presence of Kgoshi Mpaketsane's image in this text testified to his importance among the Lemba. The caption that labeled him "chief" clarified exactly what his importance consisted of while also linking him with the Venda-based Lemba Cultural Association, which could be interpreted to imply that he was chief of all of the Lemba people in South Africa, not just those in his own and surrounding villages.

By calling on K. K. Sekhukhune, Kgoshi Mpaketsane summoned long histories of his ancestors in the Sekhukhune region. By calling on the history of the Lemba as black Jews, he evoked even longer ancestral narratives that could map onto, but were not defined by, past configurations of local power. Linking the past to the postapartheid South African present was a powerful statement that legal frameworks and state power were ever changing and that current laws and current statuses vis-à-vis the state were not necessarily legitimate. Invoking the history of the Lemba as black Jews echoed his strategy with the Ralushai Commission, but whereas before his evidence had been rejected, DNA was a new form of evidence whose power was as yet untested. If the Ralushai Commission could question that he was who he said he was in part because they questioned that Lemba people were who they said they were, then DNA, he hoped, could neutralize the doubts and transform his standing.

What mattered throughout Kgoshi Mpaketsane's presentation of evidence was Lemba difference—historical, cultural, and biological. This was why he called upon K. K. Sekhukhune, utilized research by le Roux, invoked his historical authority to convene circumcision ceremonies, and spoke of Lemba DNA. He knew that his rights to land use and to control of circumcision hinged on his ability to prove that he was a traditional leader, which in turn depended on his ability to prove cultural distinctness: his experience with the Ralushai Commission had made it clear that without his ability to convince South African authorities of Lemba difference, he could not persuade them of anything else. As he utilized genetic data alongside other forms of evidence to defend himself, Kgoshi Mpaketsane was ultimately making claims on the state about the status of the Lemba and his own authority in relation to them.

Unfortunately for him and his supporters, there was a disconnection between what he felt he needed to prove and what the court was actually charging him with. From a legal perspective, the trial was over as soon as he pleaded guilty. It was not the reason for cutting the protected indigenous trees but the fact of his having cut them that was the court's concern. And it was not his ability to convene a circumcision school and to facilitate safe circumcisions that was in question for the court, but rather that his current legal status vis-à-vis traditional leadership disqualified him from taking the actions that were not only allowed, but required, of traditional leaders.

The irony of protecting the land rights of an indigenous tree at the expense of what he saw as his own rights to the land was not lost on Kgoshi Mpaketsane. One evening, months later, he called me over to his gate as I walked past on my way home from visiting one of his relatives. He told me that his being recognized as a chief by the Pedi people has been important for the survival of the Lemba people in this area, and that it troubled him that the Lemba people in Venda do not receive the same type of acknowledgment. He continued, "The Lemba people, we must be like the Khoisan people. We must be a tribe like the Khoikhoi." Khoikhoi, Khoisan, and San indigenous identities have flourished in postapartheid South Africa; in 2001 the National Khoisan Consultative Conference formed as an umbrella group to advance their collective claims as indigenous peoples, and a number of individuals have been prominent international and local activists for indigenous rights to land, livelihoods, and intellectual and cultural property since the late 1990s.[22] Khoisan peoples had also been prominent for decades as research subjects in genetic ancestry studies; in fact, the Lemba DNA study published in 1996 was a side project conducted by South African researchers whose primary research was with the DNA of Khoisan-speaking peoples.[23] But what bore on Kgoshi Mpaketsane's situation most directly was how land and indigeneity worked together toward group recognition. A ≠khomani San land claim was awarded in 1999 in a public ceremony that emphasized the success of postapartheid land restitution and characterized the claimants as an indigenous people now reborn as a nation through their (partial) return to their ancestral land (Huizenga 2014, 147).[24] For Kgoshi Mpaketsane, Khoisan peoples were exemplary because like the Lemba, they struggled for postapartheid rights and recognition based on identity and cultural heritage. But unlike the Lemba, their successes were achieved explicitly in the name of African indigeneity.

Kgoshi Mpaketsane brought up Khoisan people again at the end of 2006, when I was about to leave South Africa after twelve months of continuous ethnographic research. By then, he had invested considerable time and energy into working with me, and he hoped that my research, like Tudor Parfitt's and Magdel le Roux's, could be applied toward his recognition efforts. But he was concerned about how much my project diverged from his own. He told me that what I *should* be interested in was the *culture* of the Lemba people: he explained that this meant "the customs and the chieftainship *inside*." For him, chieftainship was the content of both culture and customs, and these three concepts were inseparable from one another. If I failed to adequately study the chieftainship, which I risked doing by spending months in Venda with members of the Lemba Cultural Association, then I had failed to adequately study Lemba culture.

He went on, "*That* is the material. When you come to a certain tribe, even the Khoikhoi people, you can go here, you can see, this is the senior leader of the Khoikhoi like here, but in Venda, there is no such thing in Venda. Because in Venda, there is no chief in Venda of the Lemba people, you understand." Kgoshi Mpaketsane used the language of tribes and custom, which were linked to colonialism and apartheid, because it reflected his experience of the terms of postapartheid recognition and exclusion. He saw the Khoikhoi as both outliers and exemplars: outliers because their recognition hinged not on chieftaincy but on a broader construct of leadership and links to land, exemplars because they achieved recognition through being first on the land

and through being perceived as culturally and biologically different from others—characteristics that for Kgoshi Mpaketsane described his own struggle and that of Lemba recognition more broadly.

When Kgoshi Mpaketsane spoke of the Khoisan, shortly after submitting as legal evidence a book that described Lemba DNA as potential proof that they were a lost tribe of Israel, he reformulated both indigenous and diasporic forms of belonging. By tying his claims not only to oral history but also to historical, documented time, he reframed the primordial narratives that diasporic and indigenous belonging so often invoke. And by presenting Lemba DNA as evidence of Lemba ethnic difference from other black South Africans, he both made genetic Jewishness African and grounded his citizenship claims in science. Ultimately, Kgoshi Mpaketsane's appearance in court was a means through which he pursued political and cultural citizenship in postapartheid South Africa—not only for himself but also for his people—and he did so by utilizing forms of evidence that to others signaled *either* diaspora *or* indigeneity. His reference to Khoisan indigeneity as a tribal status that Lemba people could emulate echoed his emerging sense of what it would take to become recognized in postapartheid South Africa, something that he expressed at his trial through K. K. Sekhukhune's testimony and his emphasis throughout on Lemba historical, cultural, and biological difference.

Difference after DNA: Traditional Culture and National Recognition

Despite his loss in court, by 2004 Kgoshi Mpaketsane felt confident that recognition of his chieftaincy was imminent. Three factors led him to be hopeful. First, he was not alone in his efforts to transform his relationship to the postapartheid state. For the most part, he had the support of other Lemba people. He also had the backing of other unrecognized traditional leaders in the Limpopo province with whom he had formed an organization to press the government to release the Ralushai Commission's findings so that they could be either implemented if the commission had found in their favor or challenged if it had not. Second, he had become more adept at presenting diverse evidence of his claims: in addition to oral history, he now had the sworn court testimony of acting Pedi kgoshikgolo K. K. Sekhukhune, and he had started to think of DNA and indigeneity as evidentiary technologies that together might finally make the critical difference. Third, the legal ground kept shifting, with new laws, new commissions, and ample opportunities for Kgoshi Mpaketsane to tweak his evidentiary strategy.

Particularly significant were three national bills that were passed in 2000, 2003, and 2004. The Promotion of Access of Information Act (2 of 2000) provided an avenue to contest the secrecy of the Ralushai Commission findings. The Traditional Leadership and Governance Framework Act (41 of 2003) nationalized the effort to entrench chieftaincy in rural areas: it stipulated that each province must pass its own legislation regulating traditional leadership, it formalized the institutions' rules and reach, and it resulted in a new body, the Nhlapo Commission, which had a task similar to that of the Ralushai Commission, but on a national scale. The Communal Land Rights Act (CLARA, 11 of 2004), which was passed just a week before Kgoshi Mpaketsane appeared in court, aimed to establish secure land tenure in rural areas through elaborated community ownership rights. Like his 2004 court case, these legal changes provided new points of access through which Kgoshi Mpaketsane could appeal for recognition directly to the South African state.

The Ralushai Commission's findings had been so controversial that not only had they not been implemented, they were also treated as classified information for years after they were published as a government document in 1998. There were several reasons for the controversy. Because the commission was convened prior to any national consensus on the postapartheid status of chieftaincy, it had the potential to inform national policy; however, because it was limited to one province, the commission was considered unfair to those in other provinces. Also, because it relied on ethnological accounts of the rules of succession to determine when manipulations had taken place, successful applicants had to make their cases by appealing to past ethnologists' overly rigid ideas of custom, culture, and tradition, even when succession had actually been flexible in practice. Moreover, because the commission's findings tended toward strict interpretations of customary practices, they consistently found female petitioners ineligible to inherit leadership positions, which was at odds with the new South African constitution that guaranteed equal rights for women. Finally, although restoring the leadership positions of those who had been wrongfully removed during apartheid sounded good on paper, stripping still-acting leaders of their titles, their status, and their livelihoods proved to be too politically delicate to put into practice, and even to make publicly known (Oomen 2005).

Kgoshi Mpaketsane, along with other applicants to the Ralushai Commission who were seeking recognition of their chieftaincies (as opposed to most applicants, who were pressing to be appointed as rightful traditional leaders in established chieftaincies in which the position was occupied by someone else), formed a group through which they proclaimed themselves to be unrecognized traditional leaders. Bolstered by the Promotion of Access of Information Act of 2000, they began the following year to write letters to government officials seeking access to the Ralushai Commission findings that pertained to each of them. Initially shuffled between different departments and officials, their requests were finally definitively denied in 2002, and they challenged that decision by bringing a case against South Africa's minister for provincial and local government to the high court in Pretoria. The court ruled in their favor in 2003, but the minister appealed. The decision was upheld in September 2004, and a month later, Kgoshi Mpaketsane and his colleagues finally gained access to the Ralushai Commission's decisions about their cases.[25]

Armed now with a clear statement of why the Ralushai Commission had rejected his claims, Kgoshi Mpaketsane began gathering evidence for a better outcome with the Nhlapo Commission, and he updated his land claim based on CLARA's expanded parameters. On the latter, success seemed imminent: he successfully filed a community claim for secure land tenure, and although the commission could not compensate him for lost land because he and his people still lived on the land they claimed, it recommended that a title deed should be issued to the Mpaketsane community. He remained focused on the transformative potential of the Nhlapo Commission, which expanded the scope of the Ralushai Commission in four ways: it was national and not just confined to one province, it was intended to be binding, it was empowered to recognize traditional leaders who had no legal precedents for their claims, and it therefore potentially had the power to recognize traditional communities that had never before existed as legal entities. The new commission seemed to have the potential to provide exactly the kinds of recognition and therefore justice that Kgoshi Mpaketsane had sought in the 1990s.

The Ralushai Commission had made it clear to him that to become recognized, he needed to demonstrate his difference; his 2004 court appearance suggested to him that Lemba DNA might be effective if it could be reworked as not just evidence of difference, but also evidence of territoriality; and his July 2005 land claim dismissal/recommendation reiterated that Lemba recognition might be best obtained through land. In his application to the Nhlapo Commission, his evidence repeatedly emphasized difference, which he seamlessly linked with territoriality. Selecting "boundary dispute between two traditional authorities" rather than "claim to a new traditional leadership position," he wrote, "We have been the existing tribe, independently from other tribes, but we were marginalized when others were recognized because of our resistance to apartheid laws. . . . Our neighbor, Kgoshi

Maesela, claims the sole ownership of the farm, because of his recognition by the apartheid government. . . . Our tribe has been residing on the farm before the said tribe."[26]

His entire claim was submitted on letterhead that reproduced the Lemba Cultural Association symbol of an elephant inside a Star of David, alongside the heading "Balepa-Ba-Mpaketsane Tribal Authority." This cover letter refuted the Ralushai Commission's objections point by point and prominently referenced a series of annexures attached as evidence. The first of these included a tribal resolution, signed by ten members of the royal family and thirty members of the tribal council that declared Nkgwatau Mack Mpaketsane as their undisputed traditional leader "in terms of our customary law." Next was Kgoshi Mpaketsane's seven-generations-long royal genealogy (see chapter 4). The third set of annexures presented written versions of Lemba and Mpaketsane oral history, including short statements that had been submitted as part of the land claim and a six-page outline of a presentation given at a recent "Lemba Youth Cultural Conference" in Indie.[27] The presentation emphasized migration and leadership history, as well as characteristics of Lemba culture: circumcision, dietary restrictions, proper greetings, religion, trade, music, and language. The fourth set compiled seventeen different letters of invitation, most from the local municipality but some from provincial departments, asking for Kgoshi Mpaketsane's presence, as a chief, to represent his community. One of these, from the Provincial Department of Agriculture and Environment's Sekhukhune district representative, requested his attendance along with all other beneficiaries whose communities "received egg-laying chickens for poverty relief." Another, addressed to him as "The Honourable Kgosi Mpaketsana," invited him to a "meeting of all traditional leaders in Fetakgomo." These letters proved that it was not only his own people and other unrecognized traditional leaders but also local government officials who de facto recognized his chieftaincy.

The final series of annexures, and the bulk of the evidence, invoked the Lemba as black Jews. This is where Lemba DNA transformed most directly into evidence of postapartheid recognition. Here the *American Society of Human Genetics* article by Amanda Spurdle and Trefor Jenkins (1996) appeared in full, alongside one page of an unidentified newspaper article that linked the Lemba with Ethiopian Jews, an article by Magdel le Roux (1997) that explained the Lemba as "African 'Jews' for Jesus," and excerpts from her book that presented the photo of Kgoshi Mpaketsane, described the findings of the genetic study for which Parfitt collected samples in 1997, explained the significance of Mohlotloane as a sacred river that was the site of initiations and rain-making ceremonies, and described Lemba circumcision rituals. Together, this was the evidence that Kgoshi Mpaketsane felt certain would be transformative.

But there was a problem. Like the Ralushai Commission and the land claims commission, the Nhlapo Commission faced delays related to inadequate funding and personnel and a volume of applications that far exceeded even fully funded and fully staffed capacity.[28] Frustrated by the slow pace, dismissive of the process, and emboldened by their high court success that gave them access to their Ralushai Commission findings, Kgoshi Mpaketsane and the sixty other members of the unrecognized traditional leaders organization pressed the provincial government to deal with them as a group whose grievances required collective redress, rather than as merely individuals whose grievances should be dealt with case by case. They hoped that together they might be able to demand recognition directly from the provincial government. For Kgoshi Mpaketsane, this meant that even while he invested his hopes in evidence that spoke to his claims alone, he invested his time in strategies of solidarity that eschewed evidence altogether.

In February 2006, I attended a meeting between Sello Moloto, then premier of the Limpopo Province, and seventeen representatives of Kgoshi Mpaketsane's group (figure 3.2). Moloto sidestepped their demands by appealing to the commission as "the only competent body" to sort out what he called the "technical legal problem" of traditional leadership. Meanwhile, another representative from the premier's office endorsed the postapartheid spirit of the commission. He explained, "It is a very open process; this is more than democracy," as if to emphasize that in his view, the unrecognized traditional leaders really had nothing to complain about.

The group regarded this as an important meeting where they hoped their status might be changed: they imagined that the provincial premier of all people would have that authority. The goal for the premier, however, was to deflect responsibility. He saw it as a question not of whether he *could* personally and immediately affirm them (in fact, he could not) but rather of whether he *should* do so. In other words, for Kgoshi Mpaketsane's group, rights in postapartheid South Africa remained a question of struggle and achievement, and for these representatives of the ANC government, they had become a question of bureaucratic procedure and therefore a project of deflection. For the group, democracy meant airing a grievance that could then be successfully remedied: it was about having voice and agency. For the premier's office, democracy was delegation to commissions of inquiry, which as a political form had by then become a characteristic product of the postapartheid state, regardless of whether each one adhered to democratic principles.

FIGURE 3.2 Members of the unrecognized traditional leaders' organization pose for a group photo before their meeting with the Limpopo Premier Sello Moloto in February 2006. Kgoshi Mpaketsane is standing fourth from the left. Kgoshi Malaga, another unrecognized Lemba traditional leader, is also pictured (*kneeling, first from left*). Photograph by author.

The group members were extremely unhappy that Moloto and the others dismissed their political claims as technical and procedural issues and that the commission's case-by-case investigations undermined their group solidarity. After the meeting, the group drove an hour from the provincial capital back to what had been the capital of the apartheid-era Lebowa "homeland." Far from the spacious boardroom where the meeting with the premier took place, we sat cramped together in the back room of a restaurant owned by a friend of several group members. Sitting on folding chairs with plates of porridge and stewed meat balanced on overturned beer crates, we debriefed.

Kgoshi Mpaketsane and others reiterated that they were a group; in their eyes, the question was not which of them should be considered legitimate chiefs, but why the postapartheid government was taking so long to instate them. They felt they were being marginalized by the very government policies that they imagined were the vehicles of postapartheid justice. Another group member explained, "As much as lesbians can marry each other, traditional leaders must exercise their rights because the Bill of Rights says we must practice our traditional culture. . . . If lesbians can be allowed, why can't we be allowed?" The South African constitution is known for its expansive Bill of Rights, and indeed the right to practice traditional culture was protected alongside many other rights, including guaranteed equality regardless of sexual orientation.[29]

When lesbians are invoked alongside traditional leadership, it is usually done to emphasize the "Africanness" of traditional leaders, against the supposed "un-Africanness" of lesbians (Hoad 2007). This comment was similar to those made by many recognized traditional leaders, as well as political and religious leaders, during 2006 debates about the Civil Union Bill, which legalized same-sex marriage in South Africa. In that context, many African leaders denounced homosexuality as "un-African" (Robins 2008). While that sentiment may have been shared by many of the unrecognized traditional leaders in Kgoshi Mpaketsane's group, the comment about lesbians in the context of their situation calls for a more complicated reading. By indexing marginalization, cultural rights, and the rights of minority groups more generally, these unrecognized traditional leaders framed recognition in and of itself as an issue of postapartheid justice, and by additionally citing the rights of lesbians, they were demonstrating that theirs should be among the new rights guaranteed by the postapartheid constitution. They wanted the right to practice "traditional culture": but for them, getting that right would put them not in the past but rather would ensure that they remain integral to the future of the nation.

Hence, by 2006, Kgoshi Mpaketsane had developed a complex array of strategies for becoming recognized, each responding to the increasingly narrow vision of justice articulated through postapartheid commissions and programs and to what had and had not worked over the preceding decade. Recognition of Lemba difference had long been the goal, but it also became one means to achieve the goal. Kgoshi Mpaketsane worked hard alongside his colleagues toward accessing rights to traditional culture that were generalized and collective, but he also believed it was land and DNA that in combination would attest to his people's particularity so that they might gain cultural rights, and with those rights, ethnic recognition. In this context, DNA became useful through a remapping: instead of evidence of diasporic belonging, DNA as evidence of difference mapped onto South African belonging and the land and chieftaincy claims that, if successful, could secure it.

Citizens and Subjects in Postapartheid South Africa

For Kgoshi Mpaketsane, becoming legally recognized as a traditional leader would mean realization of the full postapartheid citizenship that he had so far been denied. It remains an open question, however, if the same could be said for other rural residents who had no personal claim to traditional authority. In effect, two systems of representation coexist throughout contemporary rural South Africa: traditional leadership and local municipalities. These were both emphatically supported by most residents of India as parallel mechanisms for flexibly advancing their interests, depending on which most aligned with a particular grievance or need.[30] In practice, traditional authorities and local politicians alike were as likely to be despotic as they were democratic and vice versa, and their coexistence could provide recourse in either case. Having one recognized and one unrecognized traditional leader in the village threw off this balance.

Because Kgoshi Mpaketsane was unrecognized, he was perhaps more accountable to his people than he might have been if he did not need their support to push forward in his legal appeals. At the same time, because his people wanted to be recognized as Lemba as much as he did, they had to either continue to support him or accept Lemba subordination to the recognized Maesela chieftaincy. Decades of distrust had solidified two distinct groups of people who felt they could have a voice with their own traditional leader—perhaps even more of a voice than they might have in municipal politics—but not with the other. This was not inevitable and was not the case in many other multiethnic villages. But here, multigenerational rivalries and unequal legal status continued to constrain postapartheid possibilities.

In the early postapartheid years, the Mpaketsane-Maesela conflict manifested as land use issues, such as whether and where to build a clinic or install a borehole for water. Since Kgoshikgolo Sekhukhune and the local municipality alike continued to treat both Mpaketsane and Maesela chieftaincies as legitimate, this meant that they both had to sign off for any projects to move forward. Ultimately, they could not agree on the precise details of whose section of the village the clinic and the borehole should occupy, so they never gave approval. The clinic was built elsewhere, in another village, and the borehole never materialized.

The applications to various commissions and the arrest that brought Kgoshi Mpaketsane to court in 2004 were other ways that village residents paid the price for contested legal recognition: the fines imposed, as well as the lawyer, were expensive. As a recognized traditional leader, Kgoshikgadi Maesela drew a small government salary. In contrast, Kgoshi Mpaketsane survived on income from three sources: social welfare grants from the government that he and his wife received for each of their three children who were still young enough to qualify, the assistance of extended family members who were employed or were eligible for government old-age pensions, and the donations of the constituents who considered him to be their chief, even if the government did not recognize him as such. It was the last group, many of whom were women, who bore the brunt of these expenses: while some of his people earned wages, most sacrificed portions of their own government old-age pensions and child poverty grants to support what they saw as their community and their community's legitimate representative.

Rather than view his court appearance as an unwelcome expense or as a site of criminalization, Kgoshi Mpaketsane and his supporters saw it as a critical point of access to the state. His constituents' collective willingness to pay for fines and lawyers was a testament to their support of Kgoshi Mpaketsane personally and of chieftaincy generally, and it demonstrates that the goal of state recognition of Lemba traditional leadership was shared across gender and class lines. Paying the legal fees was an investment in their future, akin to how these same people paid monthly dues to burial societies that they formed with neighbors and friends. The idea behind these societies, which are ubiquitous in South Africa, is that if you made a regular investment in easing the costs of your fellow members' bereavements, you were guaranteed to have support when you and your family needed it. The payments Kgoshi Mpaketsane's supporters made toward his legal fees were similarly motivated: they hoped that eventually, when he became recognized, he would be in a position to advance their interests through his access to state resources that seemed to all of them to be reserved only for recognized traditional leaders.

Kgoshi Mpaketsane knew that to be recognized as a chief, he had to continue to act like a chief, no matter the repercussions. So when minor disasters happened, such as a March 2006 rainstorm that washed out the one road into the village, leaving everyone stranded for days, he was present among the mixed Mpaketsane and Maesela group that gathered with shovels to rebuild it when the local municipality failed to respond quickly enough (figure 3.3).[31] When new opportunities arose to form a company that could potentially own the rights to platinum in and around the village, he did so, in consultation with

FIGURE 3.3 Kgoshi Mpaketsane (*upper right, in white shirt and blue jeans*) and others survey the flood-damaged road while John Mpaketsane and Selina Carry Mohuba (*foreground*) begin rebuilding work. Photograph by author.

his people, and together they speculated about potential future profits and how they would be divided.

Nowhere was acting like a chief more important, though, than when it came to bodily ritual. When his supporters or their relatives died, Kgoshi Mpaketsane consulted on funeral arrangements and took part in the burials, and he used burial as an incentive to his people to continue to support him. The majority of chieftaincy meetings in 2000 and 2001, for example, were devoted to discussions about expanding the Lemba cemetery, fining anyone who failed to contribute their labor to the project, and establishing a payment of one thousand rand to be paid by the family of any deceased person who had failed to adequately support Kgoshi Mpaketsane and yet was to be buried in his cemetery. In a speech recorded in his meeting minutes on December 31, 2000, he said, "I can see that there are some who are disrespectful, but that disrespect will come to an end. . . . From today onwards, the keys to the cemetery will be kept at the chief's kraal. The chief's kraal will have supreme power over the cemetery. . . . We are going to leave the past in the past; governance will proceed; let us rebuild our nation, the Balepas of Ngwatau."[32] Although his ability to enforce burial restrictions was limited, and his people knew it, it remained a powerful rhetorical tool. "If you don't obey the king, you disrespected him and therefore he won't allow you to be buried in his burial yard as you don't belong to him. Where will you be buried, as everyone belongs to a particular nation?" he asked at one of his royal kraal meetings in December 2005.

Like burial, circumcision was a powerful way of negotiating cultural belonging and local leadership. So each time Kgoshikgadi Maesela exercised her government-granted legal authority to hold a circumcision ceremony, Kgoshi Mpaketsane knew that he had to respond. His monthly meeting on May 7, 2006, was almost entirely devoted to a discussion about circumcision. Kgoshikgadi Maesela had filed an application to convene an initiation school that winter, and now Kgoshi Mpaketsane and his supporters, who were still paying off his 2004 illegal circumcision fines, had to decide whether they would do the same. Before the meeting, anticipating that the attendees would not want to back down from Kgoshikgadi Maesela's challenge, Kgoshi Mpaketsane explained to me that he wanted to take the government to court if they again refused to approve his initiation school application. He told me that he has the right to practice his culture, and the 1996 circumcision law was denying him that right. The ANC government is no good, he explained, because while they claim that there is democracy, they have simply continued with the apartheid chiefs and have not appointed any new ones, so it is just like the apartheid government.

The meeting began with a prayer, everyone on their hands and knees in the dirt around the small shade tree at the edge of Kgoshi Mpaketsane's yard. We started more than two hours late, and the benches where the men sat positioned them directly in the pounding sun, but nevertheless once discussion began, they were as animated and engaged as the women sitting on the ground in the shade of the tree. After a half-dozen people had advocated for the need to go ahead with the initiation school, Kgoshi Mpaketsane called for a vote on a tribal resolution that would authorize him to submit the illegal application and to file a case against the government if the application was denied. The plan was approved and the meeting adjourned.

Soon after, rumors began to circulate: a Maesela woman, it was said, had told two Mpaketsane women that Kgoshi Mpaketsane would be able to hold the circumcision ceremony only if he applied directly to Kgoshikgadi Maesela for permission. But when Kgoshi Mpaketsane convened a court at his kraal to determine what precisely had been said and who should be punished, the two Mpaketsane women who were alleged to have been involved clarified that actually, they had not heard the Maesela woman say what she had been reported to have said. The ruling was that the Maesela woman did not *state* but only *asked* whether Mpaketsane families wishing to send a boy to that year's initiation school must apply through Maesela, so there were no further inquiries or consequences.

Everything moved forward as planned, but once the boys were away on the mountain that July, Kgoshikgadi Maesela decided to up the ante. She got a court order that authorized the police to come and forcibly remove the Lemba boys from the mountain. In the end, it did not go that far, because Kgoshi Mpaketsane and his supporters decided to speed up the initiation, quickly complete the circumcision ceremony, and bring the boys down from the mountain before the date that the police were scheduled to arrive. But each new convening of a circumcision ceremony left them vulnerable. Only recognized traditional leaders could legally hold circumcision schools, but for unrecognized traditional leaders, failure to hold circumcision schools was perceived as akin to abandoning their efforts to become recognized. Despite the fact that Kgoshi Mpaketsane's father had held circumcision ceremonies for Lemba boys, and that Kgoshi Mpaketsane himself had done so throughout the 1990s, Lemba people had to either break the law or acknowledge that Kgoshikgadi Maesela was the only legitimate authority in the village.

For Prince Mpaketsane, the eldest brother of John Mpaketsane, her despotism toward Lemba people was a failure of postapartheid democracy—but also one that could be addressed by the same democratic convictions that had motivated the anti-apartheid struggle. He explained to me,

> Because Maesela is having that letter . . . she says now the mountain where these people are initiating is hers; you see now that is Maesela there and so Mpaketsane is not allowed to do so. . . . We are also the inhabitants of the area, we must all, South Africa belongs to all those who live in it, ne? And we also say India Village belongs to all those who live in it. Why? South Africa itself, according to the charter there, according to the legislation, the freedom charter. It says South Africa belongs to all those who live in it. Why can't India belong to all those who live in it? . . . But Maesela does not want. Because she even say, when we go in courts, she even tell the court that we are her subjects [and] we are just ungovernable!

To Prince, the 1955 Freedom Charter stood as the unrealized promise of post-apartheid citizenship: Kgoshikgadi Maesela might think she could claim the mountain, but South Africa belongs to all who live in it. He argued for a joint jurisdiction in which Maesela and Mpaketsane people each had their own recognized traditional leader who would be equal rather than subject to one another.

But for Kgoshi Mpaketsane, it was cultural difference, inclusive of both circumcision and chieftaincy, evidenced by genetic ancestry, and resulting in recognition of himself and his people that could positively transform their present struggle. One day in 2006, frustrated that he had received an invitation to an LCA event that was not addressed specifically to him as Kgoshi, he questioned how they could speak of "culture" without supporting chieftaincy. "Just ask them about this question because they speak about *the culture*," he implored me. He continued,

> What does *the culture* mean? Because the Lemba people is the black Jew in Africa. So they are called the black Jew, according to DNA. We don't doubt, you see. But when coming to chieftainship, the Jew, they have the chieftainship and they have the circumcision school from long ago. *That* is our culture. To make circumcision. Like now, these Ndebele people, they are accusing us. Why we must practice our initiation. But it is not the first time. It is for long time. Yes, according to our history. We have records. . . . When we were in Yemen, we would take the boys to the mountain during that time. . . . I can show each and everybody if somebody want to accuse me like that lady now, Maesela, yes, we can take some documents to show some judge in court, yes, because there is many people who are interested to make research of the Lemba people like Magdel le Roux, like you, like Tudor Parfitt, like Mathivha now he's passed away.

In Kgoshi Mpaketsane's hands, Lemba DNA, conflated with researchers' interest in the Lemba and their conclusions about Lemba history and culture, became evidence of his community's cultural and territorial rights and of his position as leader of his community. These kinds of rights are what critics of postapartheid rural policies cite as an impediment to democracy that renders people subjects of a chief rather than citizens of a state. But for Kgoshi Mpaketsane, DNA was the pathway to recognition, and recognition was the pathway to a postapartheid citizenship that was fully realized rather than merely promised.

History, Indigeneity, and the Limits of Genetic Evidence

The links among land, chieftaincy, and ethnic difference that shaped Kgoshi Mpaketsane's postapartheid politics were informed by more than a century of dispossession, subjugation, and local political turmoil. In this way, history became not only an explanation for how local struggles began and why they mattered but also an important resource that might shape their future resolution. Kgoshi Mpaketsane made this clear to me as we drove together to Polokwane on the day of the meeting between his unrecognized traditional leaders group and the premier of the Limpopo Province. He was upset because he had seen me interacting with a wide range of people in the village, including those who did not support his chieftaincy. Reprimanding me for my promiscuous research methods, he explained,

> Take the old people, sit them down in front of me, take the history, and go to another village and do the same thing. You didn't do a meeting with the old people. You must not mention Maesela or ask Maesela the history of Maesela and Mpaketsane. You must not take history from them because you are going to contradict my history. You must be like Magdel le Roux and Tudor Parfitt. They came here to take the history of the Lemba people only. They did not make relationships with the Maesela people. I am not satisfied with your research.

Kgoshi Mpaketsane wanted two things from me: he wanted me to "take the history" of the Lemba people as it might be told by elders in his presence, and he wanted me to stop talking to Maesela people so that I would not accidentally access information that might call that version of history into question.

Kgoshi Mpaketsane's stakes in a straightforward history of Lemba people—a history modeled on the work of scholars who approached the Lemba as a possible lost tribe of Israel, and one that included an Mpaketsane chieftaincy that went back generations and that was best approached as if Maesela people simply were not there—were in part about his own desires to secure his status as Lemba chief, but they were also a result of his sophisticated understanding of how authority was contested in the past and the legal frameworks that mediated disputes in the present. His appeal to me to talk to specific people only, and only in his presence, made it very clear that he knew how fragile such an approach to history was. As Kgoshi Mpaketsane would have it, the history of the Lemba people was completely distinct from that of Maesela people—that is, it should be presented as distinct; implied in his imperative to not contradict his history was a belief that Lemba history was not as distinct from Maesela history as was politically necessary.

Hardly monolithic, as an imperative to "take the history" might imply, history as Kgoshi Mpaketsane understood it was something to be crafted. It not only mediated day-to-day interactions between neighbors who were also often relatives, it was also a potent means of making claims on the state. This is what made Lemba genetic ancestry so promising. Lemba genetic ancestry helped craft a historical narrative that was less vulnerable to contradictory assertions and interpretations. It rendered significant only a percentage of Lemba men who manifested the desired marker and then generalized from them to all Lemba people: all other Lemba people and all of their neighbors fell out of the frame. Lemba genetic ancestry was so promising because by its very existence, it evidenced Lemba difference from others and rendered irrelevant Lemba differences among themselves.

Commissions and courts were the points of access to the state, so evidence became the key to successful transformation. For Kgoshi Mpaketsane, genetic ancestry was a technology of recognition, and recognition in turn was a means of achieving citizenship. Here it was citizenship that was at stake: without legal recognition, he and his people would be subject to another chief in their village, and with it, they argued, they would be able to exercise their rights and practice their culture as was guaranteed in South Africa's postapartheid constitution. Kgoshi Mpaketsane's transformative efforts—including not only his applications to government commissions and programs but also court appearances, ongoing conflicts with neighbors, and the formation of an advocacy organization for unrecognized traditional leaders—illustrate how in the early twenty-first century, Lemba DNA became selectively incorporated into long-existing political struggles. At the same time, two postapartheid political emphases—traditional culture in relation to chieftaincy, and authentic firstness in relation to land—prompted Kgoshi Mpaketsane's consideration of a nascent concept of African indigeneity, something that was subsequently embraced more explicitly by the Lemba Cultural Association (see chapter 5). Kgoshi Mpaketsane never used the word "indigenous" to describe Lemba people, but he actively invoked the concepts and peoples that were rapidly coming to define indigeneity in Southern Africa. Together, DNA and indigeneity thus constituted new forms of evidence that Kgoshi Mpaketsane utilized in his attempts to transform his as-yet unsuccessful strategies to achieve South African recognition for himself and his people. As he merged genetic evidence with traditional, cultural, and indigenous rights claims, he reconfigured the contours of how postapartheid citizenship could be enacted.

Here were two different kinds of grounded claims: Mohlotlwane linked Lemba cultural history simultaneously to past and present southern African landscapes, and Lemba DNA grounded that history in scientific certainty; whatever the content of Lemba claims, now they were—or, according to Kgoshi Mpaketsane, they should be—beyond argument. At first glance, Kgoshi Mpaketsane's definitive linking of first settlement and DNA is counterintuitive because the former emphasized belonging in this specific South African place, while the latter spoke to belonging that went beyond Africa completely. But both forms of evidence potentially allowed for expansive belonging in which they could be simultaneously and authentically "of" more than one place. Mohlotlwane was significant precisely because it inscribed migration histories into local geographies, thus marking this place as belonging to Lemba people. Then DNA substantiated Lemba people as a collectivity that held together biologically across disparate places. Kgoshi Mpaketsane felt that genetic evidence should make the critical difference toward becoming recognized because he viewed it as the one form of evidence that could not be contested by government officials or local rivals. He saw Lemba DNA as scientific proof of Lemba difference and therefore of their distinct existence—prerequisites for the forms of recognition and resources that he sought.

The multigenerational struggle for state recognition of Lemba chieftaincy was the primary reason that Kgoshi Mpaketsane agreed to take part in Lemba genetic studies when volunteers were solicited. He hoped that the study would lend scientific credibility to his ongoing struggle for state legitimation. Thus his struggle was not new, but it engaged novel forms of evidence as well as novel political and legal contexts in postapartheid South Africa. As Lemba DNA, in the hands of geneticists and those who reported on or otherwise represented their work, became publicly detached from the Southern African contexts in which Lemba people lived, in the hands of Kgoshi Mpaketsane it also became reterritorialized when he invoked this genetic archive as evidence of Lemba difference for the purposes of his postapartheid claims. The resonance between Kgoshi Mpaketsane's claims about rights, culture, and identity and discourses of indigeneity demonstrates explicit attempts to reframe Lemba difference—both biogenetic and cultural—as part of Africa, rather than defined against it.

Mpaketsane's mobilization of genetic evidence in his applications is a form of genetic citizenship (Heath, Rapp, and Taussig 2004) in which genetic difference formed the basis of making particular claims on the state in the name of inclusive citizenship. Invoking genetic difference in this way explicitly claimed it as potential evidence for postapartheid citizenship. Following his father, who pursued citizenship from the apartheid South African state by seeking recognition of his chieftaincy as a way to access a form of Lemba legitimacy that was tethered to rural land claims, Kgoshi Mpaketsane persevered in the process of seeking state recognition. Knowing that his family's efforts had already outlasted one government, he reasoned that continuing to file his applications was a better bet than acknowledging the laws and the mission of each commission that in the moment of application could not recognize him. Lemba DNA stood out for Kgoshi Mpaketsane as valuable evidence because of its permanence. Like his own perseverance, he valued DNA as a permanent record that could outlast changing political imperatives to ultimately, eventually, deliver justice in the form of state recognition.

Both DNA and indigeneity emerged here as ways to invoke authenticity and time depth toward legally demonstrable difference, but such difference continually failed to deliver the forms of recognition that Kgoshi Mpaketsane and his interlocutors sought. To date, none of Kgoshi Mpaketsane's applications have been successful. The Communal Land Rights Act that seemed so promising ultimately was struck down as unconstitutional. The Nhlapo Commission was underresourced and overwhelmed by the number of claims that were submitted. In the end, it decided only high-profile cases, such as the dispute between K. K. Sekhukhune and Rhyne Thulare as to who was the legitimate Pedi kgoshikgolo; all other cases were allocated to new provincial commissions, and it was unclear when their work would proceed. These failed efforts illuminate the limits of DNA as a politically transformative technology and demonstrate the challenges of applying a politics of indigeneity to postapartheid political projects of ethnic recognition and rural sovereignty.

ANCESTRY, ANCESTORS, AND
CONTESTED KINSHIP AFTER DNA

When I lived in India Village in 2005 and 2006, there was a funeral or tomb-stone unveiling to attend nearly every weekend. Unlike the funerals, which took place the first weekend following someone's passing, the tombstone un-veilings could be planned in advance so that mourners who lived and worked elsewhere could arrange to be there. So it was with Oriah Ratsoma's tombstone unveiling in April 2006. Ratsoma had been an anti-apartheid leader: for a time he was the regional treasurer of the then-banned ANC and the chairperson of the local ANC-affiliated Fetakgomo organization.[1] His commitments came with sacrifices both personal and familial. At one point, he was jailed for three months and tortured, and he lost his son, who had joined the armed struggle in the early 1960s and never returned. Oriah Ratsoma's history ensured that this tombstone unveiling was particularly well attended.

It seemed everyone I had met in this part of South Africa was there, along with many more people whom I was meeting for the first time. Waiting for the official program to begin, I sat under a shady tree with Ratsoma's elderly widow, Jane, and other women. Some lived nearby and visited together often, and others were connecting again after some time. The program began, and we made our way to where the master of ceremonies, Oriah Thobakgale, a nephew of Oriah Ratsoma and his namesake, had started to address the gathering crowd.

Thobakgale, whom I had never met or seen before, introduced me to his audience before I was able to introduce myself to him. "He is here to see the

African culture of the black Jews!" he exclaimed. There was no space for me to reply; he immediately launched into an anti-apartheid struggle song and the crowd joined in, singing while dancing in a circle, joyfully kicking up dust from the dry earth. The singing and dancing continued for about an hour, interrupted by various speakers, each of whom eulogized the deceased and led prayers. Family members spoke, including Phoko John Mpaketsane, who as my host had incorporated me into his household as his son. Kgoshi Mpaketsane spoke too, not just as a family member, but also in his official capacity as Lemba chief and in acknowledgment that Oriah Ratsoma had been a royal adviser to his father throughout the latter's own chieftaincy from the 1940s until his death in 1989. And ANC comrades, both locals and those who had traveled from other provinces for the event, spoke to honor Ratsoma's contributions to the struggle against apartheid.

Multiple forms of relatedness were on display at the unveiling, invoking multiple scales, from the interpersonal and familial to the local, national, and transnational. Thobakgale and others who also lived near Pretoria or Johannesburg performed their familial ties and local belonging: he and the other Lemba people there were "blood relatives," he later told me, and though he lived and worked elsewhere, it was the village Sealane—just on the other side of the mountains but seventy-five kilometers away by road—that was home. "When I say home, I mean here," he explained.[2] From near and far, ANC comrades affirmed the links between present party politics and the anti-apartheid struggle: the relatedness that they performed was not to blood and home, but to state power and fellow party members. Finally, my presence there prompted Thobakgale to invoke the genetic relatedness of Lemba people to Jews elsewhere, and a "home" that signaled, broadly, Africa vis-à-vis the rest of the world.

Inspired by the varied ways that people enacted relatedness at Oriah Ratsoma's tombstone unveiling ceremony, and the varied audiences that their speeches, songs, and prayers invoked, this chapter asks what we can learn about genetic ancestry by looking at it alongside other means of figuring relatedness. I am especially interested here in the coemergence of relatedness and legitimacy. How, by whom, under what circumstances, and with what consequences was relatedness affirmed or contested? This chapter departs from the other chapters in this book by examining not how genetic ancestry articulated with forms of belonging such as diaspora, citizenship, and indigeneity, but rather how one interconnected group of Lemba people, all of whom embraced as a genetic fact that they have Jewish blood, worked through their own politics of relatedness with one another. Given that genetic ancestry was very much available as a technology of relatedness, it is notable when it might have been but was not invoked. I therefore ask: When does genetic ancestry matter, and when do other forms of relatedness matter more? This chapter, then, is about not only the afterlives of genetic ancestry, but also the liveliness of genealogy.

Signe Howell's concept of kinning (2003, 2006) is instructive here. Kinning is the process of incorporating any new person into existing kinship concepts and connections. Howell emphasizes that all new persons become kin via active incorporation—not just spouses or adoptees who have prior relations elsewhere to others, but also fetuses and newly born infants whose status as kin we might take for granted. Relatedness, in this view, is always an achievement. Placing kinning at the center of kinship calls attention to process, practice, and politics. It reinforces feminist and queer shifts in anthropological approaches to gender and kinship beginning in the 1970s that troubled dichotomies between female and male, nature and culture, and domestic and public spheres. These shifts made it possible to understand relatedness as dynamic and contingent rather than as a collection of culturally variable but ultimately rigid systems based on the "facts" of biological reproduction.[3] This literature makes it clear that such binary distinctions are themselves cultural rather than natural and that kinship is thus always a matter of negotiation. This chapter likewise shows how even within supposedly straightforward forms of biogenetic and reproductive kinship, people engage in the active process of kinning, both as a means to make relations, as in Howell's work, and also as a means to unmake them: kinning practices in both senses illustrate how relatedness mattered and the wide range of what relatedness could be made to accomplish.

In chapter 3, I argued that when Kgoshi Mpaketsane repurposed Lemba genetic studies from evidence that the Lemba were linked to Jews to legal proof that they were a distinct South African ethnic group with a distinct traditional leader, he was shaping a genetic afterlife. In this chapter, I explore the fact that DNA was not his only line of evidence, the South African state was not his only audience, and "the Lemba" were necessarily more varied than genetic ancestry could account for. This chapter deeply explores the kinning practices of one interconnected group of Lemba people, families, and clans. At issue was a controversy about the legitimacy of Kgoshi Mpaketsane's position; at stake were his and others' investments in the idea of royal blood and the incommensurably different means of establishing it. Peoples' assertions, their doubts, and their subsequent actions together call into question what it means to be related and when and how it matters.

In being the subject of questions and concerns about his legitimacy, Kgoshi Mpaketsane was in good company. Similar controversies were regionally and nationally widespread and perhaps inevitable given the contentious colonial, apartheid, and now postapartheid status of chieftaincy throughout rural South Africa. The account that follows should therefore not be taken as reason to doubt this particular traditional leader, but rather as an indication of some of the questions raised by the entrenchment of hereditary positions of power in the midst of democratic transformations. There is a case to be made, in fact, that it was the state's failure to legally recognize Kgoshi Mpaketsane's chieftaincy that fostered familial conflict and created an opening for biogenetic relatedness to take on new significance. I take the position that the form and content of these intimate contestations should be read as a commentary about the multivalence of local legitimacy, and also as a means of opening up theoretical questions about genetic ancestry and genealogical production in practice.

This chapter explores the complexity and contingency of relatedness in practice because, I argue, it is precisely this complexity and contingency that are obscured through genetic ancestry, whether the direct-to-consumer tests that people purchase to learn about their ethnic and national past or the scientific studies like the ones that Lemba people participated in that aim to create global maps of racial and ethnic origin and supposed one-way migratory paths. Against the apparent promise of genetic ancestry, these stories remind us that relatives—even "blood relatives"—are not found, but made and unmade.

Relatedness as Political Practice

I did not set out to do a kinship study, but in interview after interview I found myself deeply drawn in to complicated accounts of who was firstborn and who came later, which wife was married first and so was senior to other wives and which children were from which mother, and which marriages were between cousins and which involved non-Lemba women—and of these, who was from the Sekhukhune royal kraal, who was from subordinate royal lineages, and who was not part of a royal lineage at all. I pieced together different people's narratives when details converged, such as which people were known as traditional healers, where people had been born, and where they were buried. And I puzzled over how to account for people who seemed to skip generations because those whom I could not help but identify as their biological parents had only stood in to "raise seed" on behalf of deceased, childless, or sonless ancestors, so they were not regarded as the parents at all.

Oriah Ratsoma's widow, Jane, was part of a relationship like this. Born in 1924, she worked as a nanny in Johannesburg for nearly two decades, beginning

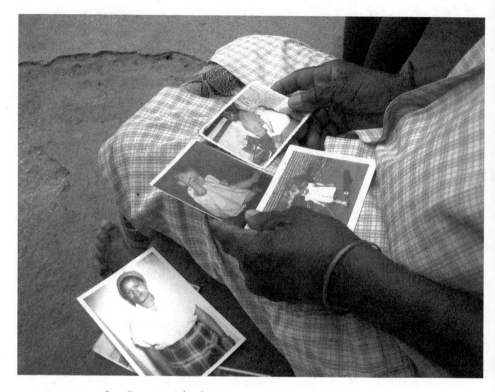

FIGURE 4.1 Jane Ratsoma, at her home in 2006, displays photographs of herself and her charges from her time working as a nanny in Johannesburg from the mid-1940s to the mid-1960s. Photograph by author.

when she was twenty (figure 4.1). That was where she and Oriah met, and in 1962 she left Johannesburg for his natal village, India. She and Oriah had had only two children, she told me, one of whom died at eight months old and the other a miscarriage. Yet there were several children and young adults in her household. When I asked who they were, she introduced me to her wife and explained that she, Jane, was the woman's husband on behalf of her son; Jane had paid *lobola*, and she and her wife had married in 1984. Her wife took the surname Ratsoma, as did her children, both those she had on her own prior to this marriage and the others who were born later. To Jane, these were all her grandchildren, and it did not concern her who may have played a role in their conception ("boyfriends, it's all mixed up," she explained). What I understood as their biological paternity was irrelevant, and what mattered was who claimed them and whose name they could pass on in the future.

Jane Ratsoma's family underscored that genealogies were never just metaphorical representations of biological relationships. Rather, they were thoroughly political assertions. For the most part, the genealogies that people shared with me corresponded in their overlaps, but interpretations of them did not. Embedded in the divergent interpretations were differing views on what makes a lineage distinct from others, what makes a chief or a leader, and whether legitimacy within local chieftaincy politics was at odds with legitimacy as Lemba people.

Family, Lineage, Clan: One Story of Mpaketsane, Peta, and Ratsoma

There were many Lemba lineages throughout this region, but the disputes among Lemba people about Kgoshi Mpaketsane principally concerned three: Mpaketsane, Peta, and Ratsoma. A number of different narratives spun out from the same tangled genealogies. But untangling which ancestors belonged to which lineages, and which were the ancestors who mattered, was less a question of accuracy and more a question of politics. At stake here were contested claims to and about significant common ancestors who were part of these genealogies, and one of the ways that these claims were expressed was through differing accounts of how each lineage related to the others.

For example, I learned from John Mpaketsane's mother, Morweshadi Mpaketsane, that the original Mpaketsane, Ratsoma, and Peta people were actually three brothers from the same mother. Mpaketsane took on that name because he wore spectacles—in Sepedi, the word for spectacles is *dipeketsana*. He was the elder brother to the one who became known as Ratsoma. The brothers were traders at that time, dealing in metal wires, but it was Mpaketsane who organized the business: he sent out the one who would be called Ratsoma to do the actual trading. This brother would come back with food or money that he had received in exchange for the metal wires, giving most of it back to Mpaketsane and keeping the rest for himself, but he ultimately grew tired of the arrangement. He decided, "I can't stay. I must go and sell for myself; I must go and hunt for myself." So he became Ratsoma, from the Sepedi word for hunt, *tsoma*.

Morweshadi had no origin story for the name "Peta" and indeed regarded it as the original name while the other two could have come into use only after the Peta/Mpaketsane/Ratsoma ancestors had migrated from Tshivenda-speaking regions to Sepedi-speaking ones. But following her explanation of the meaning of Mpaketsane and Ratsoma, I wondered if the origin of "Peta" might have been the Tshivenda word *peta*, which means to fold up cloth, or *mpeta*, which is a tree that "is medicine to fold up people's hearts and make them stop quarreling" (Van Warmelo 1989). I could not confirm this theory, but the words could easily have been associated with traditional healers, a role that many from all three lineages had held.

For Morweshadi Mpaketsane, the three lineages were both different *and* the same—different because they had diverged, and the same because they had the same roots. This difference/sameness was reflected in another way by Professor Mathivha's account of Lemba clans: he listed Mpaketsane, Peta, and Ratsoma as part of the Mhani clan (Mathivha 1992).[4] But unlike Mathivha's account, Morweshadi's was not primarily a means of cataloguing as many Lemba surnames as possible so that they might find themselves and one another and know their histories. Instead, her story naturalized the relationship between Peta, Mpaketsane, and Ratsoma, while it also affirmed the primacy of Peta, the agency of Mpaketsane, and the subordinate status of Ratsoma.

It is, of course, relevant who Morweshadi herself was in relation to each of these lineages. She had been born in the nearby village Mogabane in 1939, the child of a father from the Peta family with roots two generations back in Sealane (his grandfather had left Sealane and founded Mogabane with his six wives) and a mother from a branch of the Mpaketsane family who had stayed in Sealane when others left to live in what became known as India.[5] She herself came to India when she married Reuben Mogaisi Mpaketsane, the younger half-brother of the then-Kgoshi Mpaketsane, the deceased father of the Kgoshi Mpaketsane whom I knew. When they married, they were carrying forward generations of cross-cousin Lemba endogamy, something which many elders held up as ideal, many younger people rejected, and most scholarly work and media about the Lemba presented as both a traditional and an ongoing practice that culturally substantiated Lemba links to Jews while also biologically preserving evidence of those links.

As a daughter of Peta, a wife of Mpaketsane, and a granddaughter of Mpaketsane, and only more distantly related to Ratsoma, Morweshadi believed, as did many of her siblings, that Peta and Mpaketsane were basically the same, but that Ratsoma had been more the same with them in the distant past than they were in the present. It is no surprise, then, that Morweshadi was one of Kgoshi Mpaketsane's biggest supporters and one of the most insistent that India/Ga-Maesela belonged to Mpaketsane.[6] Yet, Morweshadi's and Kgoshi Mpaketsane's accounts of the relationship among these three lineages differed markedly.

Royal Genealogy: "There Is No Chief without the Small Kraals"

Kgoshi Mpaketsane framed almost all of our conversations in terms of his chieftaincy, his attempts to get that chieftaincy recognized by the government, and his struggles against those who did not support his efforts. When I asked him about Morweshadi's story, he dismissed it. He was not interested in common origins and divergent paths. Rather, he emphasized hierarchical arrangement, which was the basis, he explained, for understanding "what the chieftainship is." He went on, "King Sekhukhune is the senior surname at Sekhukhune royal kraal, but there is a certain surnames like Mampuru . . . they fall under King Sekhukhune. . . . Like Mpaketsane, Peta, . . . Ratsoma and all these, they fall under Chief Mpaketsane, you see? Because there is no chief without the small kraals."

To illustrate this further, he pulled out his copy of Peter Delius's *The Land Belongs to Us: The Pedi Polity, the Boers and the British in the Nineteenth-Century Transvaal* (1984). The book is a social history. Based on interviews and archival research, it presents a story of how the Pedi polity came to power in the eighteenth and nineteenth centuries. Key to their strategy was the *lebone*, or "candlewife" system, which incorporated other groups through marriage to high-status Pedi women from the ruling Maroteng lineage. These women, now given the titles Lebone (candle), Setima-mello (extinguisher of fires), and Mohumagadi (chief wife), cemented mutual support between Pedi leadership and the incorporated group (Delius 1984, 55; 1996, 163).

The presence of a candlewife secured a man's leadership position as a chief, but it also signaled his and his followers' subordinate status to the Maroteng kgoshikgolo (paramount chief or king). This is what Kgoshi Mpaketsane meant when he said, "There is no chief without the small kraals." Delius's account shows how this kinning practice was central to the rise of the Pedi polity. Kinning in the sense that I am using it, as a technology of both making *and* unmaking relations, was central to the fall of the Pedi polity as well. Two factors played decisive roles: an alliance between the British and Swazi armies, and intrafamily assassinations within the Maroteng ruling family.

But when Kgoshi Mpaketsane showed me his copy of Delius's book, he did not emphasize the extent to which leadership could ultimately hinge on elimination of rival kin. Instead, he pointed me toward the genealogy of the Maroteng royals (the Pedi kings) that appears in a chart at the book's beginning (figure 4.2). We were again in the front room of his two-room house, site of many of our visits and most of our formal interviews. This particular occasion was in late October 2006, just weeks before I returned to the United States after a year in South Africa, and we were both making our final attempts to finish my research.[7] My attempts focused on asking him more directed questions to fill in the gaps I thought were left by my ethnographic observation and open-ended interviewing methods. His focused on explaining what my research should look like once it was published as a book.

He implored me, book in hand, to be like Peter Delius. He said,

> You see, Mr. Peter Delius . . . so that man, he can sit down with the old man and the old woman with the Pedi people, right at the Pedi Royal Kraal at Mohlaletse, to get this picture of King Sekhukhune the first to make like that. Because these people, they are the custodians. But why, Noah, when coming to chieftainship of the Lemba people, why don't you make that like Peter Delius? . . . You must take the chieftainship of the Lemba people; you must set aside.

He pointed to the genealogy chart in Delius's book and told me to use it as a model. He was very specific: "Write in your book, when it gets published, you see, you must take the Mpaketsane chieftainship: this is the first chief, second chief, what what, until the last one."

As a further guide, he referred me to the genealogy chart that had been a required part of his application for legal recognition of his chieftaincy through the Nhlapo Commission. His instructions were explicit and his rationale clear: "You can take this genealogy, you put it there [in your book], then from there, each and everybody can see the book inside: here is the chiefs; you see the genealogy of the Mpaketsane people, fall under the Lemba people."

In Kgoshi Mpaketsane's framing, the genealogy of the Mpaketsane people who fall under the Lemba people had its parallel in how the Pedi royal genealogy was presented as the Maroteng people who lead and therefore define the Pedi. He had bought Delius's book at the Sekhukhune Royal Kraal, and he explained, "Each and every chief got it, because you must read the history of your forefathers at Sekhukhune Royal Kraal because it is our forefathers there; you must know the history of the Pedi people. That is why I bought this book. So now you must take my genealogy, that's what I'll give you, that is a mission of mine."

For Kgoshi Mpaketsane, the urgency of including his royal genealogy in my book served two purposes. First, because the Nhlapo Commission was still pending, he hoped that my published work might be available in time to further substantiate his legitimacy as a traditional leader and the long history of his royal lineage—the commission, however, later chose to decide only contested kingships and not smaller-scale traditional leadership disputes, so I was unable to contribute to Kgoshi Mpaketsane's recognition efforts in that way.[8]

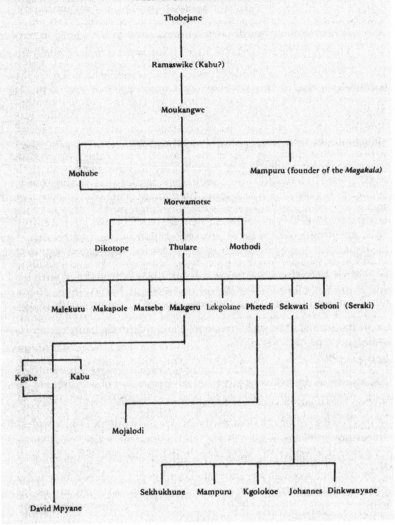

FIGURE 4.2 Skeleton genealogy of the Maroteng Royal from Peter Delius's 1984 book *The Land Belongs to Us: The Pedi Polity, the Boers, and the British in the Nineteenth Century Transvaal.*

Second, he hoped that my hypothetical future book could demonstrate to his neighbors the significance of Lemba people in South Africa, just as Delius's book about the Pedi did. Whether this book will have that effect remains to be seen.

Per his instructions, Kgoshi Mpaketsane's royal genealogy appears here, doing double duty (figure 4.3). For Kgoshi Mpaketsane and his audiences in South Africa, the chart shows the historicity and legitimacy of his position as a traditional leader. For me, the chart and Delius's together suggest that there is an important comparison to be made between royal genealogies and genetic ancestry.

Royal genealogies were political legitimation, and Kgoshi Mpaketsane knew this better than most. What his chart and Delius's had in common was that they were orderly, linear representations that naturalized the transfer of power from father to son even as they pointed toward ways in which that transfer had been or might be called into question. Delius limited his genealogy to Maroteng royals whom he mentioned in his book, and he charts fathers and children (mostly, but not exclusively, sons), omitting royal wives because legitimacy in this case flowed patrilineally. Delius's genealogy culminates with Sekhukhune I and his brothers. We see that Sekhukhune was the firstborn son of Sekwati, who gained power despite being a younger son of Thulare, who was himself the second child of Morwamotse, and that in the oldest generations, the lineage is singular: Moukangwe descends from Ramaswike, who descends from Thobejane. In the text, we learn details about migrations and rivalries, but the skeleton genealogy is just that: the bare bones of how inherited contemporary local power came to be.

In Kgoshi Mpaketsane's royal genealogy chart, legitimacy was underscored by repetition of names. This was not just a rhetorical device: naming a child after an ancestor called that ancestor into direct relation with the child, bringing the past actively into the present. Thus the Kgoshi Mpaketsane whom I knew was listed as Kgoshi Nkgwatau (3), firstborn son of Kgoshi Mothakge (3), who was the firstborn son of Kgoshi Nkgwatau (2), who was the son of a regent named Mogaisi on behalf of Mogaisi's brother Kgoshi Mapampole, who were both sons of Kgoshi Mothakge (2), who was the firstborn son of Kgoshi Nkgwatau (1), who was the only listed child of Kgoshi Mothakge (1).

In keeping with this pattern, Kgoshi Mpaketsane had named his firstborn son Mothakge in anticipation of the latter's eventual position as Kgoshi Mothakge (4). And unlike in Delius's genealogy, royal wives were listed, some also with their title "mohumagadi": for Kgoshi Mpaketsane, legitimacy flowed both patrilineally and matrilineally. The royal wives, too, had repeating names:

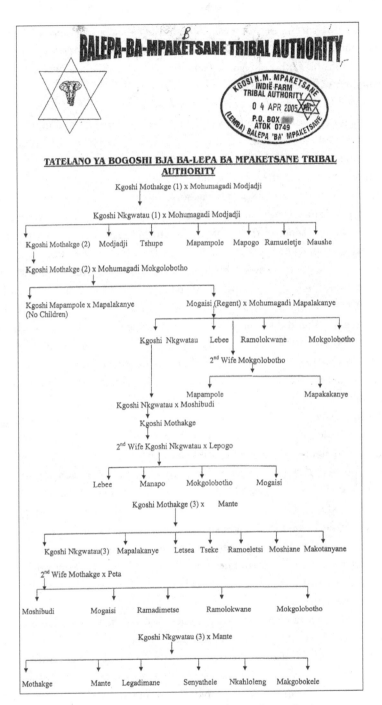

FIGURE 4.3 Kgoshi Mpaketsane's royal genealogy as depicted in his April 2005 submission to the Nhlapo Commission.

Kgoshi Mpaketsane—again, designated in the genealogy as Kgoshi Nkgwatau (3)—had a daughter, wife, and mother all named Mante, and in the earliest generations listed, Kgoshi Mpaketsane's namesake Kgoshi Nkgwatau (1) had a daughter, wife, and mother all named Modjadji.

As a rubric for understanding local power structures, these repeating names for daughters were even more significant than the repeating names for sons, because while the son's names simply established the legitimacy of lineage, the daughters' names established legitimacy in the broader frameworks of local politics. Modjadji is the name of the Lobedu Rain Queen royal lineage, which was established around 1800 and has remained one of the only and most well-known matrilineal royal houses in southern Africa (see Krige and Krige 1943). The name's presence in the earliest generations of Kgoshi Mpaketsane's royal genealogy signaled early alliances between the Mpaketsane people and what would have been a newly established, female-ruled kingdom. It also signaled that in those generations, Mpaketsane people were outside the region of Pedi dominance, something that Kgoshi Mpaketsane confirmed.[9] Mante was likewise a name that did not originate among Lemba people, though in this case, it signaled their local legitimacy in Pedi structures of power. Kgoshi Mothakge (3)'s wife Mante—the mother of the Kgoshi Mpaketsane whom I knew, Kgoshi Nkgwatau (3)—came from the Pedi royal family. This status designated her as a candlewife.

Candlewives were not married to just one person, but to the entire community, which would contribute lobola on behalf of their leader to marry a sister or daughter of the Pedi kgoshikgolo (Delius 1984). They affirmed their acceptance of Pedi leadership, and in return, their own leader's authority was affirmed. Thus when Kgoshi Mpaketsane told me that he bought Delius's book "at Sekhukhune Royal Kraal because it is our forefathers there," he meant not only that he viewed Pedi leadership as legitimate—something he confirmed when he married Mante, the candlewife who cemented his legitimate leadership as a subordinate chief under the authority of the Pedi king—but that he himself descended in part from the Sekhukhune royal lineage via his mother, also named Mante.

Skeleton genealogies, repeating names, and candlewives were all kinning practices that Kgoshi Mpaketsane needed as he navigated intertwined forms of legitimacy on the terms of the state, in relation to local power structures that predated and continued alongside state forms of authority, and in the eyes of those whom he claimed as his people. He presented his genealogy as a simple matter of paternal descent from chiefs and maternal descent from the Sekhukhune royal kraal, and in doing so, he appealed to both Lemba and Pedi histories:

because he was unrecognized, he needed the support of his own people and of recognized local traditional leaders, including the Sekhukhune royal family.

But there was another repeating matrilineal name in Kgoshi Mpaketsane's genealogy—Mapalakanye. And it turned out that as important as Modjadji may have been in the past and Mante was in the present in shoring up the legitimacy of the Mpaketsane chieftaincy by proving Lemba links to local power structures, Mapalakanye was even more significant within internal Lemba chieftaincy debates. Unlike Modjadji and Mante, Mapalakanye was a name that originated among Lemba people, and it was just as consequential to questions about the legitimacy of Kgoshi Mpaketsane's chieftaincy as was the history of incorporation into the Sekhukhune royal family.

Mapalakanye appears on Kgoshi Mpaketsane's genealogy chart four times: she was Kgoshi Mpaketsane's eldest sister from the same father and mother, and she is listed in three iterations in earlier generations. Two of these represent the same person: as Kgoshi Mpaketsane's paternal great-grandmother, she appears first as the wife to a chief who died with no heirs and second as the wife of the one chosen to replace him after he died; this latter union produced Kgoshi Mpaketsane's grandfather. Her name appears once more as that grandfather's sister from the same father and a different mother. Kgoshi Mpaketsane did not elaborate on who Mapalakanye was or where she came from, but that turned out to be the key to understanding the problems that a branch of the Ratsoma family had with the Mpaketsane chieftaincy. While she may have been an important source of his lineage's authority, she was also a primary factor in why Kgoshi Mpaketsane's chieftaincy was disputed by some of his own relatives.

Entangled Genealogies: Mpaketsane, Peta, and Ratsoma Revisited

Modite Ratsoma hesitated at first to talk to me when I approached him at a wedding in Apel the day after Oriah Ratsoma's tombstone unveiling. He had seen me at the unveiling, introduced himself, and invited me to visit with him in Apel sometime in the future. But he also knew that I was working closely with Kgoshi Mpaketsane and that what he had to tell me was contentious and potentially subversive. I had been hearing about Modite and his brothers for months and that they did not support Kgoshi Mpaketsane's chieftaincy. I did not know why, and our first conversation further confused me.

After reintroducing ourselves, his desire to make his perspective known overcame his hesitation, and he got right to the point. "We don't have a chief;

we've got only a leader," he told me, referring to Lemba people. He continued, "Like [Nelson] Mandela [who famously stepped down after a single five-year term], after five years we will choose another. We [either the Lemba people or South Africa] are like you [the United States], only a leader." I asked him who was the leader now, and his answer made me realize that not only was chieftaincy versus leadership at stake but also kinship—specifically who could claim whom as their ancestors and what made a lineage royal. He told me,

> We don't have [a leader] now. My grandfather was the leader of *Bashavhi* at Israel, at Venda [both Israel and Venda signal a distant past].[10] King Sekhukhune said, 'Let me get my daughter to be your wife [a reference to the candlewife system].' They [ambiguous: either his ancestors specifically or more broadly the local Lemba community at the time] said, 'No, because if we do that, all the children, they will die. . . .' We've got a very long history. My grandfather was the first to leave that side. King Sekhukhune said to stay there [at the place named Mohlotlwane by Lemba people and later known as India]. Our grandfather was a medicine person to King Sekhukhune during the war.

Modite's comments merged the past and the present as the pertinent time frames, and he seemed to regard both hereditary and elected leadership as important institutions to safeguard.

I was left with more questions than answers. Why would marrying King Sekhukhune's daughter cause all the children to die? What concerns about relatedness were embedded in his statement, and whose concerns were they? How did they overlap with or differ from the stories about Lemba genetic ancestry and other forms of Lemba connectedness that I had been learning from members of the Lemba Cultural Association and from Kgoshi Mpaketsane and others in India/Ga-Maesela?

Modite invoked genetic ancestry much as other Lemba people did. That same day, he told me, "'We are the black Jews' is what they told us. They found the blood and the"—he paused and mimed a cheek swab sample—"are the same. That is why we're different from other people." As confusing as Modite's initial statements were, it was clear that while DNA for him proved Lemba-Jewish connections and Lemba difference from others, it was not a relevant form of evidence for thinking through local political legitimacy.

In the months that followed this encounter and after considerable discussion between Kgoshi Mpaketsane, John Mpaketsane, and John's brothers, it was decided that I would be allowed to interact further with the Ratsoma brothers in Apel. In total, I stayed with Modite, his wife, and their children at their home for about two weeks, spread over several visits in May, August, and September 2006. These visits included Modite's tours of the area and introductions to people whom he thought I might find interesting, such as the women who ran an organization called the Rural Woman's Association. They managed vegetable garden cooperatives in what was otherwise a food-insecure and produce-poor area, and they organized adult literacy and computer skills courses. He showed me his welding workshop, which is one of the ways he had made a living since returning to Apel after several years in the 1960s working in a kitchen in Gauteng. And he showed me his religious paraphernalia: a faded poster of William Branham, an American mid-twentieth-century Christian evangelist, hung on his dining room wall; a collection of Branham's Spoken Word Fellowship Ministries prayer booklets; audiocassette recordings of Branham's sermons; and a 1963 issue of *Life Magazine* that featured Branham. Modite had joined this church in 1976 despite his proximity to a Roman Catholic mission a few doors down from his home, the fact that most of his relatives belonged to the Zion Christ Church (zcc), and affirmation from Professor Mathivha in the early 1970s that the stories he had heard from his father that the Lemba are black Jews were true. Over meals throughout my visits there, our conversations balanced talk about Brother Branham with discussions of Modite's history, both personal and genealogical.

Modite was born in India village in 1942, but when he was a child, his family moved to a nearby white-owned farm to work as laborers. As young teenagers, he and each of his brothers—including the two youngest, who were born after they moved away—had returned to India for circumcision and initiation, although they continued to live elsewhere. Despite this ongoing connection to the place of their father's birth, as adults, Modite, most of his brothers, their father, and several uncles moved to Apel, which was about fifteen kilometers from India. The draw was that unlike India and most other local villages, Apel had a health clinic, a taxi rank, and a relatively large population: it was better serviced and better connected than anywhere else nearby.

Modite and his siblings learned their family history from their father, Senyathela Mack Ratsoma, who died in 1989, and from an uncle, Mapogo Mack Ratsoma, who died in 2005. My first visit to this part of Apel had been to attend the March 2006 unveiling of Mapogo's tombstone. From that first conversation with Modite through my final interview with his youngest brother, Sekomane, the Ratsoma brothers in Apel always came back to their great-grandfather, Senyathela Ratsoma, the namesake of their father: because I first learned about him from Modite and his brothers, I will refer to him from their perspective, as Great-Grandfather Senyathela.

Great-Grandfather Senyathela was a healer and an associate of Sekhukhune I (1814–1882), the Pedi king who fought colonial forces, after whom the region is named: locals continue to call it Sekhukhuneland or Sekhukhune.[11] Great-Grandfather Senyathela's exact dates of birth and death were unknown, and no one ever mentioned to me who his parents or earlier ancestors were. But when I asked, his descendants estimated that he must have been born sometime in the first quarter of the nineteenth century, since he was a contemporary of Sekhukhune I. He may have come from what is now Zimbabwe, or perhaps from the area around what is now the South African border town Musina. By the 1870s, Great-Grandfather Senyathela had traveled south and had met Sekhukhune I, who enlisted his help in his military campaigns due to the strength of his medicine.

Modite's younger brother Sekomane, a teacher by profession, explained that it was Great-Grandfather Senyathela's work as a healer and his favored status with Sekhukhune I that brought him to the place where he eventually settled:

> So now, after Sekhukhune has overpowered the whole Transvaal . . . when everything come to be settled, my great-grandfather went from Mohlaletse [the center of Pedi power, the site of the Sekhukhune royal kraal] . . . to India, where [he was] the first person to arrive. . . . The reason was that he was looking for medicines . . . around the mountains down to India. When he arrived there he found the place very much good for living, that he can stay there. . . . So now, immediately after that he went back to Sekhukhune and he say, "Sekhukhune, I've got a very good place where I can stay if possible." So now, Sekhukhune gave him that permission that he can stay there. He even sent a group of people to make a road from that India up to Mohlaletse that side so that whenever they need him, they must get him. . . . He's the first one who came and then immediately after that he went to collect his wives.

With this narrative, Sekomane placed Great-Grandfather Senythathela squarely in the center of the history of not only his own genealogy but also of the Lemba presence in India village and therefore any claim that Lemba people might have to that place. According to Sekomane, it was Senyathela's work as a healer seeking ingredients that brought him there, his status as a healer to Sekhukhune I specifically that facilitated his permission to settle, and his bringing in of his wives that established the site as a village. This was where the Mpaketsane people entered into Sekomane's story. He continued,

> [Great-Grandfather Senyathela] had two wives. So now thereafter he went to them and go and call them to come and stay with him. . . . So

when he came to stay . . . at India, the people of Ga-Mpaketsane, Ba-
Mpaketsane people, they came to stay at [Sealane] so thereafter, one of
these Mpaketsane people get to India to marry my great-grandfather's
daughter. . . . The man who married my great-grandfather's first
daughter passed away. So now immediately after that . . . she go back to
India to her father now . . . because her husband passed away.

This widow who returned to her father's house was Mapalakanye, Kgoshi
Mpaketsane's paternal great-grandmother. But while Mapalakanye is prominent on Kgoshi Mpaketsane's royal genealogy, her father—Great-Grandfather
Senyathela from the perspective of Modite and Sekomane Ratsoma—does not
appear at all, though Kgoshi Mpaketsane did acknowledge him as a significant
ancestor when he named his fourth-born child after him.[12] Likewise, in Sekomane's story, Kgoshi Mpaketsane's royal ancestor Kgoshi Mapampole (Mapalakanye's first husband) appears only as "one of these Mpaketsane people," and
her second husband, identified on Kgoshi Mpaketsane's genealogy as "Mogaisi
(Regent)," is absent entirely.

Sekomane continued, explaining that when Mapalakanye returned to her
father's village, she did not come alone: "Some of the people of Peta, they came
with her. . . . So now when she came back to India, her father told her that
she must stay there because, well, I don't know whether she was able to feed
herself or if it was because of other things, she was forced to get back to her
father. Well, they stayed there until my grandfather was born and then my
father was born; they were together there." Echoing but inverting Morwashadi
Mpaketsane's story of the interrelationships between Peta, Mpaketsane, and
Ratsoma, Sekomane framed the relationship between the Mpaketsane and
Ratsoma lineages as one of patronage, here originating not from common descent but from marriage: when Senyathela Ratsoma's daughter was widowed,
not only did he welcome her back as his child, he also accepted some of her
new (Peta) relations as additional children. For Sekomane, the idea that the
death of Mapalakanye's husband forced her dependence on her father eclipsed
the potential significance of the fact that she apparently returned to India with
followers (the people of Peta).

Royal Ancestors

Mpaketsane royal history looked quite different when it was told not as the
primary story as in Kgoshi Mpaketsane's genealogy chart, but as incidental
to the history of Senyathela Ratsoma and his descendants. John Mpaketsane

tried to prepare me for this version of genealogical history leading up to my visits to Apel. As part of the royal family, John fully supported Kgoshi Mpaketsane's chieftaincy. However, where both Kgoshi Mpaketsane and the Ratsoma brothers emphasized the separateness of their lineages from one another and deemphasized and even omitted relatives who complicated that narrative, John Mpaketsane, like his mother, Morweshadi, knew that the lineages were intertwined, and so the story of one was necessarily the story of both.

We were together at home, and John and his brothers had just discussed whether I should be further exposed to the Ratsoma brothers' perspectives on regional Lemba history. This was in May 2006. At the time, John had a college degree from UNISA and a thriving career as a professional nurse; he was also in the process of completing a UNISA distance learning honors degree and in the midst of running what was ultimately an unsuccessful campaign for district ward councillor on a United Independent Front (UIF) minority ticket against the ANC candidate. So whenever he took time out from this busy schedule to explain something to me, I knew it was important. John felt that if I went to Apel, then I needed to understand whom I was talking to, genealogically speaking. As he began his explanation, he turned to a blank page of my field notebook to chart out a genealogy, and as Modite Ratsoma had done in our earlier encounter and as both Modite and his brother continued to do throughout my visits with them, John Mpaketsane started with Senyathela (figure 4.4).

John agreed with Modite and Sekomane that it was Senyathela's relationship with Sekhukhune I that enabled Lemba people to settle in India/Ga-Maesela, and he also agreed with Kgoshi Mpaketsane that the Mpaketsane people were the first to settle India. He reconciled this contradiction by claiming Senyathela as an Mpaketsane ancestor. He explained,

> There was nobody here, there was nobody using the land who was re-garded as the *owner* of the land. . . . The Mpaketsane people fought the wars for Sekhukhune. Our grandfathers were the traditional doctors for the chief Sekhukhune. . . . Our grandfather fought. He's the one who helped Sekhukhune to be a victor . . . and then because of his magics, our grandfather's magic, because he was a very good doctor . . . the one who was called Senyathela. He's an uncle to my father's father; my grand-father's mother is Mapalakanye and then Mapalakanye is the daughter to Senyathela. . . . He's the father to Mapalakanye who was married by Mpaketsane, and that Mpaketsane then born Ngwatau who is the father to my father . . . and the father of the current chief. And that Ngwatau

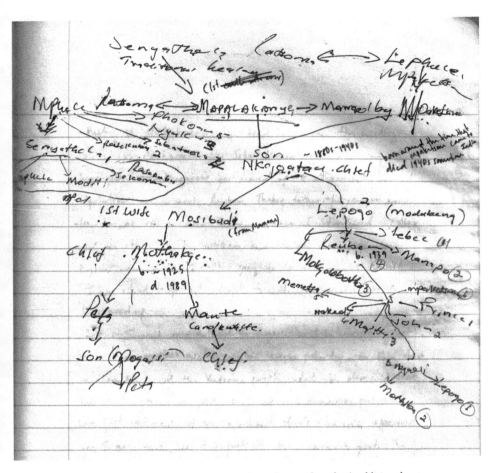

FIGURE 4.4 Phoko John Mpaketsane's genealogy chart with author's additional notes, May 2006.

married two wives, the mother to chief's father and the mother to my father.

For John Mpaketsane, Mapalakanye's marriage into Mpaketsane and the children, grandchildren, and great-grandchildren that resulted transformed Senyathela into an Mpaketsane grandfather. In other words, although he started as an uncle, Senyathela became an Mpaketsane grandfather because his grandson was an Mpaketsane chief. Thus Senyathela Ratsoma, "the one who helped Sekhukhune," for John Mpaketsane became not just the great-grandfather to Modite and Sekomane Ratsoma but "our grandfather" collectively.

As we sat huddled over my notebook, John continued to explain who was related to whom and how, writing new names on his chart along with arrows indicating relationships and using the pen in his hand for emphasis when I did not understand to whom he referred; I added my own notes as he spoke.

In John's genealogy, placement of names and directionality of arrows showed who was important and why. Senyathela Ratsoma appeared at the top, labeled "Traditional healer," but he was linked with a two-way arrow to Lephuele Mpaketsane, father of the man who married Mapalakanye and identified by John as Senyathela's cousin. Mapalakanye was centered on the page, just under her father and father-in-law, and she was surrounded by arrows. She was linked on one side with a two-way arrow to her elder brother Mphele Ratsoma, who appeared on her left, and on the other side at the end of a one-way arrow showing that she is the daughter of Senyathela. She was the origin of a one-way arrow to Lephuele's son Mpaketsane along with the words "married by." Finally, she was joined to Mpaketsane through two lines that converged on their son Nkgoatau, labeled "son" and "chief." Modite and his brothers appeared crowded in the upper left, showing that they were (also) the great-grandchildren of Senyathela via a direct paternal lineage, and that their grandfather Mphele and Mapalakanye were siblings. The remaining space on the page was devoted to the descendants of Mapalakanye's son, Chief Nkgoatua, via his two wives. On the left was the family of the first wife, culminating in "Mogaisi," who still lived at the time next to the nearby Atok platinum mine, and "Chief" (Kgoshi Mpaketsane). On the right was the family of the second wife, culminating in John and his siblings.

Compared to Kgoshi Mpaketsane's royal genealogy chart and the Ratsoma account of their patrilineal right to a privileged relationship to India and to the Sekhukhune royal family, John's genealogy chart was heavily populated. It emphasized multiple forms of relationships that could not register on Kgoshi Mpaketsane's chart because they departed from the narrow requirements of state recognition, and that also did not register with Modite and Sekomane Ratsoma because their complex interrelationality exceeded the only relationality the Ratsoma brothers cared about: their direct lineal descent from Senyathela via two generations of firstborn sons.

Yet, like other genealogy charts and genealogical stories, John Mpaketsane's genealogical map was also highly selective. While Kgoshi Mpaketsane's genealogy told the story of his ancestral claim to chieftaincy and the Ratsoma brothers' genealogy told the story of their ancestral claim to leadership that was explicitly *not* chieftaincy, John's genealogy emphasized equivalences that mediated between these competing narratives. Here, Senyathela Ratsoma was cousin, uncle, and grandfather to Mpaketsane people, and if royal authority flowed through him, then ultimately it flowed to Mpaketsane via his daughter Mapalakanye. However, authority need not flow entirely through him, because both Mapalakanye's father *and* the father to her husband (Lephuele Mpaketsane, father of the man listed only as "Mpaketsane") appeared on John Mpaketsane's genealogy chart as equivalent primary ancestors, each of whom lent their own form of legitimation to Mpaketsane claims in India.

So who was the royal ancestor? This is the wrong question, because it implies a need to reveal a genealogical truth that has been obscured—ostensibly the project of genetic ancestry. The question that mattered, similar but subtly different, was political, historical, and cultural: which ancestors made a Lemba chieftaincy possible, and how might they be claimed?

At the end of our last meeting together, Sekomane made his answer to this question clear. "In fact, to tell you the honest truth, those from Mpaketsane, they are not the chiefs," he told me. He said that if anyone had been a chief, it would have been his great-grandfather Senyathela, but "he didn't want that because in our culture, we don't have *Makgoshi*. . . . Let me say his [Kgoshi Mpaketsane's] powers were given to him by my great-grandfather." Continuing in the voice of Great-Grandfather Senyathela, he said, "Because you [Kgoshi Mpaketsane] are the son to my daughter [Mapalakanye]." For Modite and his brothers, it was Senyathela Ratsoma who mattered, not whom his daughter had married, and they therefore viewed Mpaketsane claims to be the first people at India as an instrumentalist appropriation of their own history.

Chieftaincy politics in Apel were very different from those in India, and that informed the Ratsoma brothers' readings of legitimate leadership as much as their privileging of their direct paternal ancestors over the Mpaketsane lineage with which they were entwined. Since, in their circumstances, representation, rights, and access to resources did not depend on establishing their unique group identity and first settlement, they could afford to deny that Lemba people had chiefs. For John Mpaketsane, both Senyathela Ratsoma and Lephuele Mpaketsane mattered as Mpaketsane ancestors who made Lemba chieftaincy possible. He supported Kgoshi Mpaketsane's chieftaincy, but like the Ratsoma brothers, his position made it possible to emphasize complex kinship and multiple ways to understand legitimacy.

As long as the state continued to fail to recognize his chieftaincy, Kgoshi Mpaketsane did not have that luxury. He had to stay focused on what was legitimate in the eyes of government commissions, which is to say questions of ancestry rather than attentiveness to ancestors—hence his streamlined genealogy and his inclusion of Lemba genetic ancestry studies in his submissions.

Still, although Kgoshi Mpaketsane seemed to emphasize patrilines of descent from chiefs, in the end it was the women who mattered most: Mapalakanye, not as Senyathela Ratsoma's daughter but as the mother to Kgoshi Mpaketsane's own grandfather, and Mante, the name of both Kgoshi Mpaketsane's mother and his wife, each from the Sekhukhune royal kraal.

The Pursuit of Royal Blood

Modite Ratsoma had told me, "King Sekhukhune said, 'Let me get my daughter to be your wife'; they said, 'No, because if we do that, all the children, they will die.'" One way to understand Great-Grandfather Senyathela's decision to refuse a candlewife is that he was rejecting an incorporation that would also be a subjectification: he had his own Lemba followers and the possibility of land to live on without further condition, so perhaps giving up his existing autonomous leadership to become a subordinate Pedi chief was unappealing. But what Modite emphasized instead was Lemba endogamy: this is what he meant when he said that accepting a candlewife (and therefore a chieftaincy) would result in all the children dying. Great-Grandfather Senyathela refused a Pedi candlewife so that he could remain a Lemba ancestor, with Lemba descendants.

For the Ratsoma brothers, it was the nineteenth century that mattered here. In their view, Senyathela had always been a leader, but he would have become a *royal* ancestor only if he had accepted Sekhukhune I's offer to him of a candlewife, which in any case, he declined. "That history," Modite told me, "is ours." But despite the Ratsoma brothers' contentions, in everyone's living memory, Kgoshi Mpaketsane and his father were in fact chiefs (and it seemed obvious to most people that Kgoshi Mpaketsane's father was not the first chief in the lineage, but rather inherited his position from *his* father), and to hold those positions, they had to engage not only Maroteng technologies of rule that were well established and still dominant in the nineteenth century, but also dynamics of power that had shifted significantly in the first decades of the twentieth century. It might have been possible to maintain autonomy in the 1880s and 1890s from both the Pedi king and newly established colonial rule (or at least to imagine doing so enough to refuse incorporation). But by the 1940s, when Kgoshi Mpaketsane's father was taking over his position from his recently deceased father, the best bet to maintain any autonomy in the face of an ever-encroaching white settler colonial state and a rival chieftaincy that was held in the same village by people who, everyone agreed, had found Lemba people—Ratsoma *and* Mpaketsane—there when they arrived in the early twentieth century was to be clearly acknowledged by the Sekhuhkune royal lineage as linked to them via a candlewife.

In the twenty-first century, most Lemba people could choose how and how much they wanted to claim their shared ancestors. But to be seen as a legitimate traditional leader in the milieu of twenty-first-century politics of state-recognized chieftaincy, Kgoshi Mpaketsane had to explicitly deny Ratsoma claims, and he also had to emphasize his descent from and marriage to Pedi candlewives. This came at a cost. His lack of state recognition had an echo that directly followed from the legitimacy that Pedi candlewives should have brought him, a rumor that circulated quietly but widely about another form of legitimacy that he was supposedly lacking. Here is what I heard: the reason Kgoshi Mpaketsane and his father had not been successful at petitioning the government for legally recognized status was that in each generation, they grew more distant from Lemba ancestors because they had increasingly less Lemba blood. People were worried that the Lemba chieftaincy, diluted through exogamous marriage, was no longer properly Lemba at all.

At issue were the four idioms of legitimacy that were actively in play in how people locally figured relatedness and political power. First was the legitimacy of the candlewife system: a chieftaincy could be recognized when the chief had married from the Sekhukhune royal kraal. Second was the legitimacy of Lemba blood that evidenced their status as black Jews and as an ethnic group distinct from their neighbors. Third was a different sense of blood—royal blood—and the conviction of those Lemba people who supported chieftaincy that Mpaketsane was the royal lineage. Finally—and here was where it became complicated—there was the legitimacy whereby if a woman had a child by another man before becoming married, it was not the other man but the new husband who became the known and claimed father of the existing child or children.

These four overlapping systems of legitimate kinship caused the following anxiety: What if Kgoshi Mpaketsane's firstborn son had been born to the latter's candlewife mother before she became the Lemba royal wife? That would mean that the next in line to become the chief had no Lemba blood at all. These stories speculated that the strategy of gaining local legitimacy by marrying into the Pedi royal family had backfired, and now the next generation of leadership could not even claim Lemba ancestors as his own. The people who believed these rumors worried that the reasons they had not yet been successful in getting their chieftaincy recognized were twofold: the endogamy that they claimed as a key feature that set Lemba people apart from others had been abandoned, and their ancestors were no longer with them.

This understanding of Lemba blood echoed how blood and DNA were interchangeably used to quantify relatedness and clearly followed from Lemba people's experiences with genetic ancestry research.[13] Yet, as these rumors circulated, I never heard anyone suggest that perhaps Kgoshi Mpaketsane should be compelled to take a paternity test, and if the fears were confirmed, then a younger son or someone else should be designated instead to be the future chief. The problem was too serious and too subtle for such a blunt instrument as a DNA test, even though it was discussed in similar terms as genetic ancestry.

Instead, a solution was floated that addressed endogamy and ancestors alike by looking not to the past (genetically or otherwise) but to the future. Perhaps instead of seeking a candlewife for Kgoshi Mpaketsane's son, they should instead marry him to a cousin who was genealogically linked and so an embodiment of Lemba royal blood. This infusion of royal blood might, it was hoped, result in a child who in two generations could make the chieftaincy Lemba once more.

Ancestral Returns

It is no accident that Kgoshi Mpaketsane made use of Lemba genetics to demonstrate to the South African state the legitimacy of his chieftaincy claims. Royal and genetic genealogies have much in common: they are shaped more by what they leave out than by what they include, they include less than they leave out, and decisions about whom to include are always about power and legitimacy. This raises a further question: What do the similarities between genetic ancestry research and royal genealogies tell us about what can be known via genetic ancestry and what is obscured?

Like royal genealogies, genetic ancestry is a technology of relatedness through which some are emphasized, at the expense of others who are marginalized, in order to produce a single, straightforward story that is convincing to those whom it sets out to convince. This is why genetic afterlives are so important to attend to: they disrupt these single stories, introducing multiple authorial voices which aim to reach different audiences for different reasons. What can be known via genetic ancestry are this collection of stories and the dynamics of power that differently shape each one. What is obscured is the fluid and dynamic lived experience of relatedness.

Genetic ancestry both declares and creates kinship in a way that is deceptively straightforward at all scales. At its most everyday and intimate iteration, paternity tests can pronounce people to be either related or not. But while this can have profound legal effects, it also frequently fails to be experientially transformative. Direct-to-consumer genetic ancestry testing can prompt purchasers to extend kinship beyond known histories, producing new senses of belonging to the places they are told are the points of origin of their haplogroups. But this is a belonging that often fails to be reciprocated by people in those "places of origin," who, for the most part, have not opted in to genetic methods of figuring relatedness. Genetic ancestry can appear to stand in for or supplant other ways of doing kinship (Nash 2004). But however abstracted populations may appear in published studies, they are made up of people, all of whom have stakes in relatedness in practice and how the complexities of relationality can be amplified or obscured by genetic genealogy.

Both royal genealogies and genetic ancestry are necessarily political assertions: in both cases, family trees are thoroughly cultivated and pruned to reflect the stories that matter to the storyteller and their audience. Such cultivation and pruning were as necessary to produce Kgoshi Mpaketsane as a legitimate Lemba chief as they were to produce the Lemba as a lost tribe of Israel: in both cases, lineages irrelevant to or inconvenient for the narrative were removed from view, and in the latter case, all maternal lineages entirely were cut. But those whose ancestors were pruned worried about the costs.

When I returned to India in 2010 after a four-year absence, Kgoshi Mpaketsane's chieftaincy was in crisis. I did not see him at all in my first week back. I tried to find out from others what, if anything, had become of the Nhlapo Commission and whether he was now recognized. One person told me the commission was finished, Kgoshi Mpaketsane had become recognized, and he had received a large amount of money from the government. But I saw that he, his wife, and four of their five children still lived in the same two-room house that he had occupied four years earlier, and he was now working in Burgersfort to support his family. Others noticed this too and cited his material circumstances as evidence that either the commission was not finished and he was not yet legally recognized, or it was finished and his application had been denied. Eventually, Kgoshi Mpaketsane returned from Burgersfort to see his family, and when he did I was able to hear it from him: he was not yet legally recognized. But he believed it was just a matter of time. His father had spent all of his chieftaincy unrecognized by the government and he persisted, and so would Kgoshi Mpaketsane. For him, governments could change, but his chieftaincy would remain: it was older than the postapartheid government *and* the apartheid government. Eventually, if he continued to fight for the collective future of the Lemba people as their chief, he believed that the government could help him secure that future through their acknowledgment.[14] In 2010, this seemed more important than ever because he felt his people were beginning to lose faith in his abilities.

Kgoshi Mpaketsane had grown more suspicious over the years that the rest of the royal family—John and his brothers, and even John's father who was old and increasingly frail and had never wanted to be the chief—were plotting to take his chieftaincy. This had not been an issue when I had lived there, but I knew that it had been in the early postapartheid years, when the national future of chieftaincy was an especially active and contentious question. Now in the wake of frustrated Nhlapo Commission hopes and an unclear path forward, everyone was on edge again—something that I accidentally learned about firsthand.

Upon my arrival, I noticed that the royal graveyard, which had been locked throughout all of my previous visits, was now open. I had continued to wonder about the tangled and sometimes contradictory genealogies that I had recorded, so I was curious to see which names and dates were on those royal graves; I also felt that it would be good to acknowledge the ancestors that people had spent so much time telling me about. On a visit with Kgoshi Mpaketsane at his home, I asked if I could enter the graveyard. It seemed obvious to me, given his position, that his was the authorization I would need: it did not occur to me that access might require more than one form of authority.

Kgoshi Mpaketsane told me there was no problem, I could just go to the graveyard, and he sent me there accompanied by a man who had been visiting him—a man, it turned out, whom many people did not trust. We went, and Morweshadi Mpaketsane watched me, as she often had when I lived there, from her house two doors over and slightly higher up the slope of the mountain (figure 4.5). I waved, and she looked worried. Later, she visited me at her son John's home, where I was again staying, to find out what I was doing in the graveyard and if I had been sent there by Kgoshi Mpaketsane or had asked to go. She told me that such visits properly required the permission and accompaniment of both the chief and his uncle, her husband—the former because he was the chief and the latter because the people buried there were also his parents. My asking to go made the issue less serious than if I had been sent by Kgoshi Mpaketsane, but his failure to send me first to his uncle to seek permission from him as well troubled Morweshadi.

As we spoke further, she emphasized not that the former chiefs were buried in the graveyard, but that her husband's parents were—both father *and* mother. For her, Lemba chieftaincy was important because it would continue an ideal of Lemba community that was practiced and promised by their ancestors, and she feared that Kgoshi Mpaketsane might have put that community,

FIGURE 4.5 Morweshadi Mpaketsane stands at the entrance to her home with her dog, Boss, two of her grandsons (one holding Mpho, the author's dog), and author Noah Tamarkin. Photograph by Kenny Tamarkin, 2006.

those relationships, and Lemba futures at risk by being a chief who disregarded the ancestors in this way. In 2006, there had been hope that neglected Lemba ancestors might be reengaged by reinfusing Lemba chieftaincy with Lemba blood. Now, in 2010, it seemed it was ancestors rather than ancestry that would be the best bet for the future.

On my last visit to India in December 2018, I walked again from John's house to Kgoshi Mpaketsane's, this time to introduce him to my spouse and fellow anthropologist, Juno Parreñas, who was visiting for the first time. He had built a new, much larger house, but I did not get the chance to learn if this had resulted from a change in his legal status as a traditional leader. We arrived just as he and his family were leaving; we were able to greet each other only briefly through the window of their truck before they drove away, and they would not return again until after we were gone. Juno and I continued up the hill as I so

FIGURE 4.6 Mothiba Mahlako Sylvia Mpaketsane performs a praise poem. Still image from video by author.

often had more than a decade earlier. Both Morweshadi and her husband had died, and their youngest daughter, Sylvia, now owned the house overlooking Kgoshi Mpaketsane's kraal. Sylvia greeted us as we entered her gate, and she ushered us inside.

We talked about Sylvia's recent certification as a welder and her new free-lance welding business. I pointed to a framed photo of Morweshadi that hung on the wall near the couch where we were seated and said that I missed her. Sylvia got up, took the photo off the wall, and, holding it in her hands, launched into a ten-minute praise poem, most of which I could not understand. I had known Sylvia since 2005, but this was the first time she had offered me such a performance. When she was done, we decided that she would do it again, so I could film it and she could have the recording (figures 4.6 and 4.7). Afterward, we took the recording to her brother John's house, where all of John's children were gathered, including his eldest daughter, Bella, who no longer stayed at home during the holidays now that she was married: she and her husband, Albert, had built a house in his natal village not far away (figure 4.8).

We immediately watched the video, and Sylvia, John, Bella, Albert, Juno, and I worked to construct an English translation of the praise poem. "We are the *Bashabi* [traders], we are the Lemba people, we are the nation of Mpaketsane, we are people that are like *tshipi* [steel] that is so hard that when it falls on top of another, that one bends," the poem began.[15] Next came the introduction of ancestors, one at a time, along with significant events or characteris-

FIGURE 4.7 Mothiba Mahlako Sylvia Mpaketsane performs a praise poem. Still image from video by author.

tics through which they were remembered. "We are related to Nkgwatau, we are the people of Mametja [two names for the same ancestor], who swallows big things [who withstands things that are difficult]." As Sylvia continued, her narrative voice switched from her own in the present to the Lemba people from whom Mametja Nkgwatau departed: "We stand with Mphephu and Ramabulana. How do you walk with Barwa [people of the South]? Because those people from the South are always moving in a group, they were always alert that they could be killed by other people. How do you mix up with those people?" John explained that this referred to the people of Nchabeleng, Masemola, and other nearby places to the south of the people of Mphephu and Ramabulana.

Having identified the relevant ancestor who brought them to their present place, Sylvia shifted to deeper origins and issues regarding generation and mixedness. "We come from *Mohloto*," which, John clarified, is a tree used for women's fertility medicine. The next line continued the theme of treating childlessness, though Bella and her father debated its meaning, and neither could make sense of it. "If you don't have a child, you can instead have a *kgope* [an unmarried man], because a *kgope* and a baby are just the same." The next line was equally enigmatic: "You of the Lemba, mixing the white hair and the black hair, you should mix the whole body instead of only hair on the head," John translated. Bella clarified, "So it says *Madukula*—Madukula is the Lemba people. Your problem is you've mixed everything, the Lemba people, because

FIGURE 4.8 Phoko John Mpaketsane (*center*) and his wife, Malekgale Monica Mpaketsane (*left*), his sons Edgar (*center left*) and Lington (*center right*), and his daughter Bella (*right*) in the family's dining room on Bella's wedding day, 2013. A woman pins Bella's Zion Christ Church pin to her wedding dress. Photograph by author.

they were initially a mixed race. So I think most of them, they were trying to get more into the black thing."

One might read these three juxtaposed lines as three methods of generation endorsed by the ancestors: medicinal intervention, kinning innovations that rely on methods other that sexual reproduction, and mixing more thoroughly with neighbors to be more like them. It is also impossible not to notice that the genitors here are a tree, a woman, and mixedness itself. There were clearly more ways to become an ancestor than through patrilineal descent.

In the poem, more ancestors followed, including all who were present in the living people gathered around:

We are the people of Lebee and Mapalakanye of Ratsoma. They say *Tlou* [elephant, the Lemba totem] fell on the land, it was just an open space.

Mathlapadi and Boledi [two other people] made a fire, and the bigger people just come to them to get warmth from the fire. Now I'm going to tell you who I am, me, the person who is giving you this poem. The person who is giving you this poem is Mothiba Mahlako [Sylvia's praise name] kubjana: the lady who wears the blanket with the warm side against her back. Can you hear me now? My husband is Phoko [John's praise name], Phoko is the mist, the clever man who wakes up very early. My child is Nakedi [Albert's praise name], which means a very strong animal, Khwepane, and Nakedi is the brother to Thepudi, a soldier.

Now speaking as Phoko, Sylvia continued: "I am from Thabene. There they are fighting with iron, with steel. Can you hear me, Bashabi, can you hear me?"

Sylvia then shifted back to her own voice, signaling the beginning of the end of the poem:

Me, I'm endless, I can talk forever. My mother is Morweshadi. Morweshadi is Mmakaepea of letswalo [a warm heart]. This Mmakaepea, sometimes people blame her for bad things done by others, so she was a sick person. And my father is Mogaisi, Morweshadi's husband. Mogaisi comes from Banushuana, Mogaisi who will greet his people from Moshuana. I'm related to Lepogo; I am the grandchild of Lepogo who was a king at mugodu [he secured his rule by eating goat intestines together with all of his people]. I'm related to Mmanapo.

Here Bella took over the translation: "Mmanapo is me, it's my praise name. I took it after his [John's] aunt. So yeah, [she says] I am related to Mmanapo, who is related to Chibani, who is brave. We come from Tubatse, it's a big river near Burgersfort, it's where you find these white people who chase away the rain. The people in Tubatse, when they are happy, they play the drums."

Now having gone through the story of each person present, Sylvia ended by returning to the beginning. John translated: "The old lady who gave birth to all our grandparents, who is the grand-grandmother, her name was Modjadji. She is the wife to Mametja who swallowed the big things—it means he was very strong." Bella had the last word, translating the final line: "We want to respect time, I could continue but I'm afraid of the supervisors [the praise leaders who have spoken before her], as they gave me this time and I must respect it."

Not everyone could do what Sylvia did. "We try," explained Bella, "but she's the best. Amongst the Lembas now, even everywhere they call her to make the poem. Because Morweshadi left the poem to her. Morweshadi was the best amongst the leaders, so she left the gift with her. Now it's up to her to teach somebody." John concurred, now using Sylvia's praise name: "Yeah, she [Morweshadi] left it for Mothiba. Even in Mogabane the old man wouldn't be able to recite. Only Mothiba could be able to recite." The kinds of relatedness that Mothiba, that Sylvia, brought into being offered multiple ways to understand origins, pathways, and present circumstances. The gift that passed from mother to daughter was the power to invoke the ancestors—to bring them into the present—and to affirm and legitimize the ancestral connections of the living; in other words, to build and keep relations. As Bella explained, "If we have to, we try, but it will be two or three lines, not like this. She can speak to every other ancestor that we have. Amongst us, she's the one who knows the history better than anyone." She added with affection, clearly not wanting to offend, "Well, after, of course, my dad." Everyone laughed.

LOCATING LEMBA HERITAGE,
IMAGINING INDIGENOUS FUTURES

"We are more indigenous," Ishe Lucas Thobakgale declared to the hundreds of Lemba people gathered for the annual Lemba Cultural Association conference at Sweetwaters (figure 5.1).[1] It was September 9, 2006, Thobakgale was that year's master of ceremonies, and the theme of the conference was "Let's Promote Our Culture as Our Heritage." Promoting Lemba culture had been a primary project of the LCA since it was founded in the 1940s. Promoting culture as *heritage*, however, was a new idea that emerged from the language of UNESCO.[2] Specifically, it grew from Lemba involvement in contentious plans to rebury human remains that had been excavated beginning in the 1930s from Mapungubwe, which had been designated a World Heritage Site in 2003.[3]

Like heritage, indigeneity was a new concept that immediately resonated for many Lemba people. But its meaning in South Africa was far from settled, and its association with Lemba people was complicated, not least because the genetic ancestry studies that they had participated in had illustrated Lemba links to Jews by juxtaposing Jewish and African ancestry.[4] All of the documentaries about the Lemba and their Jewish genetics likewise played on this juxtaposition, framing them as a lost tribe of Israel, definitively from outside of Africa. One of these, the Lemba episode of the History Channel's *Digging for the Truth*, was scheduled to be shown that day at the end of the formal program, but technical difficulties prevented the screening. Nevertheless, the message came across loud and clear during Richard Wade's presentation. Wade, a white South African man in his forties, was a student at the University of Pretoria

FIGURE 5.1 Ishe Lucas Thobakgale (*center*) declares Lemba indigeneity to the gathered Lemba people at the 2006 Lemba Cultural Association conference. The author (*right*) takes notes. Still from video by Pandelani Mutenda.

who was working on a master's thesis on the archaeoastronomical significance of Mapungubwe. He appeared in the *Digging for the Truth* episode along with featured expert Dr. Magdel le Roux, author of *The Lemba: A Lost Tribe of Israel in Southern Africa?* (2003), and many of the LCA executive council members who organized the conference and designed its program each year.

By the time Wade spoke, we were nearly two hours into the day's activities, and with lunch still to be served, people were beginning to fade in the heat of the afternoon. Many dozed off or spoke quietly to friends and family sitting near them as they had throughout the presentations. The opening prayer by LCA chaplain William Masala and welcome address by LCA acting president Samuel Moeti were long finished, le Roux had completed her account of historical texts that substantiated the presence of Lemba people at Mapungubwe, and singing and dancing had commenced between each item. But Wade quickly got people's attention when a few minutes into his presentation, he declared, "You're not African—I'm not African. Or am I? If I'm not African, then you're not African. . . . A lot of you have become Venda in a very short time. Some of you have become Pedi. A lot of you think you are Jewish. But in actual fact, you're Israelites. You come from the Egyptians. So who are you? This is my job: trying to work it out."[5]

Wade was not at all disputing Lemba claims to the Mapungubwe bones: on the contrary, these were claims he wholeheartedly endorsed. Rather, his statements about who was or was not African were reflective of racialized controversies that had emerged in postapartheid South Africa over who was indigenous and who was a settler, and what rights and protections should follow for each.[6] By aligning his status as not-African with the similar status of the Lemba, and by simultaneously supporting Lemba links to Mapungubwe, he was also calling into question Thobakgale's assessment that their legitimate claims to the place and to the bones scheduled to be returned there meant that they were now indigenous.

Seven years later, in August 2013, I stood on top of Mapungubwe Hill with Ishe Tswanwani Samuel Sadiki. His father had known M. M. Motenda, the founder and first president of the LCA, and for many years the elder Sadiki had been head cook at the LCA annual conference. But Ishe Sadiki became a member of the LCA only in 2007, decades after his father died and long after his own retirement from years of working as a truck driver, and he had never before seen Mapungubwe. A park guide led us up a stone path and steep wooden stairs to the top of the hill. Ishe M. J. Mungulwa, who had become president of the LCA in 2007, stayed below in the park vehicle that the guide had used for our twenty-minute drive from the visitor center and museum to the hill itself; Mungulwa was too pained by age and arthritis to make what would have been his second climb. Mungulwa and Sadiki wore beautiful black-and-purple woven yarmulkes that had been a gift several years back from a visiting Ugandan Jew from the Abayudaya community. Quietly looking out over the valley below, after being shown the reburial site on the hill, Ishe Sadiki embraced his Jewish and his African histories as together facilitating this moment (figure 5.2). His personal journey to see himself as an indigenous African Jew echoed that of Mungulwa and many other Lemba people who understood themselves in the same way. This journey and the sense of belonging that resulted encapsulate a larger story about the social significance of genetics, the convergence of race and religion, and the emergence of indigeneity as a politically salient category of postcolonial African identification.

In this chapter, I consider how the Mapungubwe reburial—as both a state project and a Lemba one—reworked indigeneity, reconfiguring ethnic recognition in the process. I enter into the project in 2006, as debates raged over how to manage multiple, competing claims to the Mapungubwe bones from different groups of people. In examining the arguments that took place among claimant groups and internally among Lemba people about how to proceed with the reburial, I will illustrate how different concepts of indigeneity were simultaneously at stake and actively being reworked in the negotiations. I then consider the reburial that took place in 2007 and my 2013 visit to Mapungubwe with Mungulwa and Sadiki to better understand how the site and the emergent concepts of indigeneity that it has fostered facilitated Lemba recognition, and what the possibilities and limitations were of the form of recognition that they achieved.

FIGURE 5.2 Ishe Tswanwani Samuel Sadiki looking out from the top of Mapungubwe Hill, 2013. Photograph by author.

As in previous chapters, genetic ancestry mattered here, in this case in relation to the possibility of establishing through DNA who could claim that the Mapungubwe bones were those of their ancestors. In what follows, I ask three related questions. What does it mean to be indigenous in postapartheid South Africa? How did Lemba people make sense of being both genetic Jews and indigenous Africans over the course of their efforts to claim and rebury the human remains from Mapungubwe? And finally, how does DNA serve as a technology of indigeneity in a context where the very meaning of indigeneity is in question?

Mapungubwe and African Indigeneity

As indigeneity has emerged as a new idiom of postcolonial African citizenship and belonging, it has reshaped imaginaries of what it means to be African and reframed the stakes of being part of an African state.[7] Two distinct kinds of indigenous claims are at work in postcolonial African contexts: those of minority groups who make claims on the state and those of the state itself. The Mapungubwe reburial facilitated both kinds of claims. This distinction between claims *on* the state and claims *of* the state can be understood through a differentiation between indigenous peoples and indigenous practices.[8]

In Southern Africa, those most commonly understood as indigenous peoples are known as San and Khoisan: at the forefront of international indigenous rights movements in recent decades, these diverse communities were historically hunter-gatherers and pastoralists, and they endured colonial enslavement and genocide as well as marginalization and subjugation at the hands of other Africans.[9] Indigenous practices can refer to Khoisan practices and knowledge, as in the intellectual property disputes that emerged between San communities and pharmaceutical companies around the medicinal uses of the *Hoodia* plant (Foster 2018).[10] But indigenous practices are also invoked as broad postcolonial state claims to precolonial traditions: this encompasses the precolonial traditions of all Africans so as to differentiate black Africans from the white descendants of European settler colonists and the postcolonial from the colonial. In this way, postcolonial state invocations of indigeneity retain the colonial idea that all Africans are natives, but they aim to reframe indigeneity from a sign of primitivity to a source of strength and cultural value (Tamarkin and Giraudo 2014).[11]

This is how the postapartheid South African state invokes indigeneity, as a reclamation of African strength and value, and this is why the Mapungubwe reburial presented such an important opportunity for Lemba people. While claims *on* the state in the name of indigeneity can face substantial challenges, the Mapungubwe reburial allowed the Lemba Cultural Association (and others) to articulate such a claim to a project that was fundamentally one *of* state indigeneity.[12] For the LCA, the two projects of indigeneity that I have identified—claims on the state and claims of the state—perfectly came together. Their status as members of a minority group positioned them alongside others making claims on the state, while their goal of demonstrating their authentic Africanness aligned them with the rhetoric of state indigeneity.

As a project of state indigeneity, the Mapungubwe reburial was an articulation of indigenous nationalism. In this sense, it echoed other postapartheid reburial projects, such as the repatriation from France of the remains of Sara Baartman, also known as the Hottentot Venus, and the reburials of people killed in the struggle against apartheid.[13] Each of these postapartheid repatriation projects recalled different aspects of the past to be recuperated as part of a nationalist indigeneity. The contrast between the Baartman and the

Mapungubwe reburials is especially instructive. Baartman's remains were returned from outside of South Africa, thus evoking repair of colonial violence, even while South Africa's museums retained their own skeletal collections (Legassick and Rassool 2015). In contrast, the Mapungubwe remains were to be returned from within South Africa, a major milestone in a national context in which museum professionals and physical anthropologists continued to resist return of remains in the name of science (Rassool 2015). Both were hailed as victories for dignity and respect. But while the reburial of Baartman's remains located that dignity and respect against a history of the sexualized racial exploitation of slavery and colonialism, the remains to be returned to Mapungubwe instead recalled the precolonial past of a far-reaching African kingdom. In this way, Baartman evoked the ability of postapartheid South Africa to overcome past injury, while Mapungubwe additionally recalled the powerful legacy of indigenous African leadership, which it projected into the present and the future.

The site itself, like many other UNESCO World Heritage sites, simultaneously stands for multiple projects of global, transnational, and national belonging. In this sense, Mapungubwe is part of three missions on three different scales. First, in line with UNESCO's mission, Mapungubwe represents an irreplaceable heritage that "belongs to all of the peoples of the world" (UNESCO n.d.). Second, as part of Limpopo-Shashe Transfrontier Conservation Area, an area of nearly five thousand square kilometers that is about half in South Africa and a quarter each in Botswana and Zimbabwe, Mapungubwe is one of several southern African initiatives tasked with the cross-border, long-term cooperative management of wildlife and natural resources (South Africa, Department of Environmental Affairs 2019). And third, as part of a national park, it falls within the South African national mission to "represent the indigenous fauna, flora, landscapes and associated cultural heritage of the country" (South African National Government n.d.).[14]

The multiple scales of Mapungbuwe's significance underscore first, that indigeneity is a juridical concept, and second, that while indigeneity has transnational implications, it is often adjudicated as a national issue. In South Africa, the postapartheid constitution and subsequent legislation set the stage for Mapungubwe controversies: together, they facilitated a form of indigenous recognition that was primarily but not only symbolic, and they did so without defining indigeneity.

The word "indigenous" appears only four times in the 1996 South African constitution. One refers to "indigenous forests," thus affirming the idea that the natural environment should be part of the national project. The other references include one to "indigenous languages" and two to "indigenous law."[15] None of these explicitly defines indigeneity or delineates precisely who might be indigenous, but all link the concept to a wide range of South Africa's people, therefore establishing indigeneity as a potentially useful and thoroughly non-specific way to articulate belonging in the postapartheid state.[16]

"Indigenous" also appears in the legislation that laid the groundwork to establish Mapungubwe as a heritage site and that provisioned for its management. This legislation, the National Heritage Resources Act (NHRA) (Act 25 of 1999), noted general procedures to identify heritage sites, established the South African Heritage Resources Agency (SAHRA) to manage and maintain such sites, and emphasized an ideal of community involvement at all levels of the heritage process, from nominating potential sites to participating in decision-making and site development.[17] Just as "indigenous" remains legally ambiguous, the NHRA also did not explicitly define "community."[18] However, the emphasis on community involvement, combined with the prominent inclusion of "indigenous knowledge" as one factor that must be considered when identifying and managing heritage resources, implicitly linked the two concepts: just as the inclusion of indigenous law in the constitution implied traditional authorities who were responsible for its adjudication, the inclusion here of indigenous knowledge implied coherent communities to whom such knowledge was endemic. It also established "indigenous knowledge" as a key point of access to the governance of heritage sites, again without clearly stating who might seek such access.[19]

Zakes Mda's 2013 novel The Sculptors of Mapungubwe points precisely to these tensions between who might be included and who excluded when answering questions about what defines a community and whose claims to indigeneity are legitimate. Based on archeologists' and historians' descriptions of twelfth-century Mapungubwe as a thriving precolonial trade center with wide-ranging trade networks, Mda creates an imaginary of the place that is characterized by unequal interaction among hunter-gatherers, a settled populace, royal elites, and traders from elsewhere.[20] Echoing reburial controversies and departing both from the neutral language of heritage and the celebratory language of precolonial power, Mda portrays this interaction as marked by inequality and violence. Mda's story indirectly references the Lemba through the inclusion of a Muslim trader named Hamisi wa Babu who, through various transgressions, proves to be the ultimate cultural outsider despite his entanglement with Mapungubwe's human and animal inhabitants.[21]

There is an echo here of Richard Wade's provocation that while the Lemba were certainly present at Mapungubwe, they were not African: following Mda,

Lemba people at Mapungubwe were not Jews but Muslims, and they were not truly part of the African cultures that thrived there, but rather always people apart. Mda's characterization echoed those of many South Africans who did not believe Lemba peoples' oral histories—the possibility of putting such doubts to rest had earlier played a large role in LCA decisions to participate in Jewish genetics studies. Now, in the space between UNESCO World Heritage and postapartheid National Park, Lemba people found another opportunity to speak against these misunderstandings of their history. But whereas their genetic studies had provided a means to address those who doubted that they were really Jews, their participation in the Mapungubwe reburial instead articulated a new kind of indigenous belonging that reconfigured what it means to be African.

Indigenous Bones, Traditional Burials, African Jews

In his book *The Silence of Great Zimbabwe*, Joost Fontein explains that the words of nineteenth-century spirit medium and anticolonial fighter Ambuya Nehanda—"Mapfupa edu achmuka" or "Our bones will rise"—became part of guerrilla training during the late twentieth-century liberation struggle, linking ancestors, liberation, the state, and the Great Zimbabwe site (Fontein 2006, 144–145).[22] Lemba people in South Africa were linked to Great Zimbabwe in the same way that they were linked to Mapungubwe. Not only did their oral history definitively put them there, but so did the early twentieth-century scholarly archive (see chapter 1). They were also linked to Zimbabwe's late twentieth-century anticolonial struggle through their active connections to their relatives north of the Limpopo. The imagery of bones rising was significant in LCA history as well. As discussed in chapter 1, in the late 1970s in the midst of unsuccessful organizing for their own homeland and subsequent repression in the Venda homeland, LCA chaplain William Masala created and circulated an image of a hand reaching out from beneath a gravestone with the caption, "Lembas are buried alive!" This was followed by another image depicting his friend and Lemba benefactor Margaret Nabarro pulling a bag full of bones out of a grave with the biblical caption, "Can these bones live again? Ezekiel 37: 11–14." The Mapungubwe bones were thus a potent symbol to claim: they resonated powerfully with both anticolonial and biblical ideas of bones. My first substantive introduction to the fact that Lemba people were claiming bones for reburial at Mapungubwe was at a July 2006 LCA executive council meeting. Echoing his apartheid-era cartoon, Chaplain Masala read from Ezekiel 37, and the chairperson told everyone that the bones from Mapungubwe that were now in Pretoria should go back where they belong.

While I was living with Lemba interlocutors in Limpopo, rarely did a weekend go by without at least one funeral to attend. Sometimes these were funerals of neighbors who were not Lemba, but when the deceased was a Lemba person, someone in the family or from the LCA would speak, either during a service in a tent set up outside the home of the bereaved family or at the graveside during the burial process. The speaker would tell the history of the Lemba people in general and of the specific patrilineal clan of the deceased as a way to honor the life of the person and to communicate to the living who they were and why it was important to be in community with other Lemba people. Burials were very much a social glue: not only did they occur frequently and provide an occasion to articulate collective histories and identities, they were opportunities to strengthen ties through the collective activities of digging graves, slaughtering goats and cows, preparing food, sitting together for hours, often over several days, and gathering small amounts of money to help cover costs.[23] Because the Mapungubwe bones were to be ceremonially reburied, they carried the weight of negotiation over belonging that characterized these everyday funerals and that indeed accompanies funerals and adheres in grave sites throughout Africa and elsewhere.[24]

In the story that I heard from LCA leaders, it was Drake Kgalushi Koka who ensured that the remains from Mapungubwe were a reburial priority among the many similar projects that demanded attention from the post-apartheid state. Koka was a cofounder of the Black Consciousness Movement along with Stephen Biko, the movement's main spokesperson who became famous as its martyr when he was murdered by police in the 1970s. Koka lived in Soweto, and the student activists who organized the demonstrations there against Afrikaans-medium instruction in 1976 went to him throughout the uprising and claimed him as a "spiritual advisor" (Magaziner 2010). Koka died in December 2005, and M. J. Mungulwa kept a newspaper article about his funeral in a file along with other news stories dating back to the 1970s that reported on the Lemba as black Jews: the earliest of these was a 1972 article from the Star with the headline "Black Semites from the Past." Mungulwa had used a pink highlighter to emphasize the Koka article's important passages, one of which noted that representatives of the Lemba people were among those who spoke at Koka's funeral and that Koka was Lemba royalty. Another explained Koka's spiritual philosophy as Africanism: "To him," the article stated, "Africa represented a very special interplay between the people and their badimo or ancestors, and an equally special interplay between Africans, nature and the environment, to which they are inextricably tied" (Mokhele 2005, 9).

Koka's role in the struggle against apartheid, his status as a spiritual adviser, and his attention to ancestors gave him political access and spiritual authority. Several years before his death, the story goes, he had a dream that the Lemba ancestors whose bones had been dug up from Mapungubwe were unsettled and would not be at peace until the bones were returned and properly laid to rest. He told President Mbeki about his dream, and Mbeki decided that this must be done. Mbeki invited members of the LCA executive committee to meet with him at his home to decide how to proceed: Professor Mathivha was there, as were F. C. Raulinga and perhaps others. Mbeki then arranged with the University of Pretoria to return the bones to the Lemba.[25] In October 2006, Chaplain Masala explained to me what happened next: "The bone of the Lemba is in Pretoria University. After the government said we must collect and fix and bury it . . . they [the LCA leaders who had met with Mbeki] said, 'Let us tell the Bavenda chiefs.'" Once informed, Masala continued, the Bavenda chiefs "went straight to Pretoria. They said, 'Where is their bone? . . . We did stay in that place; we want our bones.'"

Mapungubwe quickly emerged as the center of new controversies over who could claim to be indigenous in postapartheid South Africa and who could not. Once others made their own claims, Koka and the LCA shifted from being facilitators of the indigenous claims *of* the state (in the sense that they were willing to, as asked, collect their bones and bury them) to *potentially* indigenous claimants *on* the state (in the sense that now it was no longer certain whose bones these were, and making that determination could possibly differentiate between those who were indigenous to the place and those who were not). In other words, it was the competition that transformed Koka and the LCA into "the Lemba claimants" and indigeneity into something contested that necessarily would and should be demonstrable.

Multiple Venda royal families made claims, as did a group that called itself the Vhangona Cultural Movement; the San Council participated as well.[26] The members of the Vhangona group thought they had more of a claim to Mapungubwe than anyone else because when the Singo, accompanied by Lemba people, came down from the North and conquered them, they had already been living in the region for many centuries. As far as they were concerned, Mapungubwe was theirs because they could best prove they had lived there continuously from the time of the Mapungubwe kingdom up to the present.

While Vhangona claims might sound more valid than those of other groups, it is important to remember that the national border between South Africa and Zimbabwe is a recent invention and that the areas to the north and south of the Limpopo river are historically better understood as an interconnected region of multidirectional movement than as timeless territories of primordial peoples with fixed boundaries. Archaeology and oral history suggest that when Mapungubwe declined as a kingdom due to drought in the fourteenth century, many of its people moved north to Great Zimbabwe; there some of the same trade routes that had sustained Mapungubwe continued to flourish for another hundred years (Huffman 2005). It is entirely possible that all claimants were descendants of those who had lived at Mapungubwe, including those who remained in the region after the site was abandoned as a kingdom (represented in the present as the Vhangona) and those who migrated north but returned generations later (represented in the present as various Venda groups and the Lemba).

Government officials, in keeping with Mapungubwe as a project of state indigeneity, insisted that only one joint claim would go forward, with one reburial ceremony for all remains. They were committed to the reburial, but they were also committed to avoiding the political repercussions that would follow any decisions to advance the claims of one group over another. The Department of Environment and Tourism, the government department that was overseeing reburial plans, designated all claimant groups "stakeholders" and "indigenous groups" and arranged a series of workshops through which they were to resolve their differences. The main workshop was to be held in the week leading up to Heritage Day, September 24, 2006.[27]

A workshop agenda was sent to the LCA; it was titled "Agenda for the Meeting of Indigenous Groups to Be Involved in the Cleansing Ceremony and Reburial of the Mapungubwe Human Remains." The title made it clear to all of the groups, if it was not already, that this was an indigenous site, so all those with a claim on it were necessarily indigenous groups. The first part of the workshop was designed as an oral history project in which each "indigenous group" (listed as Vhangona, VhaLemba, Batlwanamba, and Machete) would talk about the significance for them of Mapungubwe "in an African context." This was to be followed by the drafting of the joint claim to the Mapungubwe bones and a discussion of "traditional requirements for reburial."

The subtext of the workshop agenda was that the stakeholders' competing claims had introduced three distinct controversies that the state hoped would disappear. First, there were the questions of whose ancestors the Mapungubwe bones represented and whether all stakeholders should in fact be considered "indigenous groups." The second issue had to do with which group could claim descent from the Mapungubwe royals in particular and whether that should elevate one group's claims over the others, since the site was, after all, famous because it was a stratified kingdom. And third, each claimant group now had a stake in how the bones would be reburied, but each group had different burial practices.

An archaeologist who had long been involved in the Mapungubwe reburial working group explained the controversies to me in a series of informal conversations in his office between June and August 2006. He told me that he agreed in principle that all stakeholders should be involved in the reburial plans, but in practice, this had brought up divisive questions of authenticity regarding which claims were truly legitimate. This archaeologist thought it would have been more productive and more in keeping with the spirit of World Heritage to focus not on who was a stakeholder but instead on the ways in which the site could be culturally significant for everyone, rather than just those who claimed it as the place of their ancestors. Much of his frustration was due to the competing claims from specific groups that it was their ancestors who had ruled at Mapungubwe: he saw these claims as opportunistic and primarily instrumental.[28] He believed there was insufficient evidence to link any one single group to leadership roles at Mapungubwe, that transposing contemporary identities onto ancient remains was problematic from a political perspective and nonsensical from an anthropological perspective, and that, at any rate, many Venda- and Shona-speaking people would most likely have some ancestral link to people who had at least lived, if not ruled, at Mapungubwe.

Given this expansive view of the history of Mapungubwe, I was surprised that this same archaeologist was particularly skeptical of the Lemba claimants—specifically, their assertions that they were Jewish and also that they had links to Mapungubwe. His problems with Lemba claims had as much to do with Great Zimbabwe as with Mapungubwe. He feared that Lemba inclusion in the Mapungubwe reburial might be used to argue that the site was not actually an African kingdom at all, but rather that it resulted from a precolonial, non-African presence, a claim that had circulated about Great Zimbabwe from the time of its discovery in the nineteenth century.[29]

The Lemba became part of Great Zimbabwe controversies in the 1960s. In 1967, the pro-apartheid journal *Mankind Quarterly* published an article that used two aspects of Lemba oral history—that they came from Judea and that they were part of the Great Zimbabwe kingdom—as new evidence that the site was not built by Africans. The politics of this claim, like earlier nineteenth- and twentieth-century Great Zimbabwe claims on which it was modeled, was to delegitimize African civilization and to justify colonial domination: this is one reason why the site was such a potent symbol in the struggle against colonial rule. The argument about the Lemba put forward in *Mankind Quarterly* was that they built Great Zimbabwe and were necessarily not African because they were Jews: they could not be both (Gayre of Gayre 1967). In that instance, the long-standing claims that the Lemba had built Great Zimbabwe, coupled with the stories of their Jewish and therefore non-African origins, had been taken up as proof that it was not Africans who had built it.

The archaeologist's concerns about Lemba Mapungubwe claims emerged from his knowledge of that colonial legacy. He assumed that Lemba people saw themselves much as they were seen by those who have written about them as Jews, which is to say, as not African. He feared their involvement could therefore spark a new controversy about the Africanness of this earliest southern African kingdom. Not only did he reject Lemba claims to Mapungubwe, he also dismissed the 1990s DNA studies that confirmed the Lemba as Jews, in part because he could not analytically separate those assertions from the racist motivations of the 1960s Great Zimbabwe claim. The racist logic about Great Zimbabwe that he *rejected* indicated that the Lemba could not be African because they were Jews, but his rejection recapitulated this logic in reverse: for him, the Lemba could not be Jews because they were African. He fundamentally could not reconcile the idea that they could be African and also have a Jewish history.[30]

Richard Wade's contention at the 2006 LCA conference that both he and his audience were not African echoed the Great Zimbabwe narrative that so troubled the archaeologist, if perhaps unintentionally. In light of the archaeologist's concerns and Wade's assertions, the brief note on the planning agenda for the Mapungubwe reburial, stating that it was the "African context" specifically that each indigenous group should discuss in describing how Mapungubwe was significant in their history, seemed aimed at Lemba people in particular.

Controversy erupted a few months later when, after the workshops had taken place and the joint claim had been drafted, representatives from one of the groups sent a letter to the government protesting Lemba inclusion, alleging that it occurred only because the person in charge of the project, deputy minister of the Department of the Environment and Tourism Rejoice Mabudafhasi, wanted to advance her own ethnic claims as a Lemba person. The letter requested that Mabudafhasi be replaced as head of the project, insisted that the Lemba had no valid claim to Mapungubwe, argued that Lemba people wanted only to gain access to minerals that would later be mined there, and demanded that the Lemba provide proof of their claim's legitimacy in order to remain part of the joint effort.[31]

The letter was not sent directly to Lemba people, but it eventually got back to the LCA, forcing association leaders to decide whether and how to respond. For them, the anti-Lemba sentiment that the letter communicated was all too familiar. They believed that during the apartheid years, the reason they had been denied a Lemba homeland, Lemba Tribal Authorities, and therefore government recognition of their existence as a distinct ethnic group was because many Venda people felt threatened by them and therefore undermined their claims. They recalled that in the early 1980s, the LCA conference had included a social night with a campout for youth, but it was discontinued because Venda people would come and throw stones at the participants while they slept.[32] Suspicion about Lemba people among Venda people was clear in many conversations that I had when strangers and new acquaintances learned about my research: they nearly always wanted to discuss whether the Lemba were really Jews or were essentially lying about their past to try to seem different or special.

Pandelani Mutenda, grandson of LCA founder M. M. Motenda, an emerging LCA leader, and a member of the committee working on the joint Mapungubwe claim, reacted to the letter with confident sarcasm while also echoing the language of older leaders sensitive to threats to Lemba survival. He told me, "If they want to bury them all, it is fine. We thank them for burying our people! Our ancestors were here, they were trading here, and there is nothing else that we can tell them. We were not born, even the people who speak [against Lemba people in the letter] were not there, so we close the matter. They don't want us to exist; that is the main problem."

Ishe M. J. Mungulwa felt particularly frustrated by the accusations that the Lemba sought ownership of mineral resources at the site. He explained, "It's identity only. It doesn't mean we're going to own that place." Mungulwa's daughter Tanya thought the written attack had mostly to do with the writers' own feelings of inferiority because, she suspected, they did not know their own history. She added:

There is nowhere that Lembas are claiming ownership of anything. This is xenophobia at its best. . . . The only difference between us and a lot of people is we've got our own history. And we followed it up, you know? Where it started to now. And everybody should have a history; there's nothing wrong with that. You have to understand where you're coming from so that you should know where you're going to. Now I cannot prosecute you for knowing who your grandfather and your great-grandfather is! What is wrong with them? If you don't keep your history that is your problem. Surely that is your problem. . . . They don't know anything about their forefathers. So it's very intimidating when you get somebody who knows where they're coming from and they've got their traditions which they've been following for a long time. . . . It threatens a lot of people. . . . Historically, we've never been people who want to take anything from anybody. We came here, you know, we were just trading. And some people admired some things from our culture. And we didn't have a problem with interacting with them and showing them what we are all about. Because you shouldn't only work with the Lembas; you should also help the nation that you are working with.[33]

While emphasizing Lemba trading history and the distinctiveness of their culture Tanya Mungulwa downplayed the way that Lemba people usually associated these factors with their identities as black Jews. In so doing, she subtly incorporated the assessment of others that being part of Mapungubwe while also being black Jews made Lemba claims suspect. Her father, too, thought that Lemba Jewish links should not even be part of the Mapungubwe conversation, because while these connections of course had not gone away, they were not the focus of this particular project, and mentioning them could lead other groups to ignore the aspects of their history that placed them at Mapungubwe.

Although the Mungulwas and others rejected the idea that having Jewish ancestry and having ancestral links to Mapungubwe were incompatible, they also could see that being black Jews potentially complicated their claims, so it was better to let that aspect of their history fade into the background when it came to this issue. Lemba people who minimized their Jewish links in the Mapungubwe discussions did not deny or disclaim those connections—they simply did not agree that they had to be either Jewish or African. Instead, they believed that they were both from elsewhere and fully within the emerging category of indigenous African. Lemba understanding of their history and the perceptions of others of that history ultimately represented a struggle over what it means to be African and what it means to be indigenous.

Lemba origins were not the only controversial issue in relation to the Mapungubwe claim. Also in question were which rituals and ceremonies would properly constitute the reburial process, when each of the multiple groups involved had distinct burial practices. Every group of stakeholders had to present its plans to the others for collective approval. Internally for the LCA, this was a point of contention. During meetings they debated not only whether to object to the practices of others but also which practices they should present as their own: those of the various Christian groups to which many Lemba people belonged, the more "traditional" practices that were known as specific to the Lemba but rejected by some Lemba Christians, or Jewish practices that some LCA leaders had begun to research as potentially part of their authentic past.

In the context of performative indigeneity, Lemba reburial plans became internally controversial, even though funerals were one of the primary ways that they came together, and under normal circumstances their burial practices were known and practiced among themselves without dispute.

These discussions were extremely heated. The main objections to the plans of others were that one group wanted to bury the bones in a basket, another wished to burn some of the bones, and scientists, who were regarded by the government as stakeholders, proposed interring the remains in such a way that they could be dug up again in the future for further study if new methods became available or new questions emerged. All claimant groups, including the Lemba, initially opposed this potential future unearthing. However, the various plans remained a problem, primarily because the bones, still stored at the University of Pretoria, were not actually differentiated by group, so potentially another group's burial practices could be imposed on one's own ancestors.

Because each set of plans was subject to scrutiny by the other groups, the debate over what the LCA should present as its "traditional" Lemba practice was even more contentious. Lemba people questioned their own rituals precisely because others had already questioned their Mapungubwe claims. At first, LCA members agreed that the bones set aside for Lemba people would be covered with a white cloth, and a traditional healer would be present at the ceremony. But Chaplain Masala, a lifelong Christian, objected. Citing biblical verses, he said they must bury the bones in a coffin, and furthermore, they could not lay the bones to rest without reading from the Bible during the ceremony itself.

At the same time, Masala never stopped emphasizing Lemba Jewishness, and in his view it was the publicity generated from the Jewish genetics studies and related documentaries that made people finally listen to the Lemba about where they came from, where they lived, and who they were. He was not willing to downplay one aspect of that history so that another might appear less questionable; on the contrary, he believed that since people everywhere now realized they were black Jews, the government also wanted to recognize them, as proved by the government coming to them with the reburial plans rather than the other way around. Masala told me, "We are the citizens of here. . . . Now the government did allow us and the books were written." For Masala, the Mapungubwe reburial meant that the Lemba were now truly citizens of South Africa: the books that had been written following their DNA tests showed the government who they were, so the government approached them to bury their people and thus finally acknowledged their existence, importance, and belonging within South Africa.[34]

Chaplain Masala's belief that the claims were now totally secure, no matter what, and that it was the fame of the Lemba as black Jews that brought the government to acknowledge them put him out of step with other LCA leaders who were in charge of negotiating with the other groups. As chaplain and as an elder, he believed he should be part of both the negotiations and the ceremony, because ultimately it was about burial, which was his area of expertise and authority. But the pressures of the joint claim required the LCA to come up with its own traditional cultural requirements for the reburial plan, and Masala's ideas of Lemba culture, which included reading from the Bible, were rejected by the others: the Bible was too closely associated with Christianity, and Christianity with colonialism (and, by extension, beyond the bounds of potential indigeneity).

In response to Masala's ideas, someone suggested they study Lemba traditional burial methods; this made the disagreement at the meeting much more intense. Lucas Thobakgale, the master of ceremonies at the 2006 LCA conference and a longtime executive council member who had been active in the LCA since the 1960s, exclaimed, "Why should we search how we bury Lembas when we bury Lembas every day? . . . Let's not go and seek Jews have done this, Jesus has done this. . . . We happen to be coming from the same area, but we have got our religion. . . . We will be taken as imitators, as if we do not know our identity." Thobakgale was concerned that if they conformed to some idea of traditional Jewish or Christian burial, not only would they abandon their lived cultural practices, they would also undermine their own claims in the eyes of other groups. But to answer the objections of others, they would need to emphasize not their Jewish links, which positioned them as un-African, or their Christian links, which positioned them as not indigenous enough in terms of culture and religion, but instead their Lemba traditional practices, which presumably would be both recognizably African and recognizably different from the practices of all other claimants. The tensions that erupted at the meeting and the concern with whether everyday Lemba burial practices were adequate *in the eyes of others* for the Mapungubwe reburial ceremony spoke to the pressure on the LCA to perform African indigeneity on behalf of the Lemba, all the more so because many others already thought of them as not legitimately African.

DNA as a Technology of Indigenous Belonging

The 2006 LCA annual conference was exceptionally well attended: the Mapungubwe reburial plans were generating a lot of interest. It was entirely through word of mouth that Lemba people learned that the reburial was happening and that Mapungubwe would be the subject of the conference that year. I discovered this during the weeks that I spent staying and traveling with Lucas Thobakgale. A man whom we were visiting one day explained to me, when I asked how people knew the conference theme in advance if it was not advertised, "People, they know! Because . . . as we were attending other gatherings like weddings and funerals, people would [ask], 'What's the conference this year?' and we told them, 'This is what we're going to talk about.'" So it was that hundreds of Lemba people that day in September 2006 learned that the Mapungubwe bones were definitively theirs, because DNA tests had provided the proof.

In his opening address, LCA president S. E. Moeti introduced the conference theme and the reburial project it was meant to communicate. He said, "President Thabo Mbeki honors us very much: after he hear[d] from Drake Koka that there will be no peace in the country unless the Lemba bones are reburied in the rightful way, DNA was conducted on the bones at the University of Pretoria, and it was discovered that many of the bones were Lemba bones."[35] This was just one such announcement. Just as word had spread about the conference theme, at weddings, funerals, and official gatherings throughout 2006, including those that were convened specifically to inform people about the Mapungubwe plans, Lemba leaders proclaimed, and others repeated, that the Mapungubwe bones were theirs, and DNA tests proved it—just as DNA tests had proved they were black Jews who made their way as traders into Africa centuries before Mapungubwe was established.

On October 1, 2006, Lucas Thobakgale and M. J. Mungulwa made one such presentation; Pandelani Mutenda recorded video of the event, and I was there taking notes. We were in a village in the Greater Sekhukhune district of South Africa's Limpopo Province, gathered in the kraal of Kgoshi Malaga. I did not know Malaga well, since I had not included his village as a field site, but I had met him in the context of his membership in Kgoshi Mpaketsane's unrecognized traditional leaders' group. Thobakgale likewise did not know Malaga well, but he had met him in 1996, and he had once before visited to do a presentation with the LCA, in 2001.

In 1996 Thobakgale was working as an inspector of schools with the postapartheid South African Department of Education. At one school, he recognized that some teachers had the Lemba surname Malaga, but when he told one of these young teachers that he was Lemba, that they were therefore related, and that this teacher had many more relatives in Venda, the man did not know what he was talking about. As Thobakgale explained it to me ten years later, in 2006: "'Go to the chief' [he told the young teacher]. 'Tell him there is an inspector there who says we don't belong there; we belong there. We don't belong to these people: we are Lembas.' So the young man went and told him." When weeks passed and Thobakgale did not hear from the young man's chief, he went himself: this was how he met Kgoshi Malaga.

At that first meeting, he told Malaga, "I am Thobakgale. You are my cousin." Recalling this encounter, he continued:

So I told him that they are the Lembas; there are many Malagas. . . . He didn't know about this close relationship and the extended relationship. His extended relationship went to the Sekhukhune people.[36] So I told him that look, they are there and being there they are many, and we have a conference every year and I would like you to go, and go with your people. You go and show them also how *you* live here. You shouldn't pretend to live like them that side. . . . I wanted also to educate these ones, informally, educate them to know that the Lembas are all over the world and they speak any language that is near to them, and they adopt the external elements of the culture of the people they live with.[37]

The encounter was auspicious: they met just as the Cohen Modal Haplotype study found that the Buba clan of the Lembas shared a genetic marker (the Cohen Modal Haplotype, or CMH) with Jewish priests (Cohanim, who pass along their priestly status from father to son and who claim descent from Moses's brother Aaron). The surname Malaga meant that they, too, were of the Buba clan: they were not only Lemba, they were of the clan that was primarily responsible for proving genetically that the Lembas were descended from Jews.

Kgoshi Malaga attended the 1997 LCA conference where then-president Professor Mathivha explained Lemba genetic links to Jews and attachment to Sweetwaters as an ancestral place (see the introduction). The LCA followed up in 2001 with an official visit to Ga-Malaga to give formal presentations to the entire community about the fact that they were Lemba, what that meant, and how they could be involved in the LCA.

The 2001 visit was a mutual exchange. Association secretary F. C. Raulinga gave his speech about culture as a unifying force and explained the most important aspects of Lemba culture: knowing how to greet properly, especially how to greet one's elders; praying to the Lemba god *Mwali we denga* (Yahweh), and not to ancestors or idols; male circumcision at age eight; food cleanliness, and specifically not eating pork; not eating milk and meat together and not exchanging utensils with non-Lembas; the correct position of a body for a Lemba burial (lying flat and facing north); teaching children to respect their parents; peaceful coexistence with neighbors; and an ideal of endogamy with provisions to initiate "alien" women so that they become accepted as Lemba.[38] Professor Mathivha presented the history of each clan and the Lemba migration narrative that began with them leaving Judea for Yemen and then traveling through Great Zimbabwe to South Africa. Mathivha emphasized that each time the Lemba/Sena moved, the larger group divided, which resulted in Lemba people settling all over Africa, including the Falashas of Ethiopia, the Igbos of Nigeria, and the Tutsis in Rwanda and Burundi.[39] Kgoshi Malaga introduced all the members of the royal family and presented to the LCA the Malaga genealogy and migration history, going back through seven different place names until they settled in their present kraal in 1918.

But the purpose of this October 2006 visit was to inform Kgoshi Malaga and his people about the reburial plans. Thobakgale stood in the glaring sun, microphone in hand, in front of a crowd of about eighty village residents of all ages who had gathered in Kgoshi Malaga's kraal. Kgoshi Malaga sat behind Thobakgale under a shaded canopy facing the crowd, along with his advisers, the other LCA delegates, and me. The audience included the Malaga royal family, other villagers who recognized Kgoshi Malaga as their chief despite his lack of state legal recognition, and a fair number of curious neighbors who neither considered Malaga to be their chief nor thought of themselves as Lemba people.

After reminding the Malaga people that they are from the Buba clan, which means that they are descended from Aaron, Thobakgale explained that scientific research proved most of the Mapungubwe bones belonged to *Vhashavi* (another way that Lemba people refer to themselves; it means "traders"). The link from one genetic study (the Cohen Modal Haplotype study that identified the Buba in particular as Cohanim and therefore descendants of Aaron) to another (research on the Mapungubwe bones that determined they belonged to the Lemba) was seamless.

Thobakgale continued, "We as Vhashavi, we were called since the bones of our elders are there. So our leaders went there, and we were asked what we want to do with the bones, and so we decided that we will bury in our traditional way. Conflict started when people started to say that Mapungubwe is theirs, and others said it is theirs." As he continued, Thobakgale merged the interests of the Lemba with those of the state and explained how the history of the LCA was connected to thriving in postapartheid South Africa:

> Long ago in apartheid our fathers came up with the LCA because you can't build a nation alone. That is why we are here today, and that shows that the family of Malaga are showing us the way. . . . It is important that

you know you are a Mulemba—then you can be a good South African. You young children, it is important to read about your culture and your tradition. That is why you read those stories in grade twelve that talk about different cultures. You cannot be a good South African when you don't know where you are coming from.

Thobakgale's message was that during apartheid, the LCA needed to bring together the Lemba people to build a nation, and now the LCA needed to facilitate cultural awareness among Lemba people to better participate in the nation that had been built. The nation of the Lemba had given way to the nation of South Africa, and Lemba cultural awareness was no longer a matter of survival but now a matter of good multicultural citizenship. Instead of fighting to survive as a nation, LCA promotion of Lemba (indigenous) culture as part of the (indigenous) nation-state could help the nation-state survive.

In closing out the presentation, Mungulwa explained that although the bones would be reburied in 2007, the DNA tests on the remains should not have been conducted because permission was never granted: "Our bones were taken for experimentation, which is not allowed—when a person is dead, no disturbance is allowed."[40] Nevertheless, since the results, like those of the earlier genetic studies for which they *had* given permission, aligned with what they knew about their history and provided evidence that could convince others who had called that history into question, he accepted that it was already done, and they would try to make it right by at least laying the remains of their ancestors to rest at Mapungubwe.

Later that year, we all learned something surprising: no DNA tests had in fact been done. Professor Victor Ralushai, who had been head of the 1996 Commission of Inquiry into traditional leadership disputes in the Limpopo Province and was part of the committee facilitating the joint claim and the Mapungubwe reburial, told me in July that he had heard repeatedly that the DNA had shown the Mapungubwe bones belonged to the Lemba. But when he and the rest of the committee called the University of Pretoria to find out more about these DNA tests, they were told that no such tests had been conducted. In August 2006, the archaeologist I had been meeting with told me the same thing: the committee had contacted the University of Pretoria department that was in charge of the bones until they could be reburied and was told there had been no tests. I did not fully believe them until I finally was able to interview Rejoice Mabudafhasi, the deputy minister of the environment and tourism who was in charge of the project, on November 8, 2006. I asked: Were there DNA tests that linked the Mapungubwe bones to the Lemba, or was that a rumor? She repeated what I had heard from Ralushai and the archaeologist: she had spoken to people at the University of Pretoria, and they confirmed that it did not happen.

In the book *Speaking with Vampires: Rumor and History in Colonial Africa* (2000), Luise White argues that rather than a misrecognition, rumor is an especially valuable form of historical evidence. Stories about blood-stealing European firemen, she writes, "explain what was fearsome and why" in newly colonized East African contexts. She continues: "New technologies and procedures did not have meaning because they were new or powerful, but because of how they articulated ideas about bodies and their place in the world, and because of the ways in which they reproduced older practices" (5). The Mapungubwe DNA rumors should be read in the same spirit. Like the reckonings with colonial renderings of bodies and value that White analyzes, here, too, new technologies crystallized articulations between bodies and belonging.[41]

There were different theories as to how this DNA rumor got started: it might have been in the newspaper, and some contended that Mbeki himself had said it. The archaeologist was convinced that the LCA had made up the account that DNA linked them to the Mapungubwe bones as a way to advance what he felt were dubious claims. My conversations with LCA members told a different story. On the way home from an LCA meeting in mid-November 2006, Tanya Mungulwa asked me: "Noah, do you know about the DNA test that have been conducted, isn't it?" I explained what I had learned from Mabudafhasi, who, as a relative, was a more trusted source than either of the others who had told me the same thing. She then speculated about where the rumor started. "You know, I think this DNA issue was confused," she said, "with that issue that there was some DNA test for black Jews in South Africa. I think somebody mixed up the whole issue."

In the end, it did not matter where the narrative came from, because once it had been repeated innumerable times, it became part of the larger story of the Mapungubwe reburial, significant less for its accuracy or lack thereof than for the experiential and ideological truths that made it plausible and resonant. As far as most Lemba leaders were concerned, the genetic links to the Mapungubwe bones were real and proved that they were indigenous, just as their genetic links to Jews proved that their oral history was accurate and they were who they said they were. The two DNA tests appeared equally factual in the public presentations that continued leading up to the Mapungubwe reburial: together, the tests confirmed the Lemba position that it was not a contradiction to be both Jews and Africans.

Returns: Recognition through Reburial

As it turned out, all of the care that the LCA took to present themselves as adequately indigenous did not stop other groups from objecting to their inclusion in the project, and all of the objections did not stop the Lemba from being part of it. Leaders of the LCA participated in the ceremonial release of the remains at the University of Pretoria on October 29, 2007, the cleansing ceremony at Mapungubwe to prepare the site a week later, and finally the reburial itself over the weekend of November 18, 2007. About sixty Lemba people were there, along with groups from each of the other designated stakeholder communities. The reburials at sites on the ground happened first, and only after dark on the final day did they begin the reburial at Mapungubwe Hill.[42] At each site, stakeholders performed rituals and placed small rectangular coffins in prepared communal graves.[43]

Pandelani Mutenda, speaking to me in 2013, recalled that the mood had been very good that day: people were happy because "at the end we have achieved . . . they're buried now." But throughout the negotiation process and all the way through the ceremonies themselves, that final reburial at the top of Mapungubwe Hill remained contentious. Whereas participating in the other burials indicated that one's ancestors had been part of the Mapungubwe kingdom broadly, participating in the burial on the hill indicated that one's ancestors had been Mapungubwe royalty. Three of the stakeholder communities—the Tshivhula, Ga-Machete, and Leshiba royal families—understood themselves in the present as royal, so they sent their traditional leaders and royal councils up the hill. But the other three stakeholder communities had more complicated relationships to chieftaincy: these were the San Council, the Vhangona Cultural Movement, and the Lemba Cultural Association. In this context, the existence of Lemba traditional leaders went some way toward overcoming others' objections to the inclusion of nonroyals in the burial. This was one reason for the LCA visit to Kgoshi Malaga in 2006: his participation in the Mapungubwe reburial was an embodied answer to others' questions about the existence of Lemba royalty, even as it was also a reframing of the position of royalty vis-à-vis other kinds of traditional leadership, such as the LCA presidency and executive council. Still, like genetic evidence, the evidence of chieftaincy was, from the perspective of Lemba people, a way for others to answer a question that was not their own.

While the Lemba participants in the Mapungubwe reburial did not doubt their history there, they also found it immensely satisfying to learn about archaeological evidence that confirmed their knowledge that their ancestors were present not only at Mapungubwe's surrounding communities but on the hill itself. Mungulwa, also speaking to me in 2013, recalled a professor pointing out this evidence to him:

"'Here is the kraal of the cattle; this is the place where the Lemba take circumcision for the children,'" he said, voicing the professor's explanation for my benefit. He continued with commentary on the professor's lesson:

> And then when we go there, we find that it's a lot of the scrap of the clay pot. We know that! The person who brought the clay pot in the country is the Lemba! Everywhere we go to bury, we find the scrap of the clay pots. Everywhere in Mapungubwe, even the hill! . . . So it was witness ourselves that the Lemba was here. We don't need anybody to talk about it. Because it is the material! It witness itself.

Mungulwa's attention to materiality here was an uncanny inverted echo of the uncertainty of the Mapungubwe DNA rumors: even if true, the latter were unsettling, because with no permission having been sought or granted, genetic evidence was evidence out of control. Pottery, on the other hand, was solid enough to be self-evident: every Lemba person understood that their ancestors were known for their pottery, many had living relatives who continued to craft pottery in traditional styles, and all could recognize which styles they associated with their people and which they did not.

It was not only a desire to limit the hilltop reburial to royalty but also logistical challenges that made this final event the most exclusive one. There was only one way to the top of the hill, the same steep wooden staircase that Ishe Sadiki and I climbed in 2013. Only five people could climb at a time to ensure that it would not collapse, so each stakeholder community took turns sending five people, carrying remains to the top of the hill to complete that community's rituals. Mungulwa recalled that rather than arguing over who would go first, the LCA remained quiet during negotiations and ended up going third. As they stood, coffins in hand and about to ascend, someone from another group taunted them by saying that the elephant would come and kill all these Lembas, because it would realize they were strangers there. But Mungulwa, knowing they were not strangers and that *Hashem* would see, know, and protect him, kept quiet and proceeded up the hill.[44]

Pandelani Mutenda was among those who carried the coffins, along with LCA secretary Raulinga and others. Neither Lucas Thobakgale nor Chaplain Masala attended, the latter perhaps following through on his threat not to participate if there would be no reading from the Bible. Mungulwa, as LCA president, led the Lemba portion of the ceremony at each reburial site. Mutenda told me, "Each and every grouping, they were given time to then talk on behalf of each and every group. Like the Lembas, they were given the president to talk on behalf of the Lembas. . . . He was praising the return of our ancestors back to their roots where they are and also making poems for the Lembas, all of them for the twelve clans. . . . We know that the clan that we are burying are from the twelve clans, because it was a community, it was a kingdom."

The praise poems were followed by singing *ndinde*: one of these, Mutenda explained, "shows that the *mushavi* or trader is coming, and then when he comes he is coming to trade, and when he is coming he is coming with the, I can say, with money, which will enable him to buy cattle so that he can marry with them. So we are saying we are mushavi, *bashavi*. . . . He will have to marry a wife for him so that he can become a great family." Next they proceeded to kneel at the grave, clapping. I had seen this at many Lemba funerals, and sometimes when I knew the deceased well and I was prompted to do so, I also participated in this ritual.[45] They then rose and sang as they left the graveside: "They were singing about our ancestors that they must have to go in peace . . . so that now, for the community of the Lemba, things would be very well because we have returned!" *We have returned*. With these words, Mutenda crossed over seven hundred years, collapsing the living and the dead to mark a turning point not only in the relative peace of Lemba ancestors, but also in Lemba politics of recognition in South Africa.

The different claims to Mapungubwe and the decision to incorporate all claimants on equal footing into one reburial, rather than to adjudicate which claims were valid and which were not, suggest the possibility of a category of African indigeneity in which groups such as the Lemba, who were not known as separate ethnic groups under apartheid and were not differentiated by language, could claim their ethnic distinctness through one single site. Their single negotiated claim to Mapungubwe did not mean that they had to consider themselves the same in any way except that all had ancestors who had lived there, so all were fundamentally part of the South African past that the state wanted to project into the future. Through the reburial, Lemba ancestral roots in South Africa were affirmed. Yet, these transformations could be only partial.

On August 23, 2013, I participated in another Lemba return to Mapungubwe, this time with Ishe Mungulwa and Ishe Sadiki. Mungulwa had not been there since the reburial ceremony in 2007; Sadiki had never been there before. The drive from Mungulwa's home in Shayandima to Mapungubwe was long, all the more so because we stopped to visit several relatives who were more or less on the way—and it was not only living relatives whom we passed as we drove. As we approached one hilly area that Mungulwa identified as having once been a tea plantation, he told me, "My grandfather was staying there. You cannot even find him; people are sitting on top of the graves." He had not been back there, he said, since his grandfather's burial in 1954—before the forced removals that made way for the tea plantation, owned first by white South Africans before the whole area was folded into the Venda Homeland. "All this side was Sadiki before the tea plantation," he continued. This grandfather, Musware Abdel Sadiki—a man with four wives and twenty-two children, who had been one of the elders approached by M. M. Motenda in the 1940s when he wanted to start organizing Lemba people into an association—was Ishe Sadiki's grandfather too, on his father's side, and he also had not returned to this grandfather's grave. But such a visit was not possible that day beyond this verbal memorialization: what was once a village that housed the living and the dead in relation to one another became a tea plantation and eventually a site of housing once again, built on top of formerly marked graves.

When we arrived at Mapungubwe, Mungulwa told the staff at the entrance desk that he was a stakeholder, the president of the Lemba Cultural Association. We were ushered in to meet the park management staff, who happily greeted us and brought us to the museum. As we entered, a display about the reburial was one of the first things visible. It included a photograph of Rejoice Mabudafhasi, along with her words about the project: "The symbolic handover is not just about signaling to return the dead to the Mapungubwe landscape, it is also about recognizing the importance of local custodians and beliefs, and confirms that community voices have been heard." As I read this aloud, Mungulwa read the final three words along with me. "*Have been heard!* Exactly!"

Other photos showed all stakeholders together, and a history section prominently displayed a photograph of Raulinga—identified as author of the Lemba history—alongside his historical statement.[46] Objects in the exhibit testified to Lemba links to Mapungubwe's industries: the label on the ingots declared that they were "believed to be of Lemba origin," and pottery was identified as "Lemba style." To prepare me for this visit, Mutenda had told me how important this form of recognition was: "When you go to the Mapungubwe Center, you will see all the groupings there, the pictures, all what they did in the museum. It was a symbol of saying, 'Things are settled.' Even today now, everybody, when you are coming from a far distance, they know that when they go to Mapungubwe, the Lembas are part of Mapungubwe." For Mungulwa, pottery worked as internal validation (its ubiquity provided further confirmation that the Lemba had historical roots in the area), and for Mutenda, the prominence of the Lemba in the museum worked as external validation (every visitor would see that the Lemba had been there).

When we arrived at Mapungubwe Hill, we left Mungulwa in the vehicle and walked to the top. Our guide pointed out areas that had been disturbed long ago by white treasure hunters looking for the source of the gold that had been found in graves. But, he explained, they were disappointed because the gold would have been only traded and crafted there—and mined elsewhere. "Remember these people," he explained. "They owned this land, so they moved all over as they pleased. They didn't have borders, like saying, 'That side is Zimbabwe, that side is Botswana'—they could walk all over." His invocation of land possession where borders and nations were irrelevant spoke both to a vision of state indigeneity that, in projecting itself into the past, could also become ever-more expansive and to the issue that had been at the heart of the contestations among claimant groups leading up to the reburial: ownership.

Later that night, as I drove Mungulwa and Sadiki home, Mungulwa told me about his dreams for the future. First, he said that he hopes Lemba youth will visit Mapungubwe so as to not lose this history. Then he spoke of the LCA and land ownership. The most important thing, he told me, is for the Sweetwaters land claim to be resolved so that the LCA gains the title deed, which will guarantee Lemba people a place to practice their culture without challenge. "Once they got a place for the LCA," he explained, "then each and everybody will be free."

Whatever the idea of recognition might have meant at the start of the re-burial plans and at the reburial ceremony, in 2013 it was intertwined with the open question of land ownership. This was clear in our guide's framing of the historicity of borders alongside ahistorical concepts of ownership; it was clear in Mungulwa's sense that while Mapungubwe was important to access history, it was a title deed to Sweetwaters that could generate freedom; and it was clear to me, though unremarked by Mungulwa and Sadiki, in the ways that Mapungubwe could be visited but they had no access to their grandfather's grave. Through the Mapungubwe reburial and its ongoing projects of memorialization, Lemba people became recognized as indigenous Africans, insofar as this aligned with state indigeneity. Leading up to the reburial ceremony, Mapungubwe represented the convergence of Lemba interests and state interests and the open possibilities of South African indigeneity. Now, six years later, it represented an indigenous claim that could sustain Lemba Jewish histories. But it also provided a point of reference for what had been memorialized and what still could not be.

Black Jewish Indigeneity

It was August 2013, on the day that we decided we would try to travel together to Mapungubwe later in the week, and Ishe Mungulwa and I were at his home in Shayandima, not far from Thohoyandou (figure 5.3). We had been talking already for several hours. He told me about an all-expenses-paid trip to San Francisco that he and others from the LCA had taken in 2007 to attend a conference organized by a Jewish multicultural organization called Be'chol Lashon, Hebrew for "in every tongue," and about a group of African American Hebrews that he had addressed, at Professor Ralushai's request, in 2003 at the Venda Sun Hotel.

Each meeting had yielded different visions of Jewish origins and connection that were reinforced by books the groups presented to Mungulwa. Be'chol Lashon gave him *The Everything Jewish History and Heritage Book* (R. Bank and Gutin 2003), and the African American Hebrews gave him *The Original African Heritage Study Bible* (Felder 1993). The latter particularly resonated with Mungulwa and was one spark for his rethinking the relationship between having Jewish origins and being African. As I picked up the book to investigate, he sang its praises. "This can tell you a lot of things," he said, "when the European came to this country, when they changed the boundary, when they changed to Middle East instead of Northeast Africa. Canaan is not Middle East! Middle East for where? That is the question. Because if they say Northeast Africa, they are promoting black."[47] As I continued flipping through his Afrocentric Bible, we talked about the Sweetwaters land claim, the Mapungubwe reburial, and the Lembas as both Jews and indigenous Africans.

Mungulwa recalled when "indigenous" became something to contend with: "You know when I start to hear that word [was] when I went at Mapungubwe. All along, I didn't hear that word. What is indigenous? That was a big question. And then a person from the government reply, they say so and so, and so and so, and Lemba." It was easier conceptually for the government representative to define "indigenous" as simply all of those whom they had included in the joint claim to the Mapungubwe bones than it was for many of the claimants to accept this expansive definition. This was because for the government, the indigeneity that mattered was undifferentiated state indigeneity, but for participants who were now labeled indigenous, it was an opening through which to address long-existing forms of disenfranchisement. This is why some claimants interpreted "indigenous" to mean who was first in the place or who had been there the longest without interruption, and others viewed indigeneity as a declaration of past rule and past ownership that should extend into the present. For the Mapungubwe reburial participants, being indigenous was not so

FIGURE 5.3 Lemba Cultural Association president M. J. Mungulwa at his home in Shayandima in 2013. He is surrounded by his books and plaques recognizing his contributions to the Lemba Cultural Association. Photograph by author.

much something that was claimed and achieved as it was a category of being and belonging that became available, and, once available, could not *not* be embraced.[48] Yet, as he did with Be'chol Lashon and the group of African American Hebrews, rather than accept entirely what was being presented, Mungulwa internalized what resonated and left aside what did not.

Through the Mapungubwe reburial, indigeneity provided an opportunity for the state and for the Lemba: through indigeneity, both became affirmed as legitimately African. Being indigenous in South Africa today is the space where the interests of the state and the interests of minority groups within the state converge and can be contested—it is the site of mutual intelligibility between state indigenous legitimacy and claims of marginalized groups against the state.

When I asked Mungulwa in 2013 whether he viewed Lemba people as indigenous in Africa, he answered in the affirmative: "We must be known as indigenous in Africa, because you know the time when our people crossed Phusela, the Red Sea, it was some centuries and centuries back. Now we must not be settlers here; we are indigenous!" Mungulwa's distinction between those who are settlers and those who are indigenous echoed that which Richard Wade had sought to collapse when he announced at the 2006 LCA conference that he and the Lemba were equally not African. Mungulwa's distinction directly answered anyone who would say that if the Lemba are Jews, then they originate from elsewhere and are therefore not really Africans.

For LCA leaders, the openness of indigeneity and its potential as a point of access to a form of state recognition (however symbolic) established the concept as an aspirational category that might achieve two now-intertwined goals: access to the Mapungubwe reburial and access to state recognition as a distinct and legitimate community. Their claim to the Mapungubwe bones was necessarily a claim on the state in the name of indigeneity.[49] Through Mapungubwe, the Lemba as a legally unrecognized ethnic group have experienced a limited form of postapartheid ethnic recognition predicated on their ability to connect their history to a nascent and shifting concept of African indigeneity. And the forms of belonging that Mapungubwe facilitated, limited as they were, laid the ground for Lemba people not only to accept the state project of indigeneity but also to redefine it in ways that affirmed their own histories, experiences, and values.

The Mapungubwe reburial was a pivotal event through which LCA leaders articulated Lemba claims to Jewish blood with claims to African bones, facilitating their reframing of diaspora, indigeneity, and citizenship. State actors invoked indigeneity to mark the reburial project as one of postapartheid African state legitimacy built on precolonial African power. Claimant groups opposed to Lemba participation invoked indigeneity as a question of hierarchy: Who was more indigenous, and who therefore had a legitimate claim? But Mungulwa and others in the LCA invoked indigeneity as a new language through which to claim recognition from the postapartheid South African state, given that the options that had been available to them under apartheid had failed.

In the midst of objections from other groups about Lemba inclusion in the reburial plans in 2006, Mungulwa reframed Mapungubwe indigeneity from a question of origins and ownership, which is how the objections were expressed, to something broader and more globally connected. He told me, "Now people claim Mapungubwe does not belong to Lemba, but we don't say that it belongs to Lemba, we say it was the world trade center! It was a lot of people, Portuguese, the Arabians, the other black. . . . We didn't say it's our place; it's the world trade center. It's the heritage!" In this interesting twist on dominant ideas of indigeneity in which transnational discourses of the present facilitate links to nation-states on the basis of a localism of the past, Mungulwa's Mapungubwe positioned the Lemba as part of a world trade center of the past and as a privileged part of the nation-state of the present.[50]

Like Mungulwa's embrace of Canaan as Northeast Africa, this was about calling frames of reference into question. But whereas the former challenged Eurocentric, colonial frames, here he was disrupting postcolonial nationalist frames. This was an indigeneity that marked not rootedness in what was now South Africa, but rather participation in a globally connected, precolonial place. There was nothing here that would require diasporic or settler subjects to exist in opposition to indigenous ones, because this was a conceptualization of indigeneity that rejected both origins and borders, embracing instead the mobile connectivity of trade routes and the worlds they made possible.[51]

Genetic Proof

Mungulwa had a framed certificate, dated October 29, 2007, at the center of his living-room wall. The certificate, issued by the University of Pretoria and the University of the Witwatersrand to commemorate the return for reburial of remains that they had stored since the 1930s, declared that the LCA are "bona fide descendants of Mapungubwe." During the long drive that we took together with Ishe Sadiki to the site in 2013, Mungulwa explained that in spite of this recognition, there were still stakeholders who opposed ongoing Lemba inclusion in decisions, such as whether a proposed coal mine should be allowed to operate or be denied permission because of the potential environmental impact on a sacred and historically significant site and the wildlife that freely roamed around it. He told me, "They are all claiming that they are indigenous of that place. But when they say that, they say the Lemba is not indigenous to that place; they've got no proof."

Proof, though, was in the DNA after all. As the car approached the Mapungubwe park entrance, Mungulwa praised the University of Pretoria for having dug up and stored the bones. I was confused: I thought the whole point of the reburial was to make right the injustice that had been done by disturbing the graves in the first place. But Mungulwa explained that what they did was good, because it helped to know who the bones belonged to. I asked him, "How do you know who the bones belonged to?" Without hesitating, he answered: "They took DNA."

Mungulwa had certainly heard that the 2006 DNA tests had been nothing but a rumor—he just did not believe it. His theory was that the university knew all along whose bones they had but combined them intentionally and denied the veracity of the test to prevent arguments among claimant groups, thus subverting claims *on* the state in the name of indigenous groups in favor of an undifferentiated state indigeneity.

There are three lessons to be learned from the phantom Lemba Mapungubwe DNA. First, Lemba people generated genetic meaning from tests that did not take place. This makes clear, as I have argued throughout this book, that any analysis of what DNA means cannot be limited to geneticists' work. Second, DNA (whether real or rumored) operated as a mechanism through which to bring together foreignness and Africanness, blood and bones, difference and belonging. For Lemba people in particular, then, DNA made a critical contribution to the work that their ethnic difference could do. And third, despite the expansiveness of a Lemba embrace of indigeneity, imagining genetic evidence also considerably narrowed what it would mean to be indigenous to Mapungubwe, such that DNA might substantiate the claims of some but show others that they do not belong to the place at all.

The belief that the Mapungubwe bones had been DNA-tested and proved to belong to their ancestors dovetailed perfectly with earlier experiences of the Jewish DNA studies that gave the Lemba transnational legitimacy and recognition when they were denied them by the South African state. The sign of absolute proof was DNA, and the Mapungubwe DNA proved that they were indigenous Africans. It did not actually matter that the tests were never conducted. The LCA learned this after they had already told everyone at the annual conference, at their own meetings, and at Ga-Malaga that the Mapungubwe bones were DNA-certified Lemba bones, so the story was out and remained a powerful rumor even once it had been officially denied by those who supposedly had conducted the tests.

How DNA mattered for Lemba people goes some way toward understanding how it served as a technology of indigeneity in a context where the meaning of indigeneity was in question. But the fact remains that the DNA rumors came from somewhere and resonated widely: this was not only a Lemba phenomenon. Furthermore, despite initial objections among all claimants to future DNA testing, they all eventually agreed to this condition. The boxes selected for reburying the remains and the method of sealing the burial sites ensured the integrity of the bones for potential future research, and the remains were reburied with the promise to scientists that there could be a future unearthing. This was the price of each claimant groups' recognition as indigenous. In this way, present and future scientists also became a stakeholder community whose reburial rituals were ultimately witnessed and approved by the others.

In the end, they were the only stakeholders who were not burdened with the task of standing for state indigeneity.

In his 2005 book, *Mapunbugwe: Ancient African Civilisation on the Limpopo*, Thomas Huffman asserts on the very first page that there is no genetic link between the people who lived at Mapungubwe and the Venda people who live in the region now. He then notes that "Mapungubwe people are gone, but the culture is by no means dead" (7).[52] Writing in 2011, archaeologist Maryna Steyn amends this assertion with the open possibilities of the future: "Due to the difficulties with DNA extraction from bone, contamination and cost, no DNA analyses have thus far been done on the Mapungubwe and K2 remains. . . . It is doubtful whether DNA analysis will shed light on the ancestry issue, but this may change in future" (Steyn 2011, 228).[53] Huffman's assertion that the lack of a genetic link to contemporary people in the vicinity meant that Mapungubwe people, imagined as a genetically coherent group, are gone is ultimately negated by Steyn's assertion that DNA analysis could happen in the future, and if it did, it could provide new ancestry information. As a technology of indigeneity in formation, then, DNA worked best as an unrealized future possibility.[54]

As a state heritage project, Mapungubwe promoted an idea of South African indigeneity characterized by multiethnic and multiregional coexistence, transnational trade, and the political-economic power both of elites over the populace and of a strong state over a larger region. As a project of Lemba indigenous belonging, Mapungubwe facilitated a shift in which their liminal belonging became legible as central and legitimate. And as a site where DNA continues to matter, not just as scientific research but also as research potential and as rumor, Mapungubwe underscores the importance of genetic afterlives: Mapungubwe reminds us that genetic ancestry exceeds scientific meaning and intent, even while ultimately lending scientific credibility as it circulates.

AFTERLIVES OF RESEARCH SUBJECTS

Genetic afterlives are necessarily unfinished, always newly becoming. They expand the repertoire of what DNA tells us about bodies and belonging, thus offering a means to chip away at absolutist and essentialist readings of genetic ancestry and its application to exclusionary nationalist projects. Lemba genetic knowledge production has reconfigured belonging and disrupted genetic ancestry's mappings: in Lemba hands, genetic ancestry promises openings through which to challenge racial and ethnonational boundaries. Once abstracted in genetic ancestry studies into a population that might be Jewish or might be African, Lemba people have asserted that these same studies affirmed their knowledge that their ancestors were—and that they remain—black Jews, indigenous to Africa and aligned with other Jews and Hebrews all over the world through bonds of potential mutual learning and solidarity. Lemba genetic afterlives suggest a promise of diasporic visions uninterested in singular notions of a homeland and ideals of return, and an embrace of a form of indigeneity not predicated on autochthony. By looking at Lemba genetic knowledge production, we can see that former research subjects can powerfully reconfigure dominant understandings of race and nation. But the ability to bring about categorical and conceptual shifts is highly contingent, not least on how well they align with—or alternatively, how profoundly they disrupt—state projects and scientific epistemologies.

In 2007, the same year that the reburial ceremony took place at Mapungubwe, the Lemba Cultural Association discussed and decided that there would be no future Lemba genetic ancestry studies. The decision came about because individuals—some known to the LCA, some complete strangers—began showing up with kits, ready to collect new samples. "We've had to send people away," Dr. Rudo Mathivha, now general secretary of the LCA, told me in 2013. "I mean, you just get phoned one morning, 'We're here, we're in Limpopo, we need to know where the Lemba community is, we're here to do research on this and this and this and this,' and we're like: 'We don't know about it, so just go back wherever you came from!'"

The issue caused a rift in their long relationship with Tudor Parfitt. In 2007, he asked to do another study, for reasons that were not clear to the LCA leadership. According to Mathivha, whereas in the first study the LCA had organized elders to be sampled, now Parfitt wanted to test young people. He explained it had something to do with mapping the exact migration of the Lemba, but Mathivha believed it did not add up: "I said, you've got the original samples. Obviously you haven't discarded them. Do that and as far as I know, you can map somebody's migration based on the maternal mitochondria research, but you know, you can't say, okay, for this five hundred years they lived here, for the next one hundred years they lived there. Genetics isn't going to tell you that."

Mathivha suspected that Parfitt was being pressured to use genetics to cast doubt on the earlier study, and that since fewer endogamous marriages were taking place among her generation and the next, the plan was to sample their resulting offspring to show a different result than what had been found earlier. She thought the pressure might be coming from Israel: "Word is, the high-ranking rabbis in Israel were not very happy with those results because there is no other group in the world that's got such a high incidence of the Cohanim sequence in their genetic makeup than the Lemba. So either they're feeling threatened or, you know, black people cannot be, you know, the original people. . . . It's not sitting well with them that there is a group of black people who have all this data backing their oral history, you know?"

M. J. Mungulwa, LCA president from 2013 until his death in 2018, shared Mathivha's concerns about what might motivate Parfitt or anyone else to do further studies. The DNA moratorium was one of the first things that Mungulwa wanted to talk to me about on my 2013 visit; we had not seen each other since before they had made the decision (figure E.1). He explained to me how DNA works, and how, in spite of its being used in the past to support Lemba people, it could be employed in the future by those who oppose them. "You know why, by DNA test, it is not all people who will come positive DNA. Others will be negative. That you must understand, we won't all be positive; others will be negative," he explained. "That's why we're very much

FIGURE E.1 M. J. Mungulwa (*left*) and Pandelani Mutenda (*right*) at Sweetwaters following a 2013 LCA meeting. Mungulwa was president of the Lemba Cultural Association from 2013 until his death in 2018. Mutenda became president in 2019. Photograph by author.

afraid for the researchers of opposite, the ones who would say, no this is not, they're claiming for nothing! But once they have a little mistake come out, they will say, 'We told you!' They will shed all the truth and remain [with] only the mistake." By "researchers of opposite," he meant scientists who, unlike Jenkins and Parfitt who had hoped to demonstrate Lemba links to Jews, instead hoped to disprove those connections or otherwise discredit the earlier studies.

This LCA refusal to participate in new genetic ancestry studies is also an example of genetic afterlives. Their refusal is knowledge production in that it seeks to delimit the range of narratives circulating about their DNA: they are fully aware that not all genetic knowledge production carries equal authority and that theirs could be undermined.

Mungulwa knew that ultimately it would be Lemba people who would bear the consequences if future research failed to reproduce the positive results from the Jenkins and Parfitt studies. Like Mathivha, Mungulwa felt frustrated that Parfitt would pursue new genetic research now, after having produced the study that had done so much for them by achieving the result that the LCA knew to be the truth. "Tudor is a writer; it is his job; he is getting a living out of that," Mungulwa explained. "Tudor is not one of tribe of the Lembas! If it doesn't go through, it isn't his business! His business is to sell! See? We, if we fail, it's our business."

I did not contact Parfitt to learn what his intentions had been in pursuing more Lemba genetic ancestry research and how he interpreted the rift in his long-standing relationship with the LCA. But the issues here are less about one researcher, their intentions, and the implications of their work than about the insatiable need in genetic ancestry research for more: more samples, more studies, more results to challenge the old ones. Pandelani Mutenda explained,

> You know after the DNA tested and then all the results had been released, so there were a lot of other people [who] wanted to come in and do the DNA with us. We sat down as a nation, as a community, and ask ourselves the question, why? Why repeatedly DNAs? . . . Because we don't worry about our Jewishness. We're not having a problem with that. So we find that no, we know that we're Jewish. And then we've allowed these things from the LCA for those who didn't believe. . . . Before, when DNA was allowed to be done in our community, we were doing for those who do not believe.

The problem, though, was that once the Lemba were world famous as genetic Jews, it was "the Lemba" and not the LCA per se whom new researchers pursued. Mutenda told me, "When they come, they did not want to approach the LCA, they just want to approach individuals and make research. . . . We said no, we wanted to—it was a topic [of discussion] to say, what about now if people come to make research, what is the procedure? Then we said the procedure is that each and every one who wanted to make a research about the Lemba, they must via through the general secretary. So that it must go to the [LCA] executive [board]."

But this policy proved unenforceable, and individual Lemba people, especially young ones, continued to be approached to take part in new research. "So from there," Mutenda continued, "we said OK, we see the results of DNA moving all over the world, but what about now? What should we do if some other people say we want to make a DNA? We said no. It was taken that we don't need DNA anymore. . . . Because we know that we are the Lemba Jews, there's no need." Even though the LCA did not in any official capacity speak for all Lemba people, and even though the organization could not enforce its DNA moratorium, it could at least question both the ethics and the validity of unauthorized research. "We don't worry," Mutenda told me. "Because it's not done from our Lembas. We cannot say it is a Lemba who made those DNA. Because we know that when they need DNA, they came to us. If they can go and find another one who can give DNA, how will you believe that is a Lemba? . . . Because ours we know."

The LCA's strategy of protecting its truth from predatory researchers was striking. I said to Mutenda, "It's interesting, because usually DNA is taken to prove who someone is, and what you are saying is if you have the DNA, you cannot prove that *that* DNA came from a person who is really a Lemba." He agreed,

Yes, it's very interesting, because if they don't come to LCA, they can go to whosoever they make a deal [with] and say this is for Lemba. So how can we believe? . . . They didn't come and make a DNA from my children, they go outside and make a DNA. And [we] say, "No, these are not my children," whereas they didn't take it from my children. . . . You know what, people are doing whatever they want. So it's theirs. We don't worry. Ours is on record; it is all over. And we are very happy. Those others for other people who are doing outside, the interpretation is up to them.

Mathivha, though, was less sanguine about the damage that could be done through unauthorized research. As LCA general secretary, she bore the brunt of researchers' assumptions that because the Lemba had participated in genetic ancestry research in the past, their DNA was now an infinitely available resource, no matter the purpose or the relationship (or lack thereof) between researcher and Lemba people. "The most recent was two years ago," she told me in 2013. "Somebody from Israel just sent kits." "No, request, no letter, just kits?" I asked her, incredulous. She answered:

No letter, no request. And the first I hear about it is a call from this doctor that was doing elective work at my hospital to say, "I've got the kits and I must go and collect the samples." So I was like, "What samples?" [The visiting doctor replied,] "The genetic study. This person said you will send me to the community, and I will collect." And I said, "For what purpose?" [He answered,] "We now want to date the migration of the Lemba according to the genetic studies." So I said, "That's rubbish. . . . You do not just show up in a country ready to sample people without even having talked to them. . . . I told him, "We're not like some little laboratory that's just waiting to be sampled!"

Given the challenges that Lemba people faced from predatory outsiders, Mutenda and Mathivha both knew that a more formal recognition would be necessary than the international attention brought by the Jenkins and Parfitt genetic ancestry studies or the affirmation of indigenous belonging that the Mapungubwe reburial had delivered from the postapartheid state.

For Mutenda, it was official ethnic recognition in the language of traditional culture that made the most sense. This echoed Kgoshi Mpaketsane's efforts and those of the LCA leaders in the second half of the twentieth century. "I cannot say we are recognized," he told me. "Some other people, they say the Lembas are known, they mean that as recognition. We are known throughout the whole world because of our efforts, because of the scholars. But the recognition in terms of South Africa is when we are being recognized as a *nation*. Like the Zulus, like the Vendas, like the Tsongas, Ndebeles, the San, Afrikaner, Sotho, Pedi, . . . you know, we can get that one in terms of recognition by the government."

Mutenda had a vision for how this might be achieved. He thought that the Congress of Traditional Leaders of South Africa (CONTRALESA) could be augmented so that it was not only chieftaincy but other forms of traditional leadership in culturally defined communities that would have direct representation in government through this body, or additional representative structures could exist in parallel to CONTRALESA. The idea would be for the LCA to exist as a Lemba council (like the San Council) that would then also have parliamentary representation. "Like the Khoisan," Mutenda explained. "We must have a platform from where we can view our culture, our language, everything that we wanted to be seen."

Recognition, though, was not just about being seen, but about having a substantive role in government policy regarding the rights of culturally defined communities and access to government resources in support of cultural minorities. "Recognition . . . is to say they are there as a nation. . . . In democracy, all cultures are equal! . . . When they say cultural diversity are equal, we wanted to know *how*. Or is it just in talking? But if there is a council, we . . . [will be able to] see them to be equal." For Mungulwa, a Lemba council with representation equal to or part of CONTRALESA could more effectively protect

Lemba people from predatory genetics, and it could also provide them with more concrete means to protect their heritage.

Sweetwaters and the still-pending Lemba land claim there were a case in point. "Sweetwaters is a heritage site of the Lembas. And the LCA was formed there," Mutenda told me. In addition to a secure title, he envisioned a state-built museum and library on the site to support community self-knowledge and research, a synagogue and community hall to augment the existing open-air structure that had once been described as either one of those or the other, and accommodation and infrastructure for visitors from all over the world, who had in recent years increasingly built solid mutual relationships with the LCA based on a shared interest in their mutual exchange of Jewish knowledge, history, and practice, rather than a missionary desire to tell Lemba people what they would need to know and do if they wanted to be proper Jews.

The LCA in 2013 had already achieved some progress toward this Lemba heritage goal. South Africa's National Heritage Council made a thirty-thousand-rand donation to the LCA, although to collect it, the association still had to register as a not-for-profit organization. Rudo Mathivha's vision was to find the means to have a paid Lemba staff: the LCA has always been run entirely through volunteer labor. What she emphasized about recognition, though, was not state sponsorship so much as it was state protection: "We want to engage the government to actually have statutes and acts and laws to actually protect us as a group of people, as a marginalized minority in South Africa. And to protect artifacts that are ours and our heritage, you know? Like they've made with all the other groups in South Africa."

As with the genetic ancestry researchers who now sought young Lemba people for individual participation rather than being accountable to the LCA as a community gatekeeper and protector, tour operators and the occasional entrepreneurial Lemba person also looked to profit by forging individual connections to what still remained only a tenuously protected group. Such an instance occurred when a tour operator convinced a young Lemba man to sign a contract promising access to Lemba people at their homes in villages near Mapungubwe, in exchange for direct payment for each day a tour group stayed at the site. Mathivha learned about it when the operator copied her on an email, assuming that once the contract was signed, the LCA was on board. "So I take it to the elders," she told me. "They said, 'This is invalid. It's not an LCA or Lemba contract, it's a contract between you and this guy, and no way are you going to be putting tents in any Lemba family's yard!'"

Ultimately, for Mathivha, this was not just a national issue. She believed Lemba people needed a form of international recognition that would foster their relationships and protect their interests across national borders. In South Africa, the LCA was sufficiently known and respected among Lemba people that its efforts to shut down Jewish missionary work, genetic research, and newly emerging extractive threats had largely been successful. But new threats kept appearing. For example, once the LCA severed its relationship with Kulanu, the latter organization sought out Lemba people in Zimbabwe: they established a synagogue and sponsored a young Lemba man to convert to Judaism and train in Israel to become a rabbi. Even more worrisome to Mathivha, though, was an American who tried to buy his way into the LCA in order to be able to say he was a Lemba, so that he might access mining concessions near where some Lemba people live in Zimbabwe. A group of doctors tried to do the same. "People come saying they're providing free medical care in the community. These are people we've never heard of, you know?" Mathivha told me. "They stay a few days, I guess some of them are medical doctors. Dishing out tablets, dressing up wounds, and then they go. And then the return trip is now the business partnership thing, like, 'Let's partner with the Lembas in Mbelengwa [Zimbabwe] so we can get a mining concession.' This happened with the last group that was there." She added, "My passion is to get the elders in South Africa and Zimbabwe to be one solid group, you know? I mean, they are talking to each other, they are complimenting each other, but I want them to be one structure—even though we straddle a border."

Genetic ancestry researchers and consumers of personal genetic ancestry tests alike would do well to learn from Mathivha, Mungulwa, and Mutenda's understandings of the politics and ethics of genetic ancestry. Genetic ancestry had brought international attention to Lemba people as genetic Jews, but it came with consequences, as in the unwanted attention from those who would profit from their culture or their rights, and with conditions. To be recognized as Jews, they would need to abandon Christianity or otherwise convert to an existing denomination of rabbinic Judaism. To have their oral history taken seriously, they would need to make themselves infinitely available to researchers, their DNA tested and retested, with no real sense of when it would be seen as enough.

Genetic afterlives, too, have no clear end point. Just as Lemba people must grapple with others' conclusions about who they are and what they should do—conclusions that emerge from the ongoing circulations of existing genetic studies and the media archive that they prompted—so too must they grapple with the genetic knowledge that they themselves produce. As I have shown, Lemba genetic knowledge production articulated with the politics of citizenship, diaspora, traditional and cultural rights, kinship practices, and indigeneity, all with repercussions for Lemba people who did not themselves consent to be part of genetic ancestry research—some because they had not yet even been born when samples were taken. But whereas ceding authority entirely to geneticists to interpret what genetic ancestry data prove necessarily enlists former research subjects in projects that are not their own, genetic afterlives leave open a space to introduce other stories.

Against a narrative that the genetic studies newly demonstrated that Lemba people have Jewish ancestry, that this meant that they were really Jews and not really from Africa, and that it should motivate their "return" to rabbinic Judaism and potentially to Israel, Pandelani Mutenda framed Lemba genetic ancestry as both personally inconsequential and empowering for future Lemba youth. When I asked him in 2013 what he saw as the impact of Lemba participation in genetic ancestry research, he answered,

> I knew before the DNA that I am a black Jew. . . . It's like when you ask me, "How do you feel now because it is proven that you are a Mutenda?" I would say, "I was even before, I was Mutenda!" Those are the scientific things of those people who doesn't believe, who doesn't understand. You know, people can even say that I'm staying in the northern part of South Africa, people can say, "No, you don't stay there." And then if they prove and find that really, they check from the compass, they check and find it's the northern part, they say, "How do you, what is the impact?" I say, "No, there's no impact. I was there even before."

I pressed him further: Was there an impact for others? He continued,

> Now the impact is that when it goes to the young generation of the Lemba community, it will cause them to be very, very open so that now they can realize, especially when they live amongst different cultural diversity, to say, as Lembas, really from the history that they used to tell from our forefathers, other people tried to prove it by blood. The impact is that by blood we are more than those people who are in Jerusalem today. That is the impact.

Mutenda's expansive, plural personal identities, Mathivha's incredulity when she received DNA collection kits without any formal request, and the LCA's refusal of further testing that seemed more likely to undermine than to advance their interests all point to afterlives as contested, generative sites of knowledge production. As research subjects, the Lemba are subjected to

NOTES

Introduction: Diaspora, Indigeneity, and Citizenship after DNA

1 Professor M. E. R. Mathivha, presidential address at the 1997 Lemba Cultural Association Annual Conference. The text of this speech, with the exception of the opening repetition of "shalom," which means "hello," "goodbye," and "peace" in Hebrew, was written in English but delivered to a gathered crowd of tshiVenda, Sepedi, chiShona, Afrikaans, and English speakers. The written speech was part of a Lemba Cultural Association archive compiled by F. C. Raulinga, longtime LCA secretary and briefly LCA president until his death in 2012. I was not at this event: my account of it draws on F. C. Raulinga's archive and interviews with him and others who were there. Aside from "Jews," the group names that Professor Mathivha invoked refer to Africans who have been associated with Jewish, Hebrew, or Israelite histories and identities.

2 After merging with a nearby historically white university in 2005, this is now the University of Limpopo.

3 In 1997 this province was called the Northern Transvaal. "Farm" in a South African context designates a large land area, often thousands of hectares, that is privately owned and not necessarily used for agricultural production, though in many cases, including at Sweetwaters, a portion of the land is devoted to agriculture.

4 This episode, "Lost Tribes," was one of six in the *In the Blood* series hosted by Steve Jones, then head of the Department of Genetics, Evolution, and Environment at University College London. The episode first aired in May 1996. When Jones and his BBC production *In the Blood* framed the Lemba as a lost tribe of Israel, they were echoing the framing of Tudor Parfitt's 1992 book, discussed later in this introduction.

5 Two studies that identified a "Cohen Modal Haplotype" were published in *Nature* (Skorecki et al. 1997; M. Thomas et al. 1998). The coauthors of these studies urged Parfitt to ask Lemba people with whom he had previously worked if they would agree to be part of this emerging research (Parfitt 2000). These original Cohen Modal Haplotype studies have been further scrutinized and the identified genetic sequence refined into what is now called the "Extended Cohen Modal Haplotype" (Hammer et al. 2009).

6 Parfitt sought to determine whether the Lemba were really descended from Jews by tracing, using what he learned from LCA leaders and published sources, Lemba

migration history in reverse: from late twentieth century southern Africa to the fifteenth century southern African kingdom Great Zimbabwe to sixth century B.C.E. Yemen and into biblical Israel.

7   See, for example, Brettschneider 2015; Jackson 2013; Seeman 2009.

8   Patriarchy profoundly shaped Lemba DNA, Lemba Jewishness, and Lemba leadership. The two genetic studies placing the Lemba in the international Jewish spotlight were Y chromosome studies that therefore included only Lemba men. One important way that Lemba Jewishness differed from Rabbinic Judaism was that it was paternal rather than maternal descent that made someone a member of the group. And until recently, all members of the LCA executive board were men.

9   This is the version of the story that I heard from M. J. Mungulwa in 2013. Mungulwa became LCA president following Raulinga's death in 2012.

10 For classic work on colonial representations of Africa, see, for example, Mudimbe 1988, 1994; for the ongoing reproduction of such representations, see Wainana 2005. For more on the colonial concept of "tribe," see especially C. Hamilton and Leibhammer 2016; Mamdani 1996. This particular article was written by the *Times'* controversial science writer Nicholas Wade, whose 2014 book, *A Troublesome Inheritance: Genes, Race, and Human History*, was widely condemned as poorly argued, not based on evidence, and racist. More than one hundred geneticists signed a letter to the editor denouncing the book and Wade's use of their work and that of others in the field of population genetics. They wrote, "Wade juxtaposes an incomplete and inaccurate account of our research on human genetic differences with speculation that recent natural selection has led to worldwide differences in I.Q. test results, political institutions, and economic development. We reject Wade's implication that our findings substantiate his guesswork. They do not" (Coop et al. 2014). For more on Wade's book and geneticists' responses, see Marks 2017.

11 Drawing on the work of Michel-Rolph Trouillot (1995, 2003), Yarimar Bonilla (2015) beautifully explains the kind of approach that I am working toward here: "Our interlocutors are never merely describing their world—they are perpetually analyzing and making arguments about it. The challenge then is not simply to incorporate native voices, but to engage seriously with native *arguments*" (xvi).

12 For a discussion of scientific authority and genetics, see Marks 2001.

13 The Lemba are used as an example in humanities and social sciences literatures on identity, kinship, and genetics as well as related and overlapping literatures on race and genetics. See Abu El-Haj 2011, 2012; Azoulay 2003; Brodwin 2002, 2005; Davis 2004; Efron 2013; Egorova 2010; Erasmus 2013; Imhoff and Kaell 2017; Johnston 2003; S. Kahn 2005; McGonigle 2015; McGonigle and Herman 2015; Nash 2004; Palmié 2007; Parfitt 2003; Parfitt and Egorova 2005, 2006; Zoloth 2003. They are also used in similar ways by geneticists (D. Goldstein 2008; Royal et al. 2010) and journalists (Entine 2007) writing for popular audiences.

14 "Kgoshi" is a title used by traditional leaders that translates as both "chief" and "king." It is not one's state recognition status that determines usage, but rather one's status in the eyes of one's people.

15 This framing had been a central aspect of Grenn-Scott 2002. More recently, Brett-schneider (2015) has shown that this remains an important question with much to contribute to feminist Jewish studies. For ways to think about race and identity beyond questions of authenticity, see Jackson 2005.

16 For more on indirect rule, see especially Beinart and Dubow 1995; Brubaker and Cooper 2000; C. Hamilton and Leibhammer 2016; Mamdani 1996.

17 For overviews and analyses of apartheid policies and ideologies, see especially Boonzaier and Sharp 1988; Dubow 2014; Posel 1991, 2001.

18 I thank Liz Thornberry, Meghan Healy-Clancy, Natasha Vally, Vinny Mazz, Robert Thornton, Amanda Swarr, Elliot James, Clifton Crais, and Tyler Fleming for their contributions to a clarifying Facebook discussion about terminology (Bantustan, homeland, or "homeland"). For more on the histories and politics of Bantustans, see Ally and Lissoni 2017; Beinart 2001; Beinart and Dubow 1995; Ntsebeza 2005; Posel 1991; West 1988.

19 The elders among them—men and women born from the 1920s to the early 1940s—remembered life before apartheid, lived and worked for most of their adult lives under its restrictions, and witnessed the national transformation to democratic rule. Their perspectives provide important insights about continuities across what are often regarded as distinct eras of South African history.

20 For analyses of geneticists' knowledge production in relation to Jewish race and territorial politics, see Abu El-Haj 2012; Egorova 2014; S. Kahn 2013; Parfitt and Egorova 2006. I also analyze the Lemba genetic studies in this way in chapter 2, although my primary emphasis throughout this book is on Lemba people as producers of genetic knowledge.

21 Substantial literatures have emerged around these issues over the past twenty years. For orientations, overviews, and edited collections, see especially Abu El-Haj 2007; Duster [1990] 2003; Fullwiley 2007; Gibbon and Novas 2008; Goodman, Heath, and Lindee 2003; Hartigan 2013; Koenig, Lee, and Richardson 2008; Schramm, Skinner, and Rottenburg 2012; Wailoo, Nelson, and Lee 2012.

22 See also Foster 2016; Nash 2015; K. Taussig 2009; P. Wade 2017; P. Wade et al. 2014; on coproduction, see Jasanoff 2004.

23 For more on genetic ancestry and medical research, see, for example, Epstein 2007; Fortun 2008; Fullwiley 2008; J. Kahn 2008; Montoya 2011; Pollock 2012; Rose 2006; Sunder Rajan 2006. For more on commercial ancestry testing, see Abu El-Haj 2012; Nash 2015; Nelson 2008a, 2016; TallBear 2013.

24 See also Simpson 2007, 2014, on what she calls "ethnographic refusal."

25 See also M'charek 2005a, b; Reardon 2005.

26 Biological anthropologists Bolnick (2008), Goodman (2000), and Marks (1995, 2002, 2017) have done similar work: they are inspiring advocates for an antiracist biological anthropology. This is especially important because anthropology is deeply implicated in genetic ancestry's histories and in histories of scientific racism. In the nineteenth and early twentieth centuries, physical anthropology was inseparable from race science. At the same time, anthropologists such as Boas ([1940] 1995) and Montagu ([1942] 1997) were also at the forefront of early critiques of race and

scientific racism. Biological anthropologists went on to use genetics to debunk popular beliefs that people can be divided into biologically discrete racial categories: they showed that there is more genetic variation within than between these supposedly distinct groups (Goodman, Moses, and Jones 2012). The field of research that has produced genetic ancestry in its many forms is called "anthropological genetics," although the majority of its practitioners are not anthropologists by training or professional affiliation (Abu El-Haj 2012). Meanwhile, anthropologists have continued to contribute to the unraveling of race as a biologically essentialist concept of difference; increasingly they do so while also accounting for the social and political salience and physical effects of race, racism, and processes of racialization (Hartigan 2013).

27 See especially Nash 2015; Nelson 2016; Schramm, Skinner, and Rottenburg 2012; TallBear 2013.

28 Here and elsewhere when I invoke genetic ancestry research, I am including work that is primarily concerned with genetic history and that which is primarily concerned with biomedicine: these are frequently entangled, although biomedical research more often comes to be framed as alternatively more beneficial or more dangerously racist, while genetic history is more often framed as alternatively abstracted from contemporary social politics because it examines a distant past or as an innocuous pastime when it is associated with direct-to-consumer genetic ancestry testing services and products. Nadia Abu El-Haj (2012) carefully parses genetic history not only from medical genetics but also from anthropological genetics (a field of which she sees genetic history as one part), but these careful distinctions frequently collapse when one focuses less on scientists and the specificity of how they understand their work and more on circulations of genetic ancestry research among broader publics.

29 Failure to account for the claims *of* DNA would result in two untenable choices: science could be uncritically embraced as objective truth, or it could be ignorantly rejected out of hand. In either case, scientific authority would remain absolute and unknowable, and Lemba genetic knowledge production could be dismissed as not scientific.

30 Abu El-Haj (2012) and Nash (2015) provide detailed, careful analyses of this exact issue. Hinterberger and Porter's (2015) work on "tethering" is also especially productive in understanding how such articulations are produced.

31 This same historical shift replaced the language of race with that of ethnicity in much academic and public discourse (Harrison 1995; B. Williams 1989).

32 See especially Abu El-Haj 2012; Marks 2009, 2012; M'charek 2005a; Reardon 2005.

33 In 2018, U.S. Senator Elizabeth Warren (D-MA) brought new public attention to this phenomenon. She was widely criticized for what some regarded as a "political stunt" (Zhang 2018) and later reportedly privately apologized to the principal chief of the Cherokee Nation (Herndon 2019). In the midst of the controversy, the journal *Critical Ethnic Studies* published an online resource guide for understanding the issues at stake (Keene, Nagle, and Pierce 2018).

34 See especially Duster 2006; Fullwiley 2008; Marks 2017; Olarte Sierra and Díaz Del Castillo Hernández 2013; TallBear 2013.

35 For an extended discussion of the sex and gender politics of genetic ancestry, see Nash 2015. She argues that genetic ancestry produces ideas about gendered mobility in which men can choose to migrate while women are constrained by the rules of kinship. In these imaginaries, she explains, patrilocality is imagined as universal, and everything comes down to reproductive fitness: relatively small numbers of men reproduce the most, and only those who reproduce count.

36 For more on modal haplotypes in general and the Cohen Modal Haplotype in particular, see Abu El-Haj 2012, 189–191.

37 See also Abu El-Haj 2012; Fujimura and Rajagopalan 2011; Goodman 2007; Nash 2015; Rajagopalan and Fujimura 2012; Royal et al. 2010; TallBear 2013; Templeton 2003.

38 See also Abu El-Haj 2012; Duster 2003b; Erasmus 2013; Marks 2009.

39 See also Erasmus 2017; Nash 2015. For how similar ideologies that naturalize biological reproduction among endangered species produce violence in the name of species preservation, see Parreñas 2018.

40 See, for example, D. Goldstein 2008; for more on this example, see Abu El-Haj 2012. On the phenomenon of the genetic fact, see Nelson 2008b; Wagner 2008, 121.

41 For a related argument against clear delineations between science and myth, see C. Scott 1996; see also Bardill 2014.

42 For a discussion of these dynamics in African contexts, see especially Bank and Bank 2013; C. Hamilton and Leibhammer 2016; Lekgoathi 2009; Schumaker 2001; Tilley 2010; see also Trouillot 1995.

43 For the specific text, see Stayt 1931; for a discussion of Stayt at Cambridge, see Langham 1981.

44 Some (but by no means all) Lemba people in Zimbabwe do embrace this understanding of their history (Dube 2018; Mandivenga 1989). In Zimbabwe, "Remba" is also used to designate the people known in South Africa and in the genetics literature as "Lemba."

45 See especially Berman, Eyoh, and Kymlicka 2004; Jean Comaroff 1985; Jean Comaroff and Comaroff 1991, 1997; John L. Comaroff and Comaroff 2009; Cooper 2005; Delius 1984, 1996; Fabian 1983; Grinker 1994; Gupta and Ferguson 1992; C. Hamilton and Leibhammer 2016; Hodgson 2004; Karakasidou 1997; Mahoney 2012; Malkki 1992, 1995; Mitchell 1956; Ranger 1983, 1993; Tsing 1993; Vail 1989; Worby 1994. Canessa's (2012) work on "becoming indigenous" is also relevant here. He draws on his Andean Bolivian informants' sense of identity as mutable, on Pedro Pitarch's (2010) similar analysis based on research with Tzeltal in southern Mexico, and on Henrietta Moore's (2007) reworking of Butler (1993). For more on becoming indigenous, see also Schramm 2016. João Biehl and Peter Locke (2010, 2017) have recently proposed a Deleuzian anthropology of becoming that similarly emphasizes relationality, multiplicity, and emergence. For an anthropology of becoming, see also Duclos, Criado, and Nguyen 2017.

46 This is evident in classic anthropological work such as Krige and Krige 1943 and in mid-twentieth-century ethnography such as Mitchell 1956, which located ethnic identity as an agentive urban phenomenon rather than a natural rural one.

47 See also S. Hall 1991, in which he writes, "Identities are never completed, never finished; . . . they are always, as subjectivity itself is, in process" (republished in S. Hall 2018, 69).

48 John Jackson's concept of "racial sincerity" is also an inspiration here. Racial sincerity addresses what Jackson identifies as the problematic tendency among researchers as well as within black cultural politics to search for and judge what is authentic and "real." He argues that authenticity involves external judgment and the deployment of expertise—the subject reads the object. But racial sincerity shifts the terms of engagement from subject/object to subject/subject. In other words, terms of engagement that are inherently unequal and saturated with domination can be reframed by acknowledging intersubjectivity and the sincerity of identities and of cultural practices. "Becoming" also identifies questions of authenticity and realness as problematic approaches to the production of knowledge about the Lemba. Like "racial sincerity," "becoming" works against these approaches by acknowledging intersubjectivity and sincerity. The model of racial sincerity is a powerful and important move that enables an approach to Lemba identity that does not objectify them by judging the truth of their origins, and that does not necessarily obscure their own senses of who they are, where they come from, and what that means for *them*.

49 See also the other essays in that volume, especially Kapteijns 2000; Pearson 2000; Pouwels 2000.

50 For resonant interventions against omissions of Africa from understandings of transnationalism and assumptions that culture flowed from Africa across the Atlantic but not vice versa, see Matory 2005.

51 See, for example, Mandivenga 1989; Maylam 1986; Parfitt 1992; Stayt 1931.

52 See also Wasserstrom 1995. Daniel Boyarin (2006) further argues against the existence of some stable thing that we might call "Judaism" in antiquity. The racial and religious complexities of Arab Jewish experiences in the modern Israeli state are also relevant here. See, for example, Alcalay 1993; Anidjar 2003; Domínguez 1989; Shohat 2006.

53 Although Hull (2009) centers Jews in Africa, he only unevenly considers them African Jews, and he emphasizes that Jews throughout African history had non-African origins. He does so in spite of considerable evidence, which he also cites, that being a people apart was better understood as an ideology and a norm than as a totalizing fact of peoples' lives, and that key moments of what we might understand as Jewish identity formation took place on the continent.

54 See also Olender 1992. This differs from contemporary racializations of religion in which many Jews are racialized as white and their primary racial others are Muslims, racialized as Arabs. For more on Jews and whiteness, see Azoulay 2003; Brodkin 2002; E. Goldstein 2006. For Jews as a racialized Other, see Gilman 1991. For more on the convergence of religion and race in relation to Islam, see, for example Khan 2004; Özyürek 2015; Rana 2011.

55 For more on the history of nineteenth-century race categories, see Marks 2002; for more on this in relation to South Africa, see Dubow 1995; Erasmus 2017.

56 Eric Worby (1994) calls attention to both the power and the limitations of colonial projects of ethnicity through what he refers to as "ethnocartography," the practice of producing colonial maps that marked off regions according to ethnic group. He demonstrates the subversion of these forms of knowledge production by subjects who consistently failed to identify with the ethnic name that corresponded to their place on the map. His work is particularly relevant for understanding the politics of Lemba ethnicity, although in their case it was their lack of being named on maps that they have continually contested.

57 For the role of physical anthropology in South Africa in consolidating black African racialization as primitive and representative of humanity's evolutionary past, see Dubow 1995; Kuljian 2016.

58 Most work on racialization examines either state racialization through laws that produce and govern racial categories—see, for example, Bowker and Star 1999; Goldberg 2002; HoSang, LaBennett, and Pulido 2012; Omi and Winant 1986—or racial formation through national and transnational cultural politics. For the latter, see Amrute 2016; K. Clarke and Thomas 2006; Gilroy 1991; Goldberg 2015; Hage 2000; Hartigan 1999; Pierre 2013; Schramm 2014, 2015; D. A. Thomas 2004. Lemba people have had to navigate all of these aspects of racialization.

59 Marla Brettschneider (2015) shows how these exclusions are reproduced and reinforced by scholarship on the Lemba and other black Jews that positions them as racially Other and religiously "emerging" or "Judaizing" rather than already Jewish and able to shape definitions of Jewishness based on their own histories and experiences. She is critiquing work such as Bruder's (2008) and Parfitt's (2013).

60 A key assumption underlying these question is that Jews, since they have long been a paradigmatic case of a diasporic people (Cohen [1997] 2008), are by definition not indigenous. But as Alcalay (1993) has demonstrated, such an understanding obscures the long Levantine history of Arab Jews, mistakenly asserting that Arab and Jew are mutually exclusive. So, too, with Africans and Jews.

61 For resonant approaches to political subjectivity, see Schramm, Krause, and Valley 2018.

62 For a similar point emphasizing commercial genetic ancestry testing, see Nash 2015.

63 Here I am inspired by anthropological and science studies literatures that challenge the boundaries of scientific expertise. See, for example, Dumit 2004; Martin 1994; Rapp 1999; Star and Griesemer 1989.

64 The scientific objects that are crystallized through these processes should be understood as material-semiotic (Haraway 1997). What this means here is that DNA comes to be a thing in the world as it is made meaningful, and it becomes scientifically meaningful only through becoming socially and culturally meaningful. This reading of material-semiotic draws on M'Charek (2013).

65 See also Strathern 1991.

66 This approach is inspired by Mbembe (2001), especially his theorization of emerging time and time of entanglement (14–18).

67 John Jackson's *Thin Description* (2013) resonates with Fassin's use of afterlives, though Jackson emphasizes that circulations and commentary on ethnography are real-time

phenomena such that we need to change the way we understand the temporality of ethnographic research and conceive of its authorship. The concept of afterlives is an increasingly productive analytic across a number of contexts. Ramah McKay (2012, 2018), for example, uses afterlives to emphasize how memory (and what she calls "the nostalgic humanitarian lexicon") can be critically productive. Asli Zengin (2019) and Ruha Benjamin (2018) each draw on the idea of afterlives to consider the politics of kinship and care in death for marginalized people. Yusoff (2019) talks about "the afterlives of geology" to foreground links between extractive economies, colonialism, and slavery in discussions about the Anthropocene. Afterlife in the singular has been similarly generative. For example, David Theo Goldberg (2009) writes about the afterlife of apartheid, and Daromir Rudnyckyj (2010) considers afterlife in the context of development.

68 For efforts to think through the ethical possibilities of postcolonial genetic research, see R. Benjamin 2016; Foster 2016; and South African San Institute 2017. South African geneticists have been especially proactive in thinking through these questions: see de Vries and Pepper 2012; Hardy et al. 2008; Ramsay et al. 2014; Slabbert and Pepper 2010; Soodyall 2003. For more on research ethics, genetic ancestry, and race, especially in relation to participatory research design, see Reardon 2006, 2012.

69 This resonates with how Zhan (2009) theorizes the mapping of traditional Chinese medicine and modern science.

70 For more on STS approaches to data, see Biruk 2018 and Gitelman 2013.

Chapter I. Producing Lemba Archives, Becoming Genetic Jews

1 A 1994 list of Lemba Cultural Association pioneers, written by Professor M. E. R. Mathivha, lists M. M. Motenda's full name as Maemu Mutenda Mbelengwa Hadzi. His tombstone at Sweetwaters, once his home and still the site of the annual LCA conference, lists his name as Morris Mbelengwa Motenda. Hadzi, or Hadji, is the name of his clan; likewise William Masala's clan name is Mhani. Clan names are sometimes incorporated by people as part of their names, as in William Masala Mhani or M. M. Mutenda Hadzi.

2 Sinthumule is near the town of Louis Trichardt, which was renamed Makhado in 2003. This was one of many place name changes that swept the country beginning in the mid-1990s as a way to symbolically mark the transition to majority rule. In many cases, colonial and especially Voortrekker names were replaced by the names of leaders of the anticolonial and anti-apartheid struggle. Here, the Voortrekker Louis Tregardt—who arrived in the area in the 1830s and died before the town bearing his name was founded in 1899—was overwritten by his contemporary, the Venda chief Makhado wa Ramavhoya (born in the 1840s, ruled from the 1860s until his death in 1895). This particular name change was controversial, and in 2013 it was changed back to Louis Trichardt.

3 For more on the epistemic authority of genetic facts, see especially Abu El-Haj 2012; Erasmus 2017; Nelson 2016.

4 For more on archival absences, see Burton 2005; A. Gordon [1997] 2008; C. Hamilton et al. 2002; Nuttall and Coetzee 1998; Trouillot 1995.

5 For further illustrations of this point in relation to the politics of national archives, see especially Burton 2005; C. Hamilton et al. 2002; Mangcu 2011.

6 For debates about whether Van Warmelo should be seen as an academic with a government post or as an instrument of apartheid, see Hammond-Tooke 1995; Lekgoathi 2009; Pugach 2004; Wright 2016.

7 See, for example, Schapera 1929; for more on this history, see Wright 2016.

8 Adams College was by then established not only as an incubator for political mobilization by black intellectuals and in particular African National Congress leaders, such as the organization's first president Reverend John Dube, but also as a site of segregationist and antisegregationist political theorizing (see Masilela 2011; Rich 1993).

9 This was nearly a direct quote from Jaques, who writes, "It is true that many Lemba have straight noses, rather fine features and an intelligent expression which distinguishes them from the ordinary run of natives, but on the other hand, very many of them are just like the other Bantu of this country, from among whom it would be difficult to pick them out. . . . One of my informants, old Mosheh, even had what might be termed a typical Jewish nose, a rare occurrence among real Bantu" (Jaques 1931, 245). For more on Jewish noses as an anti-Semitic trope, see Gilman 1991. Mphelo's excision of his grandfather's Christian name is an important distinction between the two versions.

10 Van Warmelo's most prolific Lemba collaborator was Wilfred Phophi; they are listed as coauthors of *Venda Law* (Van Warmelo and Phophi 1967).

11 This was a story about Shimbani, the Lemba chief who succeeded Ngwedzi, who in turn had succeeded Nkalahonye, who as the founder of the Lemba chieftaincy at Mbelengwa was also known as Mulemba. Motenda explains that all of the local chiefs used to take their wives from Lemba women, and Shimbani's eldest daughter was married to the chief of the Vhalozwi. But Shambani's daughter, fearing for her life if she refused to help her husband, decided to steal Shambani's protective medicine. The Vhalozwi then invaded, and with the protective medicine gone, Shambani was defeated. He writes, "In consequence of this they laid down the law that the daughter of a Mulemba must never again be married by a foreigner who eats carrion" (Motenda 1940, 65).

12 For more on the aesthetics of colonial racialization, see Nuttall 2005.

13 I have used Van Warmelo's spelling. The name, like the city that now bears it, is usually spelled without breaks as "Thohoyandou."

14 Van Warmelo's *Language Map of South Africa* (1952) solidified a shift from ethnological classifications based on multiple factors including history to apartheid tribal definitions based explicitly on language. This was possible because of a 1946 Native Affairs Department census that recorded peoples' language spoken. No Lemba language was reported.

15 He goes on, in a section titled "True Meaning of Zimbabwe," to assert that he is "today giving the solution to the whole scientific world" (Motenda 1958, 62). He writes, "All the intelligentsia, the scientists and the experts of the whole world have come to Zimbabwe to find out who of the ancient peoples built Zimbabwe, and have entirely failed. . . . Zimbabwe was built by skillful cunning Lemba people, as I have already pointed out to Dr. A. C. Hoffman, Director of the National Museum at Bloemfontein" (62).

16 Although pass laws and pass books had existed before in South Africa, early 1950s apartheid laws tightened restrictions and expanded control of black South Africans' movement in urban areas in particular. These laws sparked the August 9, 1956, Women's March on the Union Buildings, now commemorated as National Women's Day in postapartheid South Africa.

17 Later on in the essay, Motenda indicates that the LCA has started to try to count Lemba people, including by traveling between 1951 and 1956 to Rhodesia "hunting for our Lemba people" there (Motenda 1958, 63–64).

18 Lucas Thobakgale, another lifelong LCA leader who became a central interlocutor for this project, explained to me that in the 1970s and 1980s, informers would frequently show up at LCA meetings to see if they were politically organizing in secret. However, since LCA meetings were exclusively devoted to talking about and promoting Lemba culture, these informers always came up empty-handed. See also Buijs (1998, 677–678), who explains that the Venda "homeland" was especially repressive; political opposition was sometimes met with arrest, torture, and death, and since life in this Bantustan context was thoroughly ethnicized, Lemba people already faced job discrimination, even in the absence of any particular political agenda.

19 See James 1990; Lekgoathi 2003.

20 Technically, black South Africans were at that time cast out of the state—being assigned to a homeland meant not having South African citizenship—and so did not in a legal sense "belong" in South Africa at all (West 1988).

21 She later completed a doctoral dissertation on Marrano music (Nabarro 1974).

22 In an essay that reads the twentieth-century history of Lemba ethnic identity through the lens of Benedict Anderson's *Imagined Communities* ([1983] 1991) and Leroy Vail's *The Creation of Tribalism in Southern Africa* (1989), South African anthropologist Gina Buijs sees the founding of the LCA and its subsequent race politics as an appeal "to a distant non-African past which could be associated with a particularly successful white community in South Africa, and one which was clearly allied with resistance to apartheid" (Buijs 1998, 679). Buijs is suggesting that identifying themselves as Jews allowed them to align with whiteness in a way that was also aligned with anti-apartheid sentiment. I am not convinced that the LCA emphasis on Lemba Jewish ancestry and history was this instrumentalist, or that among Lemba people who identified in the 1940s–1980s with a Jewish past there was a sense that white South African Jews were more aligned with anti-apartheid sentiment than other white South Africans.

23 Born in Scotland, Nabarro then spent much of her life in England. She moved to South Africa with her husband when he was offered a job at the University of the Witwatersrand.

24 For more on Trefor Jenkins's role in holding the doctors to account for Biko's death, see McLean and Jenkins 2003. For more on Biko, his writings, and his legacy, see Biko and Ndebele [1978] 2017.

25 Jones 1997; Parfitt, Hale, and Espar 2000. Tudor Parfitt, who had researched Lemba origins beginning in 1987, was credited as a coauthor on the genetic study and as a coproducer of the NOVA special, in which he also starred.

26 M. J. Mungulwa saved those articles and showed them to me in November 2006.

27 These articles were also part of M. J. Mungulwa's collection. The author of the *Drum* (1986) article attributes the idea that the Lemba are a lost tribe of Israel to them. If that is correct, it may have emerged as a way to demonstrate commonality with Ethiopian Jews in a moment when the latter were internationally newsworthy.

Chapter 2. Genetic Diaspora

1 The reasons for this shift are threefold. First, screening programs for Tay-Sachs disease and for BRCA (a genetic mutation associated with increased risk for breast cancer) popularized among Ashkenazi Jews the idea that the possible prevention and early detection of disease was more important than the danger of a creeping biological essentialism (Abu El-Haj 2012; Angrist 2010; Carmeli 2004; Davis et al. 2010; Markel 1997; Mozersky 2012; Tenenbaum and Davidman 2007; Wailoo and Pemberton 2006). Second, the popularity in the United States of direct-to-consumer genetic ancestry testing has also shifted the terrain such that many people, Jews included, now embrace the industry's narrative of genetic ancestry as a harmless pastime of exploring ancestral and familial connections; this narrative necessarily downplays the dangers of biological understandings of race and ethnicity. Finally, links between biological definitions of peoplehood and Zionist politics have long histories that predate World War II, and not all Jewish scientists, particularly in the new state of Israel, were deterred by the uses to which these ideas were put in Nazi Germany (Abu El-Haj 2012; Efron 1994; Endelman 2004; Kirsh 2003; Lipphardt 2008). Articulations between DNA and Jewishness, however, have not been without controversy. While some uncritically endorse the biological definitions of peoplehood that emerge from medical and population genetics studies (Entine 2007; Ostrer 2012), others express deep discomfort with how genetic research has been designed by and for and received by Ashkenazi Jews in particular and Jews more broadly (Azoulay 2003; Falk 2010; Gilman 2006; S. Kahn 2010; Lipphardt 2012).

2 Deleuze and Guattari [1987] 2009; Ong and Collier 2005; Stewart 2012.

3 On the production of genetic diversity, see especially Fullwiley 2008; M'Charek 2005a Reardon 2005; on the epistemologies of genetic history, see Abu El-Haj 2012; on the politics of selling personal genomic ancestry, see especially Nelson 2008a; Pálsson 2012; Marks 2001; TallBear 2013; on the subjectivities of American seekers of such information see especially S. Kahn 2013; Nelson 2016; Palmié 2007; TallBear 2013.

4 I invoke "the Lemba" here because it was a general, undifferentiated "Lemba community," represented in documentaries as "the Lemba" or "the Lemba people," that most visitors sought out.

5 See also biological citizenship (Petryna 2002).

6 This approach is inspired by Michael Montoya's work on bioethnic conscription (2007, 2011). See also Nelson 2008b.

7 In addition to Fullwiley 2008 and Montoya 2007, 2011, I am especially building on Abu El-Haj 2012 and Nelson 2016.

8   There are echoes here of Ferguson 1999 and Piot 2010.

9   My phrasing "the ground of Jewish identity" is in reference to Daniel Boyarin and Jonathan Boyarin's 1993 essay "Diaspora: Generation and the Ground of Jewish Identity." It is important to note, though, that they do not see "genealogical" and "genetic" as coterminous. While genetic Jewishness, which they do not explicitly write about, implies a discernible biological link among Jews, the genealogical Jewishness that they discuss refers to being the children of Abraham, which occurs upon conversion (705). As I discuss elsewhere in this chapter, Boyarin and Boyarin are writing against a racially exclusionary Zionism that favors a territorial/autochthonous claim to peoplehood over a genealogical/diasporic claim. They note that while "the biblical story is not one of autochthony but one of always already coming from somewhere else," the Zionist narrative instead embraces autochthony, and in so doing "repress[es] memories of coming from somewhere else" (715–716). For them, "the lesson of Diaspora" is "that peoples and lands are not naturally and organically connected" (723).

10 Most transgender women have a Y chromosome, and women with intersex conditions may also have a Y chromosome.

11 Indeed, there is no definitive genetic marker that can indicate Jewishness or any other ethnically, racially, religiously, or nationally defined group, not least because all genetic markers are identified based on population frequencies, meaning that even for the most successfully predictive hypothetical marker that could exist, many individuals who view themselves and are viewed as part of the population under study would not possess the marker in question.

12 For distinctions between rabbinic and Toraitic Judaism and the importance of the latter for African Jews, see Brettschneider 2015, 30, 106.

13 LCA executive meeting minutes, August 5, 2005, F. C. Raulinga personal archives.

14 In this way, my work and hers differed from that of Parfitt and South African biblical studies scholar Magdel le Roux, whose research comparing Lemba religious and ritual practices with those of ancient Israelites aimed to explore whether the Lemba might be a lost tribe of Israel (le Roux 2003). Although Brettschneider is also Jewish and draws on ethnographic fieldwork and other interpersonal research and experience, her work does not lend itself to being read in this way because she frames it as political theory about power relations, and specifically a call to shift approaches to the study of Jews in Africa and how Jews are counted in the world, rather than as an ethnographically informed empirical study of particular groups of African Jews (Brettschneider 2015, 14–15).

15 For example, in recent years anti-Zionist Jews have compiled a Passover Haggadah that challenges the Jewish exceptionalism underpinning the holiday (International Jewish Anti-Zionist Network 2014).

16 I attended two Kulanu events in 2013, one in New York City and one in Bethesda, Maryland, that featured a young Zimbabwean Lemba man telling gathered Jews about his experience of Lemba culture and Lemba Jewishness and about his own recent formal conversion to Judaism.

17 A yarmulke is a head covering, and a tallis is a shawl wrapped around one's shoulders. Tefillin are small black boxes containing written prayers that are fixed to one's body with leather straps.

18 I draw here from Tsing 2005, specifically how different actors can come together through and for a social movement that is both the same and very different in terms of motivations and desired outcomes.

19 For more on difference in diasporic identity formation, see, for example, Edwards 2003; Jackson 2005; S. Hall 1991; S. Hall and Schwarz 2017.

20 Much of the African diaspora literature emphasizes this. See especially M. Anderson 2009; J. Brown 2005; Edwards 2003; Gilroy 1993; Patterson and Kelley 2000; D. A. Thomas 2009.

21 See, for example, the literature on African American efforts to connect with Africans as long-lost kin (Ebron 2002; Hartman 2002); this is also evident in Nelson's work, especially 2008b.

22 Jean Comaroff and Comaroff 2012; Cooper 2005; Fabian 1983; Ferguson 2006; Mbembe 2001; Piot 1999.

Chapter 3. Postapartheid Citizenship and the Limits of Genetic Evidence

1 At the time, seven rand were equal to one U.S. dollar.

2 The organizing principle of most early postapartheid legislation and policy was to address the injustices and oppressions carried out under white colonial and apartheid rule. For more on the politics of postapartheid justice, see James 2007; McEwan 2003; Oomen 2005; Ramphele 2008; Robins 2005; Shepherd and Robins 2008.

3 See especially John Comaroff and Comaroff 2018; James 2007; Mamdani 1996; Manson 2013; Oomen 2005; Tamarkin 2011; J. Williams 2010.

4 According to their own applications to the same commissions, their roots were Swazi, not Ndebele; regardless, most referred to themselves as ethnically Pedi. Alternate spellings of "Maesela" include "Maisela" and "Mayisela."

5 For more on the dynamics of postapartheid citizenship, see especially Jean Comaroff and Comaroff 2003.

6 Kgoshi means "chief," and the suffix kgadi denotes femaleness; hence kgoshikgadi is the title for a female chief.

7 This was further complicated because their two-sided dispute, defined through ethnic difference, was in effect a four-sided dispute defined through political, genealogical, and gendered contestations. Kgoshi Mpaketsane's elderly mother and a small group of other family members felt that he had taken on that role prematurely after his father's death. She sought to rule in his place as regent but had only minimal support because she had initially supported her son's installation as kgoshi. More contentious was that a number of Maesela people supported not Kgoshikgadi Maesela, who had taken over the Maesela chieftaincy when her husband died in 1995, but her nephew; they saw their support as restoring leadership to the lineage that should have had it if not for apartheid politics, which had years earlier favored Kgoshikgadi Maesela's late husband.

8 The other precolonial outcome of conflict was one group's subordination to another such that the subordinate group maintained access to land but owed various forms of tribute and allegiance to a dominant group.

9 The 1933 deed of transfer that Kgoshi Mpaketsane included in his land claim application notes that it was initially registered as Crown Grant no. 440/1896. The land was granted to Gerhardus Jozua Van Niekerk on April 19, 1896. Within the locations, land and chieftaincy were definitively linked, and chiefly authority depended on the recognition of the native commissioner, which in turn was dependent on compliance with Department of Native Affairs directives (Delius 1996).

10 Native Land Act 27 of 1913. Solomon Plaatje's 1916 critique of this law was especially influential; see Crais and McClendon 2014 for the relevant selection from Plaatje's 1916 text. Plaatje was the first general secretary of the African National Congress. The act initially granted only 7 percent of South Africa's land to natives, and this was later increased to 13 percent. The Native Land Act also prohibited natives from living on farms that fell within white areas unless they could prove they were employed there. This entrenched a tenant-farmer system. See Van Onselen 1996 for a detailed account of life as a tenant farmer. Walker (2014) further explores the historiography and ongoing legacies of the Native Land Act; see especially Beinart and Delius 2014.

11 My information comes from the Ralushai Commission report (1998, 317–320); interviews and informal conversations with Kgoshi Mpaketsane in 2004, 2005, and 2006; and an interview with the head of the commission, Professor N. V. Ralushai, that I conducted on July 31, 2006.

12 Thohoyandou is about 275 kilometers north of India village. Under apartheid it was the capital of the Venda Bantustan, which was declared independent in 1979 and dissolved in 1994.

13 The Land Claims Commission was established by the national Restitution of Land Rights Act 22 of 1994.

14 He wrote, "All fertile ploughing fields are close to us and they are ours. . . . Maesela's chief's ploughing field is allocated by our grandfathers before. Even their royal kraal (Moshate) is situated in our field where we have allocated them on their arrival here as a sign of welcome. Their place of initiation school (Seroto) is situated in the Mpaketsane's ploughing field which we have allocated them before. Original name of Indië is Mohlotlwane which is named by us." Quoted from Kgoshi Mpaketsane's Land Claims Commission application form, submitted December 29, 1996.

15 He is referring to Kgoshikgadi Maesela here in spite of the male pronoun that would indicate otherwise. Male and female English pronouns were frequently used interchangeably, particularly among those whose formal education had largely been conducted in Afrikaans.

16 Kgoshi Mpaketsane's Land Claims Commission application form, submitted December 29, 1996.

17 As evidenced in Kgoshi Mpaketsane's land claim narrative, the right to land in postapartheid South Africa was increasingly also based on the ability to convincingly demonstrate first arrival and ethnic difference. See Geschiere 2009 for a comparative analysis of first arrival as autochthony in the context of political exclusion in African and European contexts.

18 Kgoshi Mpaketsane's Land Claims Commission supplementary evidence, submitted December 29, 1996.

19 Kgoshi Mpaketsane's Land Claims Commission supplementary evidence, submitted December 29, 1996.

20 See Vincent 2008. The province was still called the Northern Transvaal at the time; I refer to it here as Limpopo for clarity.

21 At the time, Sekhukhune was enmeshed in his own struggle for state legitimacy: his status was challenged by his half-brother, Rhyne Thulare Sekhukhune III, who had been designated heir at birth but who had abdicated (temporarily, according to his supporters) in 1970 when his father died so that he could continue to attend university; the status of the entire lineage was also challenged by the Mampuru lineage, whose ancestor would have been the Pedi king in the nineteenth century had Sekhukhune I not successfully defeated him. Eventually, Rhyne Thulare Sekhukhune emerged as the recognized kgoshikgolo (King Sekhukhune III), although he died before the final decision was reached by the Nhlapo Commission in 2010. His son, Victor Thulare, is the current kgoshikgolo (King Thulare III). The Mampuru lineage claim was denied first by the Nhlapo Commission and then by the constitutional court, which ruled in favor of the commission and against the descendants of Mampuru, then again by the constitutional court, which upheld their decision on appeal on December 15, 2014.

22 Garman 2001; see also Barnard 2006; John Comaroff and Comaroff 2009; Coombes 2003; Erasmus 2017; Hodgson 2002; Robins 2001; Schramm 2016; Sylvain 2005. These are contentious politics. Erasmus (2017), for example, critiques the rise of indigeneity in South Africa, especially in relation to Khoi-San peoples. She writes that "Khoi-San is used to distinguish between Coloureds who can claim First Nation status and those who cannot" (113). She opposes the use of First Nations because of its implied hierarchies, and she likewise opposes the use of indigeneity because it "erases the ways in which the colonial category of 'the indigenous' was used to divide and rule local inhabitants" (114).

23 See, for example, Ramsay and Jenkins 1988. This was a long-standing area of inquiry for Jenkins and his colleagues that predated the genetic technologies utilized in the 1980s Lemba study. See, for example, Jenkins et al. 1975; Jenkins, Lehmann, and Nurse 1974; Nurse, Botha, and Jenkins 1977.

24 For more on the ≠khomani San land claim, see also Ellis 2010; Robins 2001.

25 In this case, the Office of the Minister for Provincial and Local Government was ordered to pay all legal fees, a decision that no doubt factored into the willingness of Kgoshi Mpaketsane's local supporters to contribute to legal costs in relation to other pending and new cases.

26 From Kgoshi Mpaketsane's submission to the Nhlapo Commission, April 4, 2005.

27 The heading says that Mpaketsane gave the presentation, but this appears to be pasted over the name of a Lemba Cultural Association representative who actually authored the document.

28 Nhlapo, personal communication, November 15, 2014.

29 For a discussion of these and related constitutional tensions, see Jean Comaroff and Comaroff 2005.

30 Thornberry (2011, 2019) notes a similar flexibility in the historical adjudication of sexual violence in the Eastern Cape. Hylton White (2015) convincingly argues that traditional and municipal authorities are not the only realms of legal practice and dispute resolution operative in contemporary rural South Africa. I highlight them here because of the relevance of municipal/state authority and the authority of traditional leaders as specific alternatives to one another when one of these two realms was invoked but other outcomes were desired.

31 A tar road was finally built in its place sometime between 2007 and 2010.

32 Balepa Traditional Authority meeting minutes, December 31, 2000, from Kgoshi Mpaketsane's personal archive. This particular action was challenged in court, and several years later, Kgoshi Mpaketsane was forced by court order to leave the cemetery unlocked so anyone could access it.

Chapter 4. Ancestry, Ancestors, and Contested Kinship after DNA

1 Details about Ratsoma are from the unveiling ceremony and subsequent interviews with the master of ceremonies, Oriah Thobakgale, and with Ratsoma's widow, Jane Ratsoma. For a history of twentieth-century ANC activity in Sekhukhuneland and the origins and affiliations of *Fetakgomo*, see Delius 1996.

2 See Hylton White 2010 for an account of some of the tensions and ambivalences around ethnoculture and ancestors that inhere in this idea of "home" for many similarly positioned South Africans.

3 Some of the most influential 1970s work sparking this rethinking of the field includes Esther Newton's *Mother Camp* (1972); Michelle Rosaldo and Louise Lamphere's edited book *Women, Culture, and Society* (1974); Gayle Rubin's essay "The Traffic in Women: Notes on the 'Political Economy' of Sex" (1975); and the volume in which Rubin's essay appeared, Rayna R. Reiter's *Toward an Anthropology of Women* (1975). This shift in anthropological approaches to kinship was solidified in the 1980s by Schneider 1984; Strathern 1988; Yanagisako and Collier 1987. Kath Weston (1991) also laid important groundwork for understanding kinship as a contingent achievement and site of struggle. For a further shift to what has been termed "the new kinship studies" (Franklin 2019), see also Carsten 2000, 2004; Franklin and McKinnon 2001; S. Kahn 2000; Rapp 1999; Strathern 1992a, b. This body of work built on and contributed to feminist and queer critiques and paid particular attention to new reproductive technologies and genetics. There is now a vast and ever-growing literature on these and related topics; see, for example, Deomampo 2016; Franklin 2013; Paxson 2004; Thompson 2005; Vora 2015. Work on queer families (Lewin 1993, 2009; Weston 1991) and adoption (Leinaweaver 2008, 2013) has been especially important toward unsettling ideas of biology and nature vis-à-vis anthropological kinship studies. Recent work by Donna Haraway (2016), which calls for a rethinking of and investment in kinship as an active practice of fostering relations with one another, rather than as an effect or reason for reproduction, underscores the political urgency of these issues. On this latter point, see R. Benjamin 2018; Clarke and Haraway 2018; Huang and Wu 2018; Murphy 2018; TallBear 2018. My focus on kinning practices in this chapter makes it

possible to decenter the narrative and practice of Lemba patriarchy that underwrite Lemba genetic ancestry and related politics. For more on the importance of women's genealogical relationships, see, for example, Yanagisako 1985, 2002; Zhan 2009.

4   Some among LCA leadership felt that Ratsoma was not from the Mhani clan at all but rather from the Hadji clan. Mhani was the clan of LCA chaplain William Masala. M. J. Mungulwa, LCA president from 2007 to 2018, was from the Hadji clan, as was Pandelani Mutenda, who became president in 2019 following Mungulwa's death in 2018.

5   Her mother was Motiba (1915–1995), daughter of Solomon Lephuele Mpaketsane. Her father was Phoko Peta, namesake of his grandfather, who founded Mogabane.

6   Her elder brother William Nakedi Peta felt similarly and frequently came to India/ Ga-Maesela to visit her and to attend Kgoshi Mpaketsane's royal kraal meetings.

7   I have returned many times since then, but this was the end of my Fulbright-funded year of dissertation field research, and at the time I had no immediate plans to return: both of us assumed that this was the end of my field research.

8   In the event that a future commission seeks to use this book in such a way, my research indicates the following: Kgoshi Mpaketsane has clearly been a de facto traditional leader since 1989, as was his father before him. Therefore, as long as traditional leadership remains something that the state categorically recognizes, it would be more justifiable to recognize Kgoshi Mpaketsane as a traditional leader than not to.

9   Kgoshi Mpaketsane initially did not emphasize the Lobedu connection, but he did indicate that Kgoshi Mothakge (1) and Mohumagadi Modjadji were the first in his lineage to move from Zimbabwe into South Africa; he thought they might be buried near Musina, by the Zimbabwe border. When I asked him explicitly about the name Modjadji and if she was related to Queen Modjadji, he explained, "It is because the Mpaketsane, they marry the wife at Modjadji Royal Kraal a long time ago. That is why the name Modjadji came in our Mpaketsane people, because this is the wife from Kgoshi Modjadji." He further explained that like the Lemba people, the Modjadji people migrated into South Africa a long time ago: "The Mpaketsane people and the Lovedu people and the Venda, the history is like a similar but it is not so much. You see? But the Lemba people, this history is unique. That is why I told you if you make a book for the history of the Lemba people you must take this genealogy."

10 *Bashavi* (traders) is another word that Lemba people use to refer to themselves. Lemba men will often greet one another with the singular *Mushavi*.

11 "Sekhukhuneland" was a colonial naming convention, and in postapartheid South Africa, this area was part of Sekhukhune District, one of the Limpopo Province's five districts.

12 This newest Senyathela did appear on Kgoshi Mpaketsane's genealogy chart along with his siblings.

13 Indigenous and American Indian Studies scholars have produced important work theorizing blood politics, sometimes in relation to the politics of genetics, but also as itself a technology of sovereignty. See especially TallBear 2013; Kauanui 2008; Sturm 2002.

14 Kgoshi Mpaketsane's persistence echoes how Hirokazu Miyazaki (2004) theorizes hope, recognition, and knowledge.

15 Among Lemba people who speak Venda, this is spelled "Bashavhi," but here I am following local spelling, which is influenced by Sepedi pronunciations.

Chapter 5. Locating Lemba Heritage, Imagining Indigenous Futures

1 "Ishe" is a term of respect used to address elder Lemba men.

2 The literature on cultural heritage in southern Africa emphasizes three things: the use of the idea of heritage toward the rhetoric of postcolonial nationalism, the convergence of the idea of culture with neoliberal capitalism, and the role of archaeology and national and international designations of sites' significance as a mechanism of "freezing" these sites in the past, limiting access through the imposition of fences and admission fees, and further alienating sacred sites from living local descendants (John Comaroff and Comaroff 2009; Fontein 2006; Meskell 2012; D. Peterson, Gavua, and Rassool 2015; Pikirayi 2011; Turner 2016; Witz, Minkley, and Rassool 2017). Each of the issues raised in the cultural heritage literature remains relevant in ongoing negotiations about Mapungubwe's management, particularly in relation to a controversial coal mine nearby (Meskell 2012; Turner 2016). Minkley, Witz, and Rassool 2017 is especially useful for thinking through the links between the "post-antiapartheid heritage complex" and indigeneity. This chapter speaks to the heritage complex that they identify but takes indigeneity rather than heritage as its problematic.

3 Mapungubwe is historically significant as Southern Africa's earliest known stratified kingdom. Rock art in the area around Mapungubwe points to occupation and use by hunter-gatherers long before the kingdom was established, and archaeological evidence suggests that by the twelfth century, royals resided at the top of Mapungubwe Hill and an estimated nine thousand others lived in villages on the ground. When researchers excavated graves on the hill and in the surrounding area, they also found gold-plated sculptures—including a now-iconic gold-plated rhinoceros that often appears in advertisements and books about Mapungubwe—and beads and pottery that linked the site to large-scale trade networks that extended to the east coast of Africa and to India and China. The Mapungubwe collection, including the human remains, was studied and stored at the University of Pretoria from the time of excavation in the 1930s until 2007, when remains from 143 individuals were finally reburied at Mapungubwe and a museum was built near Mapungubwe Hill to house many of the other materials and to welcome and orient visitors (Tiley-Nel 2011).

4 Indigeneity elsewhere is likewise not necessarily self-evident: it is a category that is at once juridical, political, and based on identity (Cattelino 2008; de la Cadena and Starn 2007; TallBear 2013). Because indigeneity as a concept is at once transnational and deeply rooted within local colonial and postcolonial histories, efforts to apply it across regions are often fraught (Hodgson 2009; Idrus 2010; Li 2000; Parreñas forthcoming; Tamarkin and Giraudo 2014). Questions about who can claim it, who wants to claim it, and whom it claims are shifting and more contentious for

some than for others, particularly where multiple forms of racialization coexist (M. Anderson 2009; de la Cadena 2000). Furthermore, accessing indigenous rights often requires a particular performance of indigenous identity that both demonstrates others' notions of authenticity and responds to prevailing national identity politics and situated histories; this can be especially pronounced in settler-colonial contexts where indigenous erasure and appropriation converge (Barker 2011; Klopotek 2011; Morgensen 2011; Povinelli 2002; Sturm 2011).

5   The quotation comes from my own audio recording. LCA general secretary F. C. Raulinga recorded Wade's statement slightly differently for the official minutes that were to become part of the LCA archive: "Mr Richard Wade said 'it is an honor to stand here. The Lembas are special people. You are Israelites who came from Egyptians. You are people who followed the star. You are traders. Your first city was Mapungubwe.'" I see this as Raulinga's corrective edit designed to extract the informative substance from Wade's speech while omitting his perhaps idiosyncratic interpretations. It is another example of how Lemba people have used archives—here LCA archives intended for internal use—to speak back to and correct others' research agendas (see chapter 1).

6   See especially Barnard 2006; Kuper 2003; Ives 2017.

7   See Tamarkin and Giraudo 2014. Some scholars reject indigeneity for its resonance with discourses of primitivity that characterized colonial designations of Africans as "natives" (Erasmus 2017; Kuper 2003; Nyamnjoh 2007). Erasmus additionally objects to indigeneity's legacy as a colonial divide-and-rule tactic (113–114; see also Witz, Minkley, and Rassool 2017). Others, though, have embraced its postcolonial possibilities (Barnard 2006; Hodgson 2011; Ndahinda 2011; Pelican 2009).

8   Rachel Giraudo and I elaborate this distinction, emphasizing how marginalized groups throughout the continent have found indigenous rights to be a productive framework through which to mitigate their disenfranchisement within postcolonial states (Tamarkin and Giraudo 2014). For an emphasis on the significance of UN indigenous rights networks to these dynamics, see also Hodgson 2011.

9   For an account of the colonial genocide of Cape San Peoples, see Adhikari 2011.

10 For more on indigenous knowledge, intellectual property, and pharmaceuticals in South Africa, see Pollock 2014, 2019. For nuanced work exploring the ambivalences of indigeneity, traditional knowledge, race, and culture in South Africa, see Ives 2014, 2017.

11 See also Minkley, Witz, and Rassool 2017. Drawing on Yusoff's (2013) work on what she calls "geologic life," to elaborate how the early twentieth-century heritage state reverberates in postapartheid state uses of indigeneity, they write, "The heritage state applied and arranged the living fossil to mark out the land as empty, located indigeneity in the prehuman without any claims to inheritance, transferred responsibility of protection to itself, and possessed territory on the land that was situated in the earth. The shift to the postapartheid state relies upon the same structures and dispositions of heritage formation but situates indigeneity as an inclusive inheritance in the earth as the genesis of human origins" (224).

12 Khoisan people, for example, have faced substantial opposition to their efforts to have their particular indigeneity recognized. In December 2017, Khoisan activists

walked from Port Elizabeth to Pretoria and undertook a hunger strike to call attention to their demands to be recognized as South Africa's "First Nation" and to have their languages elevated to national language status along with English, Afrikaans, Xhosa, Zulu, Sotho, Tswana, Northern Sotho, Venda, Tsonga, Swazi, and Ndebele. See, for example, the December 4, 2017, *Pretoria News* article "Khoisan Trio Wait for President on Lawns of Union Buildings" by Goitsemang Thlabye.

13 From the early days of postapartheid rule, academics, activists, and government officials debated and at times advanced projects that aimed to reckon with the corporeal violence of colonial and apartheid histories. This included human remains that were exploited in the name both of research, as with bones stored at universities, and of the edification and amusement of a white population, as in displays of human casts posed in naturalist dioramas at museums (Coombes 2003; Legassick and Rassool 2015; Rassool 2015; Schramm 2016). The repatriation of Sara Baartman's remains was the best known but certainly not the only example. For more on the significance of Baartman, see Crais and Scully 2009; Magubane 2003; Rassool 2015. While much of this literature focuses on archaeological and museum contexts, Rassool argues that the identification and reburial of people killed in the struggle against apartheid was also a project of indigenizing the postapartheid nation. The struggles over Native American remains provide an important comparative case, particularly in understanding the stakes of indigeneity and decolonization at work in both contexts. For a discussion of American anthropology in relation to these issues, see Starn 2004. Relatedly, see debates about Kennewick Man (D. H. Thomas 2000; J. Hamilton 2009). These debates in particular illuminate how genetic science intersects with legal frameworks and indigeneity. See also TallBear 2013.

14 Mapungubwe took on new kinds of national significance in its postapartheid protection and promotion, but it was not the first time the site was nationally designated. In its first and short-lived national iteration, it was part of the Dongola Wild Life Sanctuary that was created in 1947 to preserve the area's natural environment and then abolished as soon as the National Party came into power in 1948 (Carruthers 2006, 10). Unlike early twentieth-century South African legislation that might have protected the site because of the rock art and the shift in the 1940s to an emphasis on the area's natural rather than cultural or historical significance, it was the stratified kingdom and the artifacts found in royal graves that enabled Mapungubwe to become a national postapartheid priority under the National Heritage Resources Act, 25 of 1999).

15 Constitution of the Republic of South Africa Chapter 14, Schedule 4: Functional Areas of Concurrent National and Provincial Legislative Competence, Part A and Schedule 6: Transitional Arrangements, 26 (Local Government) 1(b). Schedule 4 establishes a framework for concurrent national and provincial legislation and Schedule 6 delineated arrangements for the transitional period after the end of apartheid. In both instances, "indigenous law" is explicitly linked to traditional leadership, though it is also subject to the rest of the constitution. For an ethnographic analysis of how this legal pluralism was enacted and contested in the decade following the end of apartheid, see Oomen 2005.

16 These references remain controversial: the one concerning indigenous languages because South Africa's list of eleven official languages excludes Khoisan ones, and those dealing with law because they are linked to concepts of traditional and rural authority, which critics feel extend colonial and apartheid indirect rule and entrench differential citizenship for urban and rural black South Africans (Mamdani 1996; Ntsebeza 2005; see also chapter 3). Here the term "indigenous" straddles a line between on the one hand protecting and fostering primarily black South African cultural practices and on the other hand subjecting a portion of that population to undemocratic rule. But neither reference delineates who is or is not indigenous or how that might be determined.

17 For a discussion of this legislation in relation to governing access and procedures for archaeological research, especially in relation to human remains, see Nienaber and Steyn 2011.

18 Others have noted the difficulties that emerge in South Africa when "community" is invoked but ambiguously or multiply defined. See especially Turner 2013.

19 The 1999 National Heritage Resources Act (NHRA) makes no mention of indigenous peoples, but indigeneity does appear twice as a concept in relation to indigenous knowledge: it is explicitly part of the definition of "living heritage," which designates "intangible aspects of inherited culture" (Preamble 2: Definitions, xxi, g), and it appears as one of six imperatives for how to identify and manage heritage resources, itself the last of a list of seven general principles for heritage resources management. This imperative states: "The identification, assessment and management of the heritage resources of South Africa must take account of all relevant cultural values and indigenous knowledge systems" (Chapter 1: System for Management of National Heritage Resources, Part 1: General Principles, 5: General principles for heritage resources management, 7, a). Interestingly, the inclusion of a concept of indigeneity in the NHRA is a departure from earlier iterations of legislation designed to protect nature, culture, and history in South Africa. The 1911 Bushman Relics Act, for example, defines its subject solely as "bushman," and the 1923 Natural and Historical Monuments, Relics, and Antiques Act, while far more sweeping in its scope, clarifies that Bushmen paintings—along with waterfalls, caves, avenues of trees, old trees, and old buildings—are part of the intended definition of "monument." This early twentieth-century singling out of "bushman" cultural products as requiring national protection reflects the different ways that San peoples have been racialized vis-à-vis other Africans. There is no doubt that San peoples were historically subjugated and dispossessed by agriculturalists; however, this history has been used rhetorically to position Africans as colonists, thus minimizing the violence and oppression of European colonialism. Richard Wade's alignment of himself and the Lemba as either not African or African evokes this framing. The 1969 National Monuments Act kept the designation "Bushmen" for rock paintings that were to be protected but expanded it in two ways: in addition to rock art it included artifacts and built structures, and in addition to "Bushmen" it accounted for the markedly less specific "any other people who inhabited or visited the Republic before the settlement of the Europeans at the Cape" (National Monuments Act of 1969, Section 12, 2A).

20 The trade networks received the greatest emphasis in the World Heritage site nomination materials (Meskell 2012, 1).

21 The name "Hamisi" is one of twelve or thirteen Lemba clan names. Sometimes Lemba people are referred to by their surnames, but sometimes by their surnames followed by their clan names, and sometimes only by their clan names. So, for example, F. C. Raulinga (LCA general secretary and briefly LCA president from soon after S. E. Moeti died in 2006 until his own death in 2009) would frequently sign his name "F. C. Raulinga Hamisi," and other Lemba people frequently called him by this extended name.

22 See also Lan 1985; Obarrio 2014.

23 These donations, frequently as small as ten rand (equivalent to less than one U.S. dollar), were meticulously written down in what one might understand as a literal paying of respects, and failures to participate in this way were often understood as intentional affronts that could damage social relationships for months or years. These financial transactions took place in addition to and alongside burial societies, which form part of a complex calculus of social support and redistribution amidst widespread precarity (Makhulu 2015). See also Golomski 2018.

24 See, for example, Geschiere 2009; Golomski 2018; Klima 2002.

25 There are, no doubt, other stories of how the Mapungubwe reburial came about, but this is how LCA leaders explained it to me in 2006.

26 Rock art at Mapungubwe was associated with San people, and the locally well known but also contested history of the region noted that Vhangona people had long inhabited the area when the Singo, accompanied by Lemba people, moved south from Great Zimbabwe in the fifteenth century and conquered them. In this way, the Singo became the dominant Venda rulers and continued in this position of dominance throughout the apartheid era: they were not among the Mapungubwe reburial claimants, since their story of migration and conquest took place centuries after the site was an active kingdom.

27 This meeting was postponed, but the agenda items were addressed at subsequent meetings.

28 Prior to the joint claim, if indeed Koka initiated the claim and the LCA was brought in before others to carry out the reburial process, then these royal bones would have been assumed to be Lemba ancestors. This was surprising, because the most famous excavations from the top of Mapungubwe Hill, where gold sculptures were found alongside human remains, found the bones in a seated position, while Lemba people were known to bury people lying flat and facing north. However, despite this discrepancy and the subsequent claims of others, some Lemba people thought that it was likely that at least some of the burials on top of the hill represented their ancestors. After participating in a state-sponsored tour of Mapungubwe, along with other representatives of claimant groups, F. C. Raulinga explained to me that they saw the burial sites and were told that some on the hill had been buried seated, but others had been buried flat. It was the latter that he identified as likely Lemba burial sites.

29 See Sanders 1969.

30 This was not an unusual position: as I discuss elsewhere in this book, scholarly debates about Lemba origins hinge on the question of whether they are really Jews or really Africans, as if these are mutually exclusive positions. Parfitt's (2000) and le Roux's (2003) books elaborate the terms of these debates. See Hendrickx (1991) for an instructive overview of twentieth-century theories about Lemba origins.

31 The mining that eventually took place there was for coal, and all parties who were part of the Mapungubwe reburial were designated "stakeholders" who had to consent to the plan prior to the mine becoming operational; they continue to have an oversight role. The stakeholder role was envisioned here as custodial: no profits from the coal mine were offered to any of the designated stakeholders.

32 This is how it was explained to me by Chaplain William Masala in 2006.

33 Xenophobic violence had recently erupted in South Africa, primarily targeting African immigrants; this was the subtext of Tanya Mungulwa's commentary. The violence had prompted many reflections on the status of being South African specifically and African in general, as well as denunciations of xenophobia. See especially Hassim, Kupe, and Worby 2008.

34 One major difference between the controversy over Lemba involvement in Mapungubwe and the obstacles that the LCA faced under apartheid was that this time, the Lemba had people in power to advocate for them. This assured their continued role in the Mapungubwe reburial project despite the doubts of people like the archaeologist with whom I spoke and the objections of other claimants. Some LCA leaders saw Koka's dream and Mabudafasi's advocacy as their primary defenses against once again being undermined by others. Chaplain Masala instead saw in the Mapungubwe project proof that the threats to the Lemba that he had so vividly depicted in the 1970s and 1980s were finally vindicated in the twenty-first century.

35 Moeti delivered his address in tshiVenda. This translation is from Raulinga's conference report.

36 Kgoshi Malaga had ancestral links to Sekhukhune people for the same reasons that Kgoshi Mpaketsane did: for generations, local Lemba chiefs' wives came from the Sekhukhune royal family, thus establishing their regional legitimacy as traditional leaders (see chapter 4).

37 In Thobakgale's account of his chance meeting with the Malaga people, there is an interesting interplay between his assurance that he knows better than they do who they are and his endorsement of the value of their particularity. He tells them he knows who they really are although they do not, but that they must retain their difference, share it with other Lembas, and not succumb to expectations that they should be culturally or linguistically like Lemba people elsewhere. When Thobakgale said that the Malaga people do not belong "there" but instead belong "there," he was pointing out that in his view, primary Lemba belonging was with other Lemba people—but when he emphasized the Sekhukhune pride that he thought Malaga should bring with him to the LCA, he was actually demonstrating a belief that the Lemba have a double belonging rather than a double exclusion. Instead of not belonging where they live and not being able to live together, as many in the LCA understood the situation

to be during apartheid, in Thobakgale's postapartheid vision, the Lemba belonged everywhere—even more so because of their difference (their difference as Lemba in the context of Sekhukhune and as Sepedi speakers from Sekhukhune in the context of the LCA). Further, Thobakgale's comment that he wanted to educate Lemba people that they are all over the world and that their language and culture adapt to the norms of their places of residence is doubly significant. It speaks to the fact that the LCA has drawn considerable strength from its multilingual, translocal, and transnational membership over the years as LCA members have faced both national and local oppressions. It also speaks to the difficulties that Lemba people have had with many of the Jews who have enthusiastically sought out connections with the Lemba based on a presumed sameness only to become frustrated at Lemba difference (see chapter 2).

38 My reconstruction of this 2001 event is based on stories that I heard in 2005 and 2006 from participants, along with documents from Raulinga's LCA archive (specifically a printed program, original speeches written in English, and Raulinga's report composed immediately after the event).

39 I heard versions of this history, which also features in documentaries about the Lemba, many times throughout my research. Raulinga repeated one version to me nearly word for word three times between 2004 and 2006. The contrasts among Mathivha's telling of this deep history to the Malaga people in 2001, Raulinga's repetition of it to me a few years later, and the retelling of a version in television documentaries as if it were the only Lemba history speak to the significance of audience and also to the role that particular Lemba men have played in conveying particular images of their history to researchers. In the first instance, Mathivha communicated to other Lemba people what he felt to be their first lesson in knowing who they are, so that they might better connect to one another as Lemba people and to the LCA as their representative organization. In the second, Raulinga made sure that I knew this first lesson inside and out since I planned to write about the Lemba (see the introduction). In the third instance, by presenting who the Lemba were as who they are, it recast them as part of ancient history, as if everything that had happened since was not also part of them (see chapters 1 and 2).

40 Disturbance of the dead was incredibly contentious in South Africa at the time and to a large extent still is. This played out through debates about return of remains held at museums and universities, as well as in the context of urban development, as with the remains uncovered during a construction project on Prestwich Street in Cape Town (M. Hall 2009; Rassool 2015; Schramm 2016).

41 For resonant approaches to questions of evidence in the context of colonial and other violence, see A. Gordon (1997) 2008; M. Taussig 1986; Trouillot 1995; see also J. Scott 1991. For more recent work that elaborates rumor as method, see K. Peterson 2009.

42 The story that I tell here, including details such as the number of Lemba participants, is based on how Lemba people recounted their experience of the reburial when I interviewed a number of LCA leaders in 2013. Archaeologist Johan Nel's contribution to Sian Tiley-Nel's commemorative book, *Mapungubwe Remembered:*

Contributions to Mapungubwe by the University of Pretoria (2011), offers another account, including technical details related to preparation for the reburial process and the process itself. Nel writes, "Four communal graves were excavated and prepared in the Mapungubwe National Park, managed by Marko Hutten. . . . Three of these graves consisted of subterranean brick structures at *Schroda*, K2, and Hamilton House. The remains from *Schroda* and K2 were buried in rehabilitated areas at these sites, while diverse remains from other satellite sites were buried at Hamilton House. Marko also prepared a communal grave on the summit of Mapungubwe in the general area where the original gold graves were discovered in 1933" (Nel 2011, 234–235).

43 Nel explains that instead of the stainless steel that has been used in repatriations in Canada and Australia, the coffins were made of high-density polyethylene. This was to lower costs and also to ensure maximum protection for the bones and minimum temptation for potential scrap-metal seekers (Nel 2011, 233–234).

44 Lemba people used a number of words for "God." It is interesting that in telling me this story, Mungulwa recalled this Hebrew word rather than English or Venda terms that were more often used. This suggests that while he may have downplayed Lemba links to Jews in public engagements with other claimants, in his private thoughts, these connections remained highly important.

45 Mutenda called this "making *totoma*," and he was careful to explain that this is not prayer. "They settle in the grave and then they make totoma . . . the clapping of hands. Now it's a show of saying goodbye. Some other people when they see you do like that think you might be praying. We said, 'No, it's a way of saying goodbye, only that. It's a show of respect.'"

46 Mungulwa later referred to this as one of the best parts of the museum and thought the artifacts were presented in the right way—although he explained that Raulinga was named as the author because only one person could give the history, according to the project organizers. So the LCA had discussed, written down, and approved the statement that Raulinga then gave.

47 Fran Markowitz (1996) credits Black Hebrew Israelites in Dimona, Israel, with this geographic innovation. See also Jackson 2013.

48 I am drawing here on Wendy Brown's (2002) theorizations of rights and late liberalism, and specifically her engagement with Gayatri Spivak's (1993) provocation that one cannot not want rights.

49 The politics of indigeneity demand particular performances of identity and history that demonstrate others' notions of authenticity and respond to prevailing notions of national identity and situated historical legacies (Hodgson 2004; Kirsch 1997; Li 2000; Povinelli 2002). In this case, what was demanded was a willingness to be indigenous in general, in service to state projects, even while the concept sparked other ideas.

50 South Africa's Mapungubwe drew on ancient African cosmopolitanism to bolster the transnational (and neoliberal) status of the postapartheid state; Lemba histories as traders therefore put them at the center of present-day South Africa's nostalgic self-image of its foundational past.

51 For other remappings inspired by oceanic trade routes, see Ben-Yehoyada 2017; Chari 2015, 2016; Dua 2019; Ho 2006; Vergés 2003, 2005.

52 Huffman does not cite his source here, but it seems likely that his idea that there was no genetic link came from Steyn (1994), who seems to be the only researcher who conducted any genetic analysis of Mapungubwe remains. Steyn (2011) describes her conclusions slightly differently. Instead of Huffman's "no genetic link," Steyn writes, "The genetic relationships between the K2 people and currently living groups are complex and may not be directly traceable (227).

53 Recent research on ancient DNA has shown increased capabilities to sequence what had previously been unreadable, and therefore speculation about future research could very easily become reality. See, for example, a special section in the January 2019 issue of the SAA Archaeological Record, especially Piscitelli 2019; Hofman and Warinner 2019.

54 For more on intersections between indigeneity and DNA, see Bardill 2014; Kowal 2013; Radin and Kowal 2015; TallBear 2013.

REFERENCES

Abel, Sarah. 2018. "What DNA Can't Tell: Problems with Using Genetic Tests to Determine the Nationality of Migrants." *Anthropology Today* 34 (6): 3–6.

Abrami, Leo Michel. 2010. "The Last Jew on Earth: A Modern Midrash on Jewish Survival." Accessed October 20, 2013. http://www.highholydayservices.org/PDF/TheLastJewOnEarth.pdf.

Abu El-Haj, Nadia. 2007. "The Genetic Reinscription of Race." *Annual Review of Anthropology* 36 (1): 283–300.

Abu El-Haj, Nadia. 2011. "Jews—Lost and Found: Genetic History and the Evidentiary Terrain of Recognition." In *Rites of Return: Diaspora Poetics and the Politics of Memory*, edited by Marianne Hirsch and Nancy K. Miller, 40–58. New York: Columbia University Press.

Abu El-Haj, Nadia. 2012. *The Genealogical Science: The Search for Jewish Origins and the Politics of Epistemology*. Chicago: University of Chicago Press.

Adhikari, Mohamed. 2011. *The Anatomy of a South African Genocide: The Extermination of the Cape San Peoples*. Athens: Ohio University Press.

Alcalay, Ammiel. 1993. *After Jews and Arabs: Remaking Levantine Culture*. Minneapolis: University of Minnesota Press.

Ally, Shireen, and Ariana Lissoni, eds. 2017. *New Histories of South Africa's Apartheid-Era Bantustans*. New York: Routledge.

Amrute, Sareeta. 2016. *Encoding Race, Encoding Class: Indian IT Workers in Berlin*. Durham, NC: Duke University Press.

Anderson, Benedict R. [1983] 1991. *Imagined Communities: Reflections on the Origin and Spread of Nationalism*. New York: Verso.

Anderson, Mark. 2009. *Black and Indigenous: Garifuna Activism and Consumer Culture in Honduras*. Minneapolis: University of Minnesota Press.

Angrist, Misha. 2010. *Here Is a Human Being: At the Dawn of Personal Genomics*. New York: Harper.

Anidjar, Gil. 2003. *The Jew, the Arab: A History of the Enemy*. Stanford, CA: Stanford University Press.

Anidjar, Gil. 2008. *Semites: Race, Religion, Literature*. Stanford, CA: Stanford University Press.

Arkin, Kimberly A. 2009. "Rhinestone Aesthetics and Religious Essence: Looking Jewish in Paris." *American Ethnologist* 36 (4): 722–734.

Azoulay, Katya Gibel. 2003. "Not an Innocent Pursuit: The Politics of a 'Jewish' Genetic Signature." *Developing World Bioethics* 3 (2): 119–126.

Bachar, Arik. 1986. "Are the Lembas of Makanye a Lost Tribe?" *Sunday Times*, July 6.

Baker, Cynthia M. 2017. *Jew*. New Brunswick, NJ: Rutgers University Press.

Bank, Andrew, and Leslie John Bank, eds. 2013. *Inside African Anthropology: Monica Wilson and Her Interpreters*. New York: Cambridge University Press.

Bank, Richard D., and Julie Gutin. 2003. *The Everything Jewish History and Heritage Book: From Abraham to Zionism, All You Need to Understand the Key Events, People, and Places*. Avon, MA: Adams Media.

Bardill, Jessica. 2014. "Native American DNA: Ethical, Legal, and Social Implications of an Evolving Concept." *Annual Review of Anthropology* 43 (1): 155–166.

Barker, Joanne. 2011. *Native Acts: Law, Recognition, and Cultural Authenticity*. Durham, NC: Duke University Press.

Barnard, Alan. 2006. "Kalahari Revisionism, Vienna and the 'Indigenous Peoples' Debate." *Social Anthropology* 14 (1): 1–16.

Beinart, William. 2001. *Twentieth-Century South Africa*. Oxford: Oxford University Press.

Beinart, William, and Peter Delius. 2014. "The Historical Context and Legacy of the Natives Land Act of 1913." *Journal of Southern African Studies* 40 (4): 667–688.

Beinart, William, and Saul Dubow, eds. 1995. *Segregation and Apartheid in Twentieth-Century South Africa*. London: Routledge.

Benjamin, Ruha. 2016. "Informed Refusal: Toward a Justice-Based Bioethics." *Science, Technology and Human Values* 41 (6): 967–990.

Benjamin, Ruha. 2018. "Black AfterLives Matter: Cultivating Kinfulness as Reproductive Justice." In *Making Kin Not Population: Reconceiving Generations*, edited by Adele E. Clarke and Donna Haraway, 41–66. Chicago: Prickly Paradigm.

Benjamin, Walter. (1968) 2019. *Illuminations: Essays and Reflections*. Boston: Mariner Books, Houghton Mifflin Harcourt.

Ben-Yehoyada, Naor. 2017. *The Mediterranean Incarnate: Region Formation between Sicily and Tunisia since World War II*. Chicago: University of Chicago Press.

Berlant, Lauren. 2007a. "Introduction: What Does It Matter Who One Is?" *Critical Inquiry* 34 (1): 1–4.

Berlant, Lauren. 2007b. "On the Case." *Critical Inquiry* 33 (4): 663–672.

Berman, Bruce, Dickson Eyoh, and Will Kymlicka, eds. 2004. *Ethnicity and Democracy in Africa*. Athens: Ohio University Press.

Biehl, João, and Peter Locke, eds. 2010. "Deleuze and the Anthropology of Becoming." *Current Anthropology* 51 (3): 317–351.

Biehl, João, and Peter Locke, eds. 2017. *Unfinished: The Anthropology of Becoming*. Durham, NC: Duke University Press.

Biko, Steve, and Njabulo S. Ndebele. (1978) 2017. *I Write What I Like: A Selection of His Writings*. 40th anniv. ed. Johannesburg, SA: Picador Africa.

Biruk, Crystal. 2018. *Cooking Data: Culture and Politics in an African Research World*. Durham, NC: Duke University Press.

Boas, Franz. [1940] 1995. *Race, Language, and Culture*. Chicago: University of Chicago Press.

Bolnick, Deborah A. 2008. "Individual Ancestry Inference and the Reification of Race as a Biological Phenomenon." In *Revisiting Race in a Genomic Age*, edited by Barbara A. Koenig, Sandra Soo-Jin Lee, and Sarah S. Richardson, 70–85. New Brunswick, NJ: Rutgers University Press.

Bonilla, Yarimar. 2015. *Non-Sovereign Futures: French Caribbean Politics in the Wake of Disenchantment.* Chicago: University of Chicago Press.

Boonzaier, Emile, and John Sharp, eds. 1988. *South African Keywords: The Uses and Abuses of Political Concepts.* Cape Town, SA: Philip.

Bowker, Geoffrey C., and Susan Leigh Star, eds. 1999. *Sorting Things Out: Classification and Its Consequences.* Cambridge, MA: MIT Press.

Boyarin, Daniel. 2006. "Apartheid Comparative Religion in the Second Century: Some Theory and a Case Study." *Journal of Medieval and Early Modern Studies* 36 (1): 3–34.

Boyarin, Daniel, and Jonathan Boyarin. 1993. "Diaspora: Generation and the Ground of Jewish Identity." *Critical Inquiry* 19 (4): 693–725.

Boyarin, Jonathan, and Daniel Boyarin. 2002. *Powers of Diaspora: Two Essays on the Relevance of Jewish Culture.* Minneapolis: University of Minnesota Press.

Brettschneider, Marla. 2015. *The Jewish Phenomenon in Sub-Saharan Africa: The Politics of Contradictory Discourses.* Lewiston, NY: Mellen.

Brodkin, Karen. 2002. *How Jews Became White Folks and What That Says about Race in America.* New Brunswick, NJ: Rutgers University Press.

Brodwin, Paul. 2002. "Genetics, Identity, and the Anthropology of Essentialism." *Anthropological Quarterly* 75 (2): 323–330.

Brodwin, Paul. 2005. "Genetic Knowledge and Collective Identity." *Culture, Medicine and Psychiatry* 29 (2): 139–143.

Brown, Jacqueline Nassy. 2005. *Dropping Anchor, Setting Sail: Geographies of Race in Black Liverpool.* Princeton, NJ: Princeton University Press.

Brown, Wendy. 2002. "Suffering the Paradox of Rights." In *Left Legalism/Left Critique*, edited by Wendy Brown and Janet Halley, 420–434. Durham, NC: Duke University Press.

Brubaker, Rogers, and Frederick Cooper. 2000. "Beyond 'Identity.'" *Theory and Society* 29:1–47.

Bruder, Edith. 2008. *The Black Jews of Africa: History, Religion, Identity.* Oxford, UK: Oxford University Press.

Buijs, Gina. 1998. "Black Jews in the Northern Province: A Study of Ethnic Identity in South Africa." *Ethnic and Racial Studies* 21 (4): 661–682.

Bunzl, Matti. 2007. *Anti-Semitism and Islamophobia: Hatreds Old and New in Europe.* Chicago: Prickly Paradigm.

Burton, Antoinette M., ed. 2005. *Archive Stories: Facts, Fictions, and the Writing of History.* Durham, NC: Duke University Press.

Buthelezi, Mbongiseni. 2016. "We Need New Names Too." In *Tribing and Untribing the Archive: Identity and the Material Record in Southern KwaZulu-Natal in the Late Independent and Colonial Periods*, edited by Carolyn Hamilton and Nessa Leibhammer, 586–599. Pietermarizburg, SA: University of KwaZulu-Natal Press.

Butler, Judith. 1993. *Bodies That Matter: On the Discursive Limits of "Sex."* New York: Routledge.

Canessa, Andrew. 2012. *Intimate Indigeneities: Race, Sex, and History in the Small Spaces of Andean Life*. Durham, NC: Duke University Press.

Carmeli, Daphna Birenbaum. 2004. "Prevalence of Jews as Subjects in Genetic Research: Figures, Explanation, and Potential Implications." *American Journal of Human Genetics Part A* 130A (1): 76–83.

Carruthers, Jane. 2006. "Mapungubwe: An Historical and Contemporary Analysis of a World Heritage Cultural Landscape." *Koedoe* 49 (1): 1–13.

Carsten, Janet. 2000. *Cultures of Relatedness: New Approaches to the Study of Kinship*. Cambridge, UK: Cambridge University Press.

Carsten, Janet, ed. 2004. *After Kinship*. Cambridge, UK: Cambridge University Press.

Cattelino, Jessica R. 2008. *High Stakes: Florida Seminole Gaming and Sovereignty*. Durham, NC: Duke University Press.

Chari, Sharad. 2015. "African Extraction, Indian Ocean Critique." *South Atlantic Quarterly* 114 (1): 83–100.

Chari, Sharad. 2016. "Trans-Area Studies and the Perils of Geographical 'World Writing.'" *Environment and Planning D: Society and Space* 34 (5): 149–159.

Clarke, Adele E., and Donna Haraway, eds. 2018. *Making Kin Not Population: Reconceiving Generations*. Chicago: Prickly Paradigm.

Clarke, Kamari Maxine, and Deborah A. Thomas, eds. 2006. *Globalization and Race: Transformations in the Cultural Production of Blackness*. Durham, NC: Duke University Press.

Clifford, James. 1997. *Routes: Travel and Translation in the Late Twentieth Century*. Cambridge, MA: Harvard University Press.

Cohen, Robin. [1997] 2008. *Global Diasporas: An Introduction*. Seattle: University of Washington Press.

Comaroff, Jean. 1985. *Body of Power, Spirit of Resistance: The Culture and History of a South African People*. Chicago: University of Chicago Press.

Comaroff, Jean, and John Comaroff. 1991. *Of Revelation and Revolution*. Vol. 1, *Christianity, Colonialism, and Consciousness in South Africa*. Chicago: University of Chicago Press.

Comaroff, Jean, and John Comaroff. 1997. *Of Revelation and Revolution*. Vol. 2, *The Dialectics of Modernity on a South African Frontier*. Chicago: University of Chicago Press.

Comaroff, Jean, and John Comaroff. 2003. "Reflections on Liberalism, Policulturalism, and ID-ology: Citizenship and Difference in South Africa." *Social Identities* 9 (4): 445–473.

Comaroff, Jean, and John Comaroff. 2005. "The Struggle between the Constitution and 'Things African.'" *Interventions* 7 (3): 299–303.

Comaroff, Jean, and John L. Comaroff. 2012. *Theory from the South, or, How Euro-America is Evolving toward Africa*. Boulder, CO: Paradigm.

Comaroff, John L., and Jean Comaroff. 2009. *Ethnicity, Inc.* Chicago: University of Chicago Press.

Comaroff, John L., and Jean Comaroff, eds. 2018. *The Politics of Custom: Chiefship, Capital, and the State in Contemporary Africa*. Chicago: University of Chicago Press.

Coombes, Annie E. 2003. *History after Apartheid: Visual Culture and Public Memory in a Democratic South Africa*. Durham, NC: Duke University Press.

Coop, Graham, Michael B. Eisen, Rasmus Nielsen, Molly Przeworski, and Noah Rosenberg. 2014. Letters: "A Troublesome Inheritance." *New York Times*, August 10.

Cooper, Frederick. 2005. *Colonialism in Question: Theory, Knowledge, History*. Berkeley: University of California Press.

Crais, Clifton C., and Thomas V. McClendon, eds. 2014. *The South Africa Reader: History, Culture, Politics*. Durham, NC: Duke University Press.

Crais, Clifton C., and Pamela Scully. 2009. *Sara Baartman and the Hottentot Venus: A Ghost Story and a Biography*. Princeton, NJ: Princeton University Press.

Davis, Dena S. 2004. "Genetic Research and Communal Narratives." *Hastings Center Report* 34 (4): 40–48.

Davis, Dena S., Nancy Gerson, Roselle Ponsaran, and Laura A. Siminoff. 2010. "Ashkenazi Jews: Overburdened and Overexposed?" *New Genetics and Society* 29 (3): 241–260.

de la Cadena, Marisol. 2000. *Indigenous Mestizos: The Politics of Race and Culture in Cuzco, Peru, 1919–1991*. Durham, NC: Duke University Press.

de la Cadena, Marisol, and Orin Starn, eds. 2007. *Indigenous Experience Today*. New York: Berg.

Deleuze, Gilles, and Félix Guattari. (1987) 2009. *A Thousand Plateaus: Capitalism and Schizophrenia*. Translated by Brian Massumi. Minneapolis: University of Minnesota Press.

Delius, Peter. 1984. *The Land Belongs to Us: The Pedi Polity, the Boers and the British in the Nineteenth-Century Transvaal*. London: Heinemann.

Delius, Peter. 1996. *A Lion amongst the Cattle: Reconstruction and Resistance in the Northern Transvaal*. Portsmouth, NH: Heinemann.

Deomampo, Daisy. 2016. *Transnational Reproduction: Race, Kinship, and Commercial Surrogacy in India*. New York: New York University Press.

de Vries, Jantina, and Michael S. Pepper. 2012. "Genomic Sovereignty and the African Promise: Mining the African Genome for the Benefit of Africa." *Journal of Medical Ethics* 38 (8): 474–478.

Domínguez, Virginia R. 1989. *People as Subject, People as Object: Selfhood and Peoplehood in Contemporary Israel*. Madison: University of Wisconsin Press.

Drum. 1986. "Jews Prepare to Trek: 40,000 Expected to Head for Ceremonies in Transvaal." September.

Dua, Jatin. 2019. *Captured at Sea: Piracy and Protection in the Indian Ocean*. Berkeley: University of California Press.

Dube, Edmore. 2018. "Religions and Insecurities: Heritage Contestations and Religious Praxis in Mberengwa and Masvingo, Zimbabwe." In *Rethinking Securities in an Emergent Technoscientific New World Order: Retracing the Contours for Africa's Hi-jacked Futures*, edited by Munyaradzi Mawere and Artwell Nhemachena, 237–257. Bamenda, Cameroon: Langaa Research and Publishing Common Initiative Group.

Dubow, Saul. 1995. *Scientific Racism in Modern South Africa*. Cambridge, UK: Cambridge University Press.

Dubow, Saul. 2014. *Apartheid, 1948–1994*. New York: Oxford University Press.

Duclos, Vincent, Tomás Sánchez Criado, and Vinh-Kim Nguyen. 2017. "Speed: An Introduction." *Cultural Anthropology* 32 (1): 1–11.

Dumit, Joseph. 2004. *Picturing Personhood: Brain Scans and Biomedical Identity*. Princeton, NJ: Princeton University.

Duster, Troy. [1990] 2003. *Backdoor to Eugenics*. 2nd ed. New York: Routledge.

Duster, Troy. 2003. "Buried Alive: The Concept of Race in Science." In *Genetic Nature/Culture: Anthropology and Science beyond the Two-Culture Divide*, edited by Alan H. Goodman, Deborah Heath, and M. Susan Lindee, 258–277. Berkeley: University of California Press.

Duster, Troy. 2006. "The Molecular Reinscription of Race: Unanticipated Issues in Biotechnology and Forensic Science." *Patterns of Prejudice* 40 (4–5): 427–441.

Ebron, Paulla A. 2002. *Performing Africa*. Princeton, NJ: Princeton University Press.

Edwards, Brent Hayes. 2003. *The Practice of Diaspora: Literature, Translation, and the Rise of Black Internationalism*. Cambridge, MA: Harvard University Press.

Efron, John M. 1994. *Defenders of the Race: Jewish Doctors and Race Science in Fin-de-Siècle Europe*. New Haven, CT: Yale University Press.

Efron, John M. 2013. "Jewish Genetic Origins in the Context of Past Historical and Anthropological Inquiries." *Human Biology* 85 (6): 901–918.

Egorova, Yulia. 2010. "DNA Evidence? The Impact of Genetic Research on Historical Debates." *Biosocieties* 5 (3): 348–365.

Egorova, Yulia. 2014. "Theorizing 'Jewish Genetics': DNA, Culture, and Historical Narrative." In *The Routledge Handbook of Contemporary Jewish Cultures*, edited by Laurence Roth and Nadia Valman, 353–364. New York: Routledge.

Ellis, William 2010. "The ≠Khomani San Land Claim against the Kalahari Gemsbok National Park: Requiring and Acquiring Authenticity." In *Land, Memory, Reconstruction, and Justice: Perspectives on Land Claims in South Africa*, edited by Cherryl Walker, Anna Bohlin, Ruth Hall, and Thembela Kepe, 181–197. Athens: Ohio University Press.

Endelman, Todd M. 2004. "Anglo-Jewish Scientists and the Science of Race." *Jewish Social Studies* 11 (1): 52–92.

Entine, Jon. 2007. *Abraham's Children: Race, Identity, and the DNA of the Chosen People*. New York: Grand Central Publishing.

Epstein, Steven. 2007. *Inclusion: The Politics of Difference in Medical Research*. Chicago: University of Chicago Press.

Erasmus, Zimitri. 2013. "Throwing the Genes: A Renewed Biological Imaginary of 'Race,' Place and Identification." *Theoria* 136 (60): 38–53.

Erasmus, Zimitri. 2017. *Race Otherwise: Forging a New Humanism for South Africa*. Johannesburg, SA: Wits University Press.

Fabian, Johannes. 1983. *Time and the Other: How Anthropology Makes Its Object*. New York: Columbia University Press.

Falk, Raphael. 2010. "Eugenics and the Jews." In *The Oxford Handbook of the History of Eugenics*, edited by Alison Bashford and Philippa Levine, 462–476. Oxford, UK: Oxford University Press.

Fassin, Didier. 2015. "The Public Afterlife of Ethnography." *American Ethnologist* 42 (4): 592–609.

Felder, Cain Hope, ed. 1993. *The Original African Heritage Study Bible: King James Version with Special Annotations Relative to the African/Edenic Perspective*. Nashville, TN: Winston.

Ferguson, James. 1999. *Expectations of Modernity: Myths and Meanings of Urban Life on the Zambian Copperbelt.* Berkeley: University of California Press.

Ferguson, James. 2006. *Global Shadows: Africa in the Neoliberal World Order.* Durham, NC: Duke University Press.

Fontein, Joost. 2006. *The Silence of Great Zimbabwe: Contested Landscapes and the Power of Heritage.* London: University College London Press.

Fortun, Michael. 2008. *Promising Genomics: Iceland and deCODE Genetics in a World of Speculation.* Berkeley: University of California Press.

Foster, Laura A. 2016. "A Postapartheid Genome: Genetic Ancestry Testing and Belonging in South Africa." *Science, Technology and Human Values* 41 (6): 1015–1036.

Foster, Laura A. 2018. *Reinventing Hoodia: Peoples, Plants, and Patents in South Africa.* Seattle: University of Washington Press.

Franklin, Sarah. 2013. *Biological Relatives: IVF, Stem Cells, and the Future of Kinship.* Durham, NC: Duke University Press.

Franklin, Sarah. 2019. "The Anthropology of Biology: A Lesson from the New Kinship Studies." In *The Cambridge Handbook of Kinship,* edited by Sandra Bamford, 107–132. Cambridge: Cambridge University Press.

Franklin, Sarah, and Susan McKinnon, eds. 2001. *Relative Values: Reconfiguring Kinship Studies.* Durham, NC: Duke University Press.

Fujimura, Joan H., and Ramya Rajagopalan. 2011. "Different Differences: The Use of 'Genetic Ancestry' versus Race in Biomedical Human Genetic Research." *Social Studies of Science* 41 (1): 5–30.

Fullwiley, Duana. 2007. "Race and Genetics: Attempts to Define the Relationship." *BioSocieties* 2 (2): 221–237.

Fullwiley, Duana. 2008. "The Biologistical Construction of Race: 'Admixture' Technology and the New Genetic Medicine." *Social Studies of Science* 38 (5): 695–735.

Garman, Anthea. 2001. "Khoisan Revivalism: The Claims of Africa's First Indigenous Peoples." *Rhodes Journalism Review* (August): 41.

Gayre of Gayre, Robert. 1967. "The Lembas and Vendas of Vendaland." *Mankind Quarterly* 8 (1): 3–15.

Geschiere, Peter. 2009. *The Perils of Belonging: Autochthony, Citizenship, and Exclusion in Africa and Europe.* Chicago: University of Chicago Press.

Gibbon, Sahra, and Carlos Novas, eds. 2008. *Biosocialities, Genetics and the Social Sciences: Making Biologies and Identities.* New York: Routledge.

Gilman, Sander L. 1991. *The Jew's Body.* New York: Routledge.

Gilman, Sander L. 2006. "Alcohol and the Jews (Again), Race and Medicine (Again): On Race and Medicine in Historical Perspective." *Patterns of Prejudice* 40 (4–5): 335–352.

Gilroy, Paul. 1991. *"There Ain't No Black in the Union Jack": The Cultural Politics of Race and Nation.* Chicago: University of Chicago Press.

Gilroy, Paul. 1993. *The Black Atlantic: Modernity and Double Consciousness.* Cambridge, MA: Harvard University Press.

Gitelman, Lisa, ed. 2013. *"Raw Data" Is an Oxymoron.* Cambridge, MA: MIT Press.

Goldberg, David Theo. 2002. *The Racial State.* Malden, MA: Blackwell.

Goldberg, David Theo. 2009. "A Political Theology of Race." *Cultural Studies* 23 (4): 513–537.

Goldberg, David Theo. 2015. *Are We All Postracial Yet?* Malden, MA: Polity.

Goldstein, David. 2008. *Jacob's Legacy: A Genetic View of Jewish History.* New Haven, CT: Yale University Press.

Goldstein, Eric L. 2006. *The Price of Whiteness: Jews, Race, and American Identity.* Princeton, NJ: Princeton University Press.

Golomski, Casey. 2018. *Funeral Culture: AIDS, Work, and Cultural Change in an African Kingdom.* Bloomington: Indiana University Press.

Goodman, Alan. 2000. "Why Genes Don't Count (for Racial Differences in Health)." *American Journal of Public Health* 90 (11): 1699–1702.

Goodman, Alan. 2007. "Toward Genetics in an Era of Anthropology." *American Ethnologist* 34 (2): 227–229.

Goodman, Alan H., Deborah Heath, and M. Susan Lindee, eds. 2003. *Genetic Nature/Culture: Anthropology and Science beyond the Two-Culture Divide.* Berkeley: University of California Press.

Goodman, Alan H., Yolanda T. Moses, and Joseph L. Jones. 2012. *Race: Are We So Different?* Malden, MA: Wiley-Blackwell.

Gordillo, Gastón. 2014. *Rubble: The Afterlife of Destruction.* Durham, NC: Duke University Press.

Gordon, Avery. (1997) 2008. *Ghostly Matters: Haunting and the Sociological Imagination.* Minneapolis: University of Minnesota Press.

Gordon, Robert, and Andrew D. Spiegel. 1993. "Southern Africa Revisited." *Annual Review of Anthropology* 22:83–105.

Grenn-Scott, Deborah. 2002. "For She Is a Tree of Life: Shared Roots Connecting Women to Deity: An Organic Theological Inquiry into Identities, Beliefs and Practices among South African Lemba and European-American Jewish Women." PhD diss., California Institute of Integral Studies.

Grinker, Roy Richard. 1994. *Houses in the Rain Forest: Ethnicity and Inequality among Farmers and Foragers in Central Africa.* Berkeley: University of California Press.

Gupta, Akhil, and James Ferguson. 1992. "Beyond 'Culture': Space, Identity, and the Politics of Difference." *Cultural Anthropology* 7 (1): 6–23.

Hage, Ghassan. 2000. *White Nation: Fantasies of White Supremacy in a Multicultural Society.* New York: Routledge.

Hall, Martin. 2009. "New Knowledge and the University." *Anthropology Southern Africa* 32 (1–2): 69–76.

Hall, Stuart. 1990. "Cultural Identity and Diaspora." In *Identity: Community, Culture, Difference,* edited by Jonathan Rutherford, 222–237. London: Lawrence and Wishart.

Hall, Stuart. 1991. "Old and New Identities, Old and New Ethnicities." In *Culture, Globalization, and the World System,* edited by Anthony D. King, 41–68. London: Macmillan.

Hall, Stuart. 2018. *Essential Essays.* Vol. 2, *Identity and Diaspora.* Edited by David Morley. Durham, NC: Duke University Press.

Hall, Stuart, and Bill Schwarz. 2017. *Familiar Stranger: A Life between Two Islands.* Durham, NC: Duke University Press.

Hamilton, Carolyn, Verne Harris, Jane Taylor, Michele Pickover, Graeme Reid, and Razia Saleh, eds. 2002. *Refiguring the Archive*. Boston: Kluwer Academic.

Hamilton, Carolyn, and Nessa Leibhammer, eds. 2016. *Tribing and Untribing the Archive: Identity and the Material Record in Southern KwaZulu-Natal in the Late Independent and Colonial Periods*. Pietermaritzburg, SA: University of KwaZulu-Natal Press.

Hamilton, Jennifer A. 2009. *Indigeneity in the Courtroom: Law, Culture, and the Production of Difference in North American Courts*. New York: Routledge.

Hammer, Michael F., Doron M. Behar, Tatiana M. Karafet, Fernando L. Mendez, Brian Hallmark, Tamar Erez, Lev A. Zhivotovsky, Saharon Rosset, and Karl Skorecki. 2009. "Extended Y Chromosome Haplotypes Resolve Multiple and Unique Lineages of the Jewish Priesthood." *Human Genetics* 126 (5): 707–717.

Hammond-Tooke, W. D. 1995. "Van Warmelo and the Ethnological Section." *African Studies* 54 (1): 119–127.

Haraway, Donna. 1988. "Situated Knowledges: The Science Question in Feminism and the Privilege of Partial Perspective." *Feminist Studies* 14 (3): 575–599.

Haraway, Donna. 1997. *Modest_Witness@Second_Millennium. FemaleMan_Meets_Onco-Mouse: Feminism and Technoscience*. New York: Routledge.

Haraway, Donna. 2008. *When Species Meet*. Minneapolis: University of Minnesota Press.

Haraway, Donna. 2016. *Staying With the Trouble: Making Kin in the Chthulucene*. Durham, NC: Duke University Press.

Hardy, Billie-Jo, Béatrice Séguin, Raj Ramesar, Peter A. Singer, and Abdallah S. Daar. 2008. "South Africa: From Species Cradle to Genomic Applications." *Nature Reviews Genetics* 9:S19–S23. doi: 10.1038/nrg2441.

Harmon, Amy. 2018. "Geneticists Criticize Use of Science by White Nationalists to Justify 'Racial Purity.'" *New York Times*, October 19.

Harmon, Amy. 2018. "Why White Supremacists Are Chugging Milk (and Why Geneticists Are Alarmed)." *New York Times*, October 17.

Harper, Peter. 2007. "Trefor Jenkins Interview." *Cardiff University's Special Collection and Archives (SCOLAR): The Wellcome Genetics Archives Project*. http://www.genmedhist.info/interviews/Jenkins.

Harrison, Faye V. 1995. "The Persistent Power of 'Race' in the Cultural and Political Economy of Racism." *Annual Review of Anthropology* 24:47–74.

Hartigan, John. 1999. *Racial Situations: Class Predicaments of Whiteness in Detroit*. Princeton, NJ: Princeton University Press.

Hartigan, John, ed. 2013. *Anthropology of Race: Genes, Biology, and Culture*. Santa Fe, NM: School for Advanced Research Press.

Hartman, Saidiya. 2002. "The Time of Slavery." *South Atlantic Quarterly* 101 (4): 757–777.

Hartman, Saidiya. 2007. *Lose Your Mother: A Journey along the Atlantic Slave Route*. New York: Farrar, Straus and Giroux.

Hassim, Shireen, Tawana Kupe, and Eric Worby, eds. 2008. *Go Home or Die Here: Violence, Xenophobia and the Reinvention of Difference in South Africa*. Johannesburg, SA: Wits University Press.

Heath, Deborah, Rayna Rapp, and Karen-Sue Taussig. 2004. "Genetic Citizenship." In *A Companion to the Anthropology of Politics*, edited by David Nugent and Joan Vincent, 152–167. Malden, MA: Blackwell.

Hendrickx, Ben. 1991. "The Ancient Origin of the Lemba (Mwenye): A Critical Overview of Existing Theories." *Journal of Oriental and African Studies* 3:172–193.

Herndon, Astead W. 2019. "Elizabeth Warren Apologizes to Cherokee Nation for DNA Test." *New York Times*, February 1.

Hinterberger, Amy, and Natalie Porter. 2015. "Genomic and Viral Sovereignty: Tethering the Materials of Global Biomedicine." *Public Culture* 27 (2): 361–386.

Ho, Engseng. 2006. *The Graves of Tarim: Genealogy and Mobility across the Indian Ocean.* Berkeley: University of California Press.

Hoad, Neville. 2007. *African Intimacies: Race, Homosexuality, and Globalization.* Minneapolis: University of Minnesota Press.

Hodgson, Dorothy L. 2002. "Introduction: Comparative Perspectives on the Indigenous Rights Movement in Africa and the Americas." *American Anthropologist* 104 (4): 1037–1049.

Hodgson, Dorothy L. 2004. *Once Intrepid Warriors: Gender, Ethnicity, and the Cultural Politics of Maasai Development.* Bloomington: Indiana University Press.

Hodgson, Dorothy L. 2009. "Becoming Indigenous in Africa." *African Studies Review* 52 (3): 1–32.

Hodgson, Dorothy L. 2011. *Being Maasai, Becoming Indigenous: Postcolonial Politics in a Neoliberal World.* Bloomington: Indiana University Press.

Hofman, Courtney A., and Christina Warinner. 2019. "Ancient DNA 101: An Introductory Guide in the Era of High-Throughput Sequencing." *SAA Archaeological Record* 19 (1): 18–25.

HoSang, Daniel, Oneka LaBennett, and Laura Pulido. 2012. *Racial Formation in the Twenty-First Century.* Berkeley: University of California Press.

Howell, Signe. 2003. "Kinning: The Creation of Life Trajectories in Transnational Adoptive Families." *Journal of the Royal Anthropological Institute* 9 (3): 465–484.

Howell, Signe. 2006. *The Kinning of Foreigners: Transnational Adoption in a Global Perspective.* New York: Berghahn.

Huang, Yu-Ling, and Chia-Ling Wu. 2018. "New Feminist Biopolitics for Ultra-Low-Fertility East Asia." In *Making Kin Not Population: Reconceiving Generations*, edited by Adele E. Clarke and Donna Haraway, 125–144. Chicago: Prickly Paradigm.

Huffman, Thomas N. 2005. *Mapungubwe: Ancient African Civilisation on the Limpopo.* Johannesburg, SA: Wits University Press.

Hughes, Aaron W. 2017. *Shared Identities: Medieval and Modern Imaginings of Judeo-Islam.* New York: Oxford University Press.

Huizenga, Daniel. 2014. "Documenting 'Community' in the ≠khomani San Land Claim in South Africa." *PoLAR: Political and Legal Anthropology Review* 37 (1): 145–161.

Hull, Richard W. 2009. *Jews and Judaism in African History.* Princeton, NJ: Wiener.

Hunt, Nancy Rose. 2016. *A Nervous State: Violence, Remedies, and Reverie in Colonial Congo.* Durham, NC: Duke University Press.

Idrus, Rusaslina. 2010. "From Wards to Citizens: Indigenous Rights and Citizenship in Malaysia." *PoLAR: Political and Legal Anthropology Review* 33 (1): 89–108.

Imhoff, Sarah, and Hillary Kaell. 2017. "Lineage Matters: DNA, Race, and Gene Talk in Judaism and Messianic Judaism." *Religion and American Culture: A Journal of Interpretation* 27 (1): 95–127.

International Jewish Anti-Zionist Network. 2014. *Legacies of Resistance: An Anti-Zionist Haggadah for a Liberation Seder.*

Ives, Sarah. 2014. "Farming the South African 'Bush': Ecologies of Belonging and Exclusion in Rooibos Tea." *American Ethnologist* 41 (4): 698–713.

Ives, Sarah. 2017. *Steeped in Heritage: The Racial Politics of South African Rooibos Tea.* Durham, NC: Duke University Press.

Jackson, John L. 2005. *Real Black: Adventures in Racial Sincerity.* Chicago: University of Chicago Press.

Jackson, John L. 2013. *Thin Description: Ethnography and the African Hebrew Israelites of Jerusalem.* Cambridge, MA: Harvard University Press.

James, Deborah. 1990. "A Question of Ethnicity: Ndzundza Ndebele in a Lebowa Village." *Journal of Southern African Studies* 16 (1): 33–54.

James, Deborah. 2007. *Gaining Ground: "Rights" and "Property" in South African Land Reform.* New York: Routledge-Cavendish.

Jaques, A. A. 1931. "Notes on the Lemba Tribe." *Anthropos* 26:245–251.

Jasanoff, Sheila. 2004. *States of Knowledge: The Co-production of Science and Social Order.* New York: Routledge.

Jenkins, Trefor, A. B. Lane, G. T. Nurse, and Jiro Tanaka. 1975. "Sero-Genetic Studies on the G/wi and G//ana San of Botswana." *Human Heredity* 25 (4): 318–328.

Jenkins, Trefor, H. Lehmann, and G. T. Nurse. 1974. "Public Health and Genetic Constitution of the San ('Bushmen'): Carbohydrate Metabolism and Acetylator Status of the Kung of Tsumkwe in the North-Western Kalahari." *British Medical Journal* 2:23–26.

Johannesburg Star. 1985. "Israelis Rescue Black 'Lost Tribe.'" January 19.

Johnston, Josephine. 2003. "Case Study: The Lemba." *Developing World Bioethics* 3 (2): 109–111.

Jones, Steve. 1997. *In the Blood.* Princeton, NJ: Films for the Humanities and Sciences.

Junod, Henri A. 1908. "The Balemba of the Zoutpansberg (Transvaal)." *Folklore* 19 (3): 276–287.

Kahn, Jonathan. 2008. "Exploiting Race in Drug Development: BiDil's Interim Model of Pharmacogenomics." *Social Studies of Science* 38 (5): 737–758.

Kahn, Susan Martha. 2000. *Reproducing Jews: A Cultural Account of Assisted Conception in Israel.* Durham, NC: Duke University Press.

Kahn, Susan Martha 2005. "The Multiple Meanings of Jewish Genes." *Culture Medicine and Psychiatry* 29 (2): 179–192.

Kahn, Susan Martha. 2010. "Are Genes Jewish? Conceptual Ambiguities in the New Genetic Age." In *Boundaries of Jewish Identity,* edited by Susan A. Glenn and Naomi B. Sokoloff, 12–26. Seattle: University of Washington Press.

Kahn, Susan Martha. 2013. "Who Are the Jews? New Formulations of an Age-Old Question." *Human Biology* 85 (6): 919–924.

Kapteijns, Lidwien. 2000. "Ethiopia and the Horn of Africa." In *The History of Islam in Africa*, edited by Nehemia Levtzion and Randall Lee Pouwels, 227–250. Athens: Ohio University Press.

Karakasidou, Anastasia N. 1997. *Fields of Wheat, Hills of Blood: Passages to Nationhood in Greek Macedonia, 1870–1990*. Chicago: University of Chicago Press.

Kauanui, J. Kēhaulani. 2008. *Hawaiian Blood: Colonialism and the Politics of Sovereignty and Indigeneity*. Durham, NC: Duke University Press.

Keene, Adrienne, Rebecca Nagle, and Joseph M. Pierce. 2018. "Syllabus: Elizabeth Warren, Cherokee Citizenship, and DNA Testing." *Critical Ethnic Studies*. December 19. http://www.criticalethnicstudiesjournal.org/blog/2018/12/19/syllabus-elizabeth -warren-cherokee-citizenship-and-dna-testing.

Kemp, Martin, dir. 2008. *Quest for the Lost Ark*. History Channel.

Khan, Aisha. 2004. *Callaloo Nation: Metaphors of Race and Religious Identity among South Asians in Trinidad*. Durham, NC: Duke University Press.

Khandaker, Tamara. 2018. "Canada Is Using Ancestry DNA Websites to Help It Deport People." *Vice News*, July 26. https://news.vice.com/en_ca/article/wjkxmy/canada-is -using-ancestry-dna-websites-to-help-it-deport-people.

Kirsch, Stuart. 1997. "Lost Tribes: Indigenous People and the Social Imaginary." *Anthropological Quarterly* 70 (2): 58–67.

Kirsh, Nurit. 2003. "Population Genetics in Israel in the 1950s: The Unconscious Internalization of Ideology." *Isis* 94 (4): 631–655.

Klima, Alan. 2002. *The Funeral Casino: Meditation, Massacre, and Exchange with the Dead in Thailand*. Princeton, NJ: Princeton University Press.

Klopotek, Brian. 2011. *Recognition Odysseys: Indigeneity, Race, and Federal Tribal Recognition Policy in Three Louisiana Indian Communities*. Durham, NC: Duke University Press.

Koenig, Barbara A., Sandra Soo-Jin Lee, and Sarah S. Richardson, eds. 2008. *Revisiting Race in a Genomic Age*. New Brunswick, NJ: Rutgers University Press.

Kowal, Emma. 2013. "Orphan DNA: Indigenous Samples, Ethical Biovalue and Postcolonial Science in Australia." *Social Studies of Science* 43 (4): 578–598.

Krige, Eileen Jensen, and J. D. Krige. 1943. *The Realm of a Rain Queen: A Study of the Pattern of Lovedu Society*. London: Oxford University Press.

Krut, Riva. 1987. "The Making of a South African Jewish Community in Johannesburg, 1886–1914." In *Class, Community and Conflict: South African Perspectives*, edited by Belinda Bozzoli. Johannesburg, SA: Raven.

Kuljian, Christa. 2016. *Darwin's Hunch: Science, Race and the Search for Human Origins*. Johannesburg, SA: Jacana.

Kuper, Adam. 2003. "The Return of the Native." *Current Anthropology* 44 (3): 389.

Lan, David. 1985. *Guns and Rain: Guerrillas and Spirit Mediums in Zimbabwe*. Berkeley: University of California Press.

Langham, Ian. 1981. *The Building of British Social Anthropology: W. H. R. Rivers and His Cambridge Disciples in the Development of Kinship Studies, 1898–1931*. Dordrecht, Holland: Reidel.

Legassick, Martin, and Ciraj Rassool. 2015. *Skeletons in the Cupboard: South African Museums and the Trade in Human Remains, 1907–1917*. 2nd ed. Cape Town, SA: Iziko Museum.

Leinaweaver, Jessaca B. 2008. *The Circulation of Children: Kinship, Adoption, and Morality in Andean Peru*. Durham, NC: Duke University Press.

Leinaweaver, Jessaca B. 2013. *Adoptive Migration: Raising Latinos in Spain*. Durham, NC: Duke University Press.

Lekgoathi, Sekibakiba Peter. 2003. "Chiefs, Migrants and North Ndebele Ethnicity in the Context of Surrounding Homeland Politics, 1965–1978." *African Studies* 62 (1): 53–77.

Lekgoathi, Sekibakiba Peter. 2009. "Colonial Experts, Local Interlocutors, Informants and the Making of an Archive on the Transvaal Ndebele, 1930–1989." *Journal of African History* 50 (1): 61–80.

le Roux, Magdel. 1997. "African 'Jews' for Jesus: A Preliminary Investigation into the Semitic Origins and Missionary Initiatives of Some Lemba Communities in Southern Africa." *Missionalia* 25 (4): 493–510.

le Roux, Magdel. 2003. *The Lemba: A Lost Tribe of Israel in Southern Africa?* Pretoria, SA: Unisa.

Levtzion, Nehemia, and Randall Lee Pouwels, eds. 2000. *The History of Islam in Africa*. Athens: Ohio University Press.

Lewin, Ellen. 1993. *Lesbian Mothers: Accounts of Gender in American Culture*. Ithaca, NY: Cornell University Press.

Lewin, Ellen. 2009. *Gay Fatherhood: Narratives of Family and Citizenship in America*. Chicago: University of Chicago Press.

Li, Tania Murray. 2000. "Articulating Indigenous Identity in Indonesia: Resource Politics and the Tribal Slot." *Comparative Studies in Society and History* 42 (1): 149–179.

Lipphardt, Veronika. 2008. *Biologie der Juden: Jüdische Wissenschaftler über "Rasse" und Vererbung, 1900–1935*. Göttingen, Germany: Vandenhoeck and Ruprecht.

Lipphardt, Veronika. 2012. "Isolates and Crosses in Human Population Genetics; or, A Contextualization of German Race Science." *Current Anthropology* 53 (S5): S69–S82.

Magaziner, Daniel. 2010. *The Law and the Prophets: Black Consciousness in South Africa, 1968–1977*. Athens: Ohio University Press.

Magubane, Zine. 2003. "Simians, Savages, Skulls, and Sex: Science and Colonial Militarism in Nineteenth-Century South Africa." In *Race, Nature, and the Politics of Difference*, edited by Donald S. Moore, Jake Kosek, and Anand Pandian. Durham, NC: Duke University Press.

Mahoney, Michael R. 2012. *The Other Zulus: The Spread of Zulu Ethnicity in Colonial South Africa*. Durham, NC: Duke University Press.

Makhulu, Anne-Maria. 2015. *Making Freedom: Apartheid, Squatter Politics, and the Struggle for Home*. Durham, NC: Duke University Press.

Malkki, Liisa. 1992. "National Geographic: The Rooting of Peoples and the Territorialization of National Identity among Scholars and Refugees." *Cultural Anthropology* 7 (1): 24–44.

Malkki, Liisa H. 1995. *Purity and Exile: Violence, Memory, and National Cosmology among Hutu Refugees in Tanzania*. Chicago: University of Chicago Press.

Mamdani, Mahmood. 1996. *Citizen and Subject: Contemporary Africa and the Legacy of Late Colonialism*. Princeton, NJ: Princeton University Press.

Mandivenga, Ephraim. 1989. "The History and 'Re-Conversion' of the Varemba of Zimbabwe." *Journal of Religion in Africa* 19 (2): 98–124.

Mangcu, Xolela, ed. 2011. *Becoming Worthy Ancestors: Archive, Public Deliberations and Identity in South Africa*. Johannesburg, SA: Wits University Press.

Manson, Andrew. 2013. "Mining and 'Traditional Communities' in South Africa's 'Platinum Belt': Contestations over Land, Leadership and Assets in North-West Province c. 1996–2012." *Journal of Southern African Studies* 39 (2): 409–423.

Markel, Howard. 1997. "Di Goldine Medina (The Golden Land): Historical Perspectives of Eugenics and the East European." *Health Matrix: Journal of Law-Medicine* 7 (1): 49.

Markowitz, Fran. 1996. "Israel as Africa, Africa as Israel: 'Divine Geography' in the Personal Narratives and Community Identity of the Black Hebrew Israelites." *Anthropological Quarterly* 69 (4): 193–205.

Marks, Jonathan. 1995. *Human Biodiversity: Genes, Race, and History*. New York: Aldine de Gruyter.

Marks, Jonathan. 2001. "We're Going to Tell These People Who They Really Are: Science and Relatedness." In *Relative Values: Reconfiguring Kinship Studies*, edited by Sarah Franklin and Susan McKinnon, 355–383. Durham, NC: Duke University Press.

Marks, Jonathan. 2002. *What It Means to Be 98% Chimpanzee: Apes, People, and Their Genes*. Berkeley: University of California Press.

Marks, Jonathan. 2009. "What Is the Viewpoint of Hemoglobin, and Does It Matter?" *History and Philosophy of the Life Sciences* 31 (2): 241–262.

Marks, Jonathan. 2012. "The Origins of Anthropological Genetics." *Current Anthropology* 53 (s5): s161–s172.

Marks, Jonathan. 2017. *Is Science Racist?* Malden, MA: Polity.

Marrocco, Gabriel, and Yann Joly. 2018. "Understanding the Dangers of Genetic Testing in Immigration." *CBA/ABC National*, September 27. http://www.nationalmagazine.ca /Articles/September-2018/Understanding-the-dangers-of-genetic-testing-in-im.aspx.

Martin, Emily. 1994. *Flexible Bodies: Tracking Immunity in American Culture from the Days of Polio to the Age of AIDS*. Boston: Beacon.

Masilela, Ntongela. 2011. "The Transmission Lines of the New African Movement." In *Becoming Worthy Ancestors: Archive, Public Deliberation and Identity in South Africa*, edited by Xolela Mangcu, 17–46. Johannesburg, SA: Wits University Press.

Mathivha, M. E. R. 1987. "The Lemba Characteristics." In *Minorities: Self-Determination and Integration, Conference 2–6 November 1987, Missak Centre*, 1–6. Bryanston, SA: International Freedom Foundation.

Mathivha, M. E. R. 1992. *The Basena/Vamwenye/Balemba*. Pietersburg, SA: Morester.

Matory, J. Lorand. 2005. *Black Atlantic Religion: Tradition, Transnationalism, and Matriarchy in the Afro-Brazilian Candomblé*. Princeton, NJ: Princeton University Press.

Maylam, Paul. 1986. *History of the African People of South Africa: From the Early Iron Age to the 1970s*. Cape Town, SA: Philip.

Mbembe, Achille. 2001. *On the Postcolony*. Berkeley: University of California Press.

McEwan, Cheryl. 2003. "Building a Postcolonial Archive? Gender, Collective Memory and Citizenship in Post-Apartheid South Africa." *Journal of Southern African Studies* 29 (3): 739–757.

McGonigle, Ian Vincent. 2015. "'Jewish Genetics' and the 'Nature' of Israeli Citizenship." *Transversal* 13 (2): 90–102.

McGonigle, Ian V., and Lauren W. Herman. 2015. "Genetic Citizenship: DNA Testing and the Israeli Law of Return." *Journal of Law and the Biosciences* 2 (2): 469–478.

M'charek, Amade. 2005a. *The Human Genome Diversity Project: An Ethnography of Scientific Practice.* New York: Cambridge University Press.

M'charek, Amade. 2005b. "The Mitochondrial Eve of Modern Genetics: Of Peoples and Genomes, or the Routinization of Race." *Science as Culture* 14 (2): 161–183.

M'charek, Amade. 2013. "Beyond Fact or Fiction: On the Materiality of Race in Practice." *Cultural Anthropology* 28 (3): 420–442.

McIntosh, Janet. 2009. *The Edge of Islam: Power, Personhood, and Ethnoreligious Boundaries on the Kenya Coast.* Durham, NC: Duke University Press.

McKay, Ramah. 2012. "Afterlives: Humanitarian Histories and Critical Subjects in Mozambique." *Cultural Anthropology* 27 (2): 286–309.

McKay, Ramah. 2018. *Medicine in the Meantime: The Work of Care in Mozambique.* Durham, NC: Duke University Press.

McLean, G. R., and Trefor Jenkins. 2003. "The Steve Biko Affair: A Case Study in Medical Ethics." *Developing World Bioethics* 3 (1): 77–95.

Mda, Zakes. 2013. *The Sculptors of Mapungubwe.* Cape Town, SA: Kwela.

Meskell, Lynn. 2012. *The Nature of Heritage: The New South Africa.* Malden, MA: Wiley-Blackwell.

Minkley, Gary, Leslie Witz, and Ciraj Rassool. 2017. "Heritage and the Post-antiapartheid." In *Unsettled History: Making South African Public Pasts*, edited by Leslie Witz, Gary Minkley, and Ciraj Rassool, 204–226. Ann Arbor: University of Michigan Press.

Mitchell, J. Clyde. 1956. *The Kalela Dance: Aspects of Social Relationships among Urban Africans in Northern Rhodesia.* Manchester, UK: Manchester University Press.

Miyazaki, Hirokazu. 2004. *The Method of Hope: Anthropology, Philosophy, and Fijian Knowledge.* Palo Alto, CA: Stanford University Press.

Mochama, Vicky. 2018. "DNA Testing to Aid Deportations Leaves Plenty of Room for Misinterpretation and Mistreatment." *Toronto Star*, July 29.

Mokhele, Khoto. 2005. "Tower of Consciousness: Passing of Great Africanist Reminds Us of Struggle for Social and Political Justice." *Sowetan*, December 27, 9.

Montagu, Ashley. [1942] 1997. *Man's Most Dangerous Myth: The Fallacy of Race.* Walnut Creek, CA: AltaMira.

Montoya, Michael J. 2007. "Bioethnic Conscription: Genes, Race, and Mexicana/o Ethnicity in Diabetes Research." *Cultural Anthropology* 22 (1): 94–128.

Montoya, Michael J. 2011. *Making the Mexican Diabetic: Race, Science, and the Genetics of Inequality.* Berkeley: University of California Press.

Moolman, M. 1982. "Tribe of Israel Claim." *Rand Daily Mail*, September 15.

Moore, Henrietta L. 2007. *The Subject of Anthropology: Gender, Symbolism and Psychoanalysis.* Malden, MA: Polity.

Morgensen, Scott Lauria. 2011. *Spaces between Us: Queer Settler Colonialism and Indigenous Decolonization.* Minneapolis: University of Minnesota Press.

Motenda, M. M. 1940. "History of the Western Venda and of the Lemba." In *The Copper Miners of Musina and the Early History of the Zoutpansberg*, edited by N. J. Van Warmelo, 51–70. Pretoria, SA: Government Printer.

Motenda, M. M. 1958. "The Lemba Tribe." *Bantu* 2:61–65.

Mozersky, Jessica. 2012. *Risky Genes: Genetics, Breast Cancer and Jewish Identity*. New York: Routledge.

Mphelo, Manasseh N. 1936. "The Balemba of the Northern Transvaal." *Native Teachers' Journal* 16 (1): 35–44.

Mudimbe, V. Y. 1988. *The Invention of Africa: Gnosis, Philosophy, and the Order of Knowledge*. Bloomington: Indiana University Press.

Mudimbe, V. Y. 1994. *The Idea of Africa*. Bloomington: Indiana University Press.

Murphy, Michelle. 2018. "Against Population, Towards Alterlife." In *Making Kin Not Population: Reconceiving Generations*, edited by Adele E. Clarke and Donna Haraway, 101–124. Chicago: Prickly Paradigm.

Nabarro, Margaret. 1974. "The Music of the Western European Sephardic Jews and the Portuguese Marranos: An Ethnomusicological Study." DMus diss., University of South Africa.

Nash, Catherine. 2004. "Genetic Kinship." *Cultural Studies* 18 (1): 1–33.

Nash, Catherine. 2015. *Genetic Geographies: The Trouble with Ancestry*. Minneapolis: University of Minnesota Press.

Ndahinda, Felix Mukwiza. 2011. *Indigenousness in Africa: A Contested Legal Framework for Empowerment of "Marginalized" Communities*. The Hague: Asser.

Nel, Johan. 2011. "'Gods, Graves, and Scholars': The Return of Human Remains to Their Resting Place." In *Mapungubwe Remembered: Contributions to Mapungubwe by the University of Pretoria*, edited by Sian Tiley-Nel, 230–239. Pretoria, SA: University of Pretoria Press.

Nelson, Alondra. 2008a. "Bio Science: Genetic Genealogy Testing and the Pursuit of African Ancestry." *Social Studies of Science* 38 (5): 759–783.

Nelson, Alondra. 2008b. "The Factness of Diaspora: The Social Sources of Genetic Genealogy." In *Revisiting Race in a Genomic Age*, edited by Barbara A. Koenig, Sandra Soo-Jin Lee, and Sarah S. Richardson, 253–268. New Brunswick, NJ: Rutgers University Press.

Nelson, Alondra. 2016. *The Social Life of DNA: Race, Reparations, and Reconciliation after the Genome*. Boston: Beacon.

Newton, Esther. 1972. *Mother Camp: Female Impersonators in America*. Englewood Cliffs, NJ: Prentice-Hall.

Nienaber, Willem Coenraad, and Maryna Steyn. 2011. "Republic of South Africa." In *The Routledge Handbook of Archaeological Human Remains and Legislation: An International Guide to Laws and Practice in the Excavation and Treatment of Archaeological Human Remains*, edited by Nicholas Márquez-Grant and Linda Fibiger, 501–512. New York: Routledge.

Ntsebeza, Lungisile. 2005. *Democracy Compromised: Chiefs and the Politics of the Land in South Africa*. Leiden: Brill.

Nurse, G. T., M. C. Botha, and Trefor Jenkins. 1977. "Sero-Genetic Studies on the San of South West Africa." *Human Heredity* 27 (2): 81–98.

Nuttall, Sarah. 2005. *Beautiful Ugly: African and Diaspora Aesthetics*. Cape Town, SA: Kwela.

Nuttall, Sarah, and Carli Coetzee, eds. 1998. *Negotiating the Past: The Making of Memory in South Africa*. Oxford, UK: Oxford University Press.

Nyamnjoh, Francis B. 2007. "'Ever-Diminishing Circles': The Paradoxes of Belonging in Botswana." In *Indigenous Experience Today*, edited by Marisol de la Cadena and Orin Starn, 305–332. New York: Berg.

Obarrio, Juan. 2014. *The Spirit of the Laws in Mozambique*. Chicago: University of Chicago Press.

Olarte Sierra, María Fernanda, and Adriana Díaz Del Castillo Hernández. 2013. "'We Are All the Same, We All Are Mestizos': Imagined Populations and Nations in Genetics Research in Colombia." *Science as Culture* 23 (2): 226–252.

Olender, Maurice. 1992. *The Languages of Paradise: Race, Religion, and Philology in the Nineteenth Century*. Cambridge, MA: Harvard University Press.

Omi, Michael, and Howard Winant. 1986. *Racial Formation in the United States: From the 1960s to the 1980s*. New York: Routledge and Kegan Paul.

Ong, Aihwa, and Stephen J. Collier, eds. 2005. *Global Assemblages: Technology, Politics, and Ethics as Anthropological Problems*. Malden, MA: Blackwell.

Oomen, Barbara. 2005. *Chiefs in South Africa*. Madison: University of Wisconsin Press.

Ostrer, Harry. 2012. *Legacy: A Genetic History of the Jewish People*. New York: Oxford University Press.

Özyürek, Esra. 2015. *Being German, Becoming Muslim: Race, Religion, and Conversion in the New Europe*. Princeton, NJ: Princeton University Press.

Palmié, Stephan. 2007. "Genomics, Divination, 'Racecraft.'" *American Ethnologist* 34 (2): 205–222.

Pálsson, Gísli. 2012. "Decode Me! Anthropology and Personal Genomics." *Current Anthropology* 53 (s5): s185–s195.

Parfitt, Tudor. 1985. *Operation Moses: The Untold Story of the Secret Exodus of the Falasha Jews from Ethiopia*. New York: Stein and Day.

Parfitt, Tudor. 1987. *The Thirteenth Gate: Travels among the Lost Tribes of Israel*. Bethesda, MD: Adler and Adler.

Parfitt, Tudor. 1992. *Journey to the Vanished City: The Search for a Lost Tribe of Israel*. London: Hodder and Stoughton.

Parfitt, Tudor. 2000. *Journey to the Vanished City: The Search for a Lost Tribe of Israel*. New York: Vintage.

Parfitt, Tudor. 2003. "Constructing Black Jews: Genetic Tests and the Lemba—The 'Black Jews' of South Africa." *Developing World Bioethics* 3 (2): 112–118.

Parfitt, Tudor. 2013. *Black Jews in Africa and the Americas*. Cambridge, MA: Harvard University Press.

Parfitt, Tudor, and Yulia Egorova. 2005. "Genetics, History, and Identity: The Case of the Bene Israel and the Lemba." *Culture, Medicine and Psychiatry* 29:193–224.

Parfitt, Tudor, and Yulia Egorova. 2006. *Genetics, Mass Media and Identity: A Case Study of the Genetic Research on the Lemba and Bene Israel*. New York: Routledge.

Parfitt, Tudor, Christopher Hale, and David Espar. 2000. *Lost Tribes of Israel*. South Burlington, VT: WGBH Boston Video.

Parreñas, Juno Salazar. 2018. *Decolonizing Extinction: The Work of Care in Orangutan Rehabilitation*. Durham, NC: Duke University Press.

Parreñas, Juno Salazar. Forthcoming. "Reaching the Limits of Decoloniality and Indigenous Knowledges in Southeast Asia." *History and Theory*.

Patterson, Tiffany Ruby, and Robin D. G. Kelley. 2000. "Unfinished Migrations: Reflections on the African Diaspora and the Making of the Modern World." *African Studies Review* 43 (1): 11–45.

Paxson, Heather. 2004. *Making Modern Mothers: Ethics and Family Planning in Urban Greece*. Berkeley: University of California Press.

Pearson, M. N. 2000. "The Indian Ocean and the Red Sea." In *History of Islam in Africa*, edited by Nehemia Levtzion and Randall Lee Pouwels, 37–59. Athens: Ohio University Press.

Pelican, Michaela. 2009. "Complexities of Indigeneity and Autochthony: An African Example." *American Ethnologist* 36 (1): 52–65.

Peterson, Derek R., Kodzo Gavua, and Ciraj Rassool, eds. 2015. *The Politics of Heritage in Africa: Economies, Histories, and Infrastructures*. New York: Cambridge University Press.

Peterson, Kristin. 2009. "Phantom Epistemologies." In *Fieldwork Is Not What It Used to Be: Learning Anthropology's Method in a Time of Transition*, edited by James D. Faubion and George E. Marcus, 37–51. Ithaca, NY: Cornell University Press.

Peterson, Kristin. 2014. *Speculative Markets: Drug Circuits and Derivative Life in Nigeria*. Durham, NC: Duke University Press.

Petryna, Adriana. 2002. *Life Exposed: Biological Citizens after Chernobyl*. Princeton, NJ: Princeton University Press.

Pierre, Jemima. 2013. *The Predicament of Blackness: Postcolonial Ghana and the Politics of Race*. Chicago: University of Chicago Press.

Pikirayi, Innocent. 2011. *Tradition, Archaeological Heritage Protection and Communities in the Limpopo Province of South Africa*. Addis Ababa: Organisation for Social Science Research in Eastern and Southern Africa.

Piot, Charles. 1999. *Remotely Global: Village Modernity in West Africa*. Chicago: University of Chicago Press.

Piot, Charles. 2010. *Nostalgia for the Future: West Africa after the Cold War*. Chicago: University of Chicago Press.

Piscitelli, Matthew. 2019. "Introduction: Bones and Chromosomes: Ancient DNA Revolution in Archaeology (Part I)." *SAA Archaeological Record* 19 (1): 15–17.

Pitarch, Pedro. 2010. *The Jaguar and the Priest: An Ethnography of Tzeltal Souls*. Austin: University of Texas Press.

Plaatje, Solomon Tshekisho. 1916. *Native Life in South Africa, before and since the European War and the Boer Rebellion*. London: King.

Pollock, Anne. 2012. *Medicating Race: Heart Disease and Durable Preoccupations with Difference*. Durham, NC: Duke University Press.

Pollock, Anne. 2014. "Places of Pharmaceutical Knowledge-Making: Global Health, Postcolonial Science, and Hope in South African Drug Discovery." *Social Studies of Science* 44 (6): 848–873.

Pollock, Anne. 2019. *Synthesizing Hope: Matter, Knowledge, and Place in South African Drug Discovery*. Chicago: University of Chicago Press.

Posel, Deborah. 1991. *The Making of Apartheid, 1948–1961*. Oxford, UK: Clarendon.

Posel, Deborah. 2001. "Race as Common Sense: Racial Classification in Twentieth-Century South Africa." *African Studies Review.* 44 (2): 87–113.

Pouwels, Randall Lee. 2000. "The East African Coast, C. 780 to 1900 C.E." In *The History of Islam in Africa*, edited by Nehemia Levtzion and Randall Lee Pouwels, 251–272. Athens: Ohio University Press.

Povinelli, Elizabeth A. 2002. *The Cunning of Recognition: Indigenous Alterities and the Making of Australian Multiculturalism.* Durham, NC: Duke University Press.

Pugach, Sara. 2004. "Carl Meinhof and the German Influence on Nicholas van Warmelo's Ethnological and Linguistic Writing, 1927–1935." *Journal of Southern African Studies* 30 (4): 825–845.

Rabinowitz, Aaron. 2020. "Israeli High Court Allows DNA Testing to Prove Judaism." *Haaretz*, January 24. https://www.haaretz.com/israel-news/.premium-israeli-high -court-allows-dna-testing-to-prove-judaism-1.8439615.

Radin, Joanna, and Emma Kowal. 2015. "Indigenous Blood and Ethical Regimes in the United States and Australia since the 1960s." *American Ethnologist* 42 (4): 749–765.

Rajagopalan, Ramya, and Joan H. Fujimura. 2012. "Making History via DNA, Making DNA from History: Deconstructing the Race-Disease Connection in Admixture Mapping." In *Genetics and the Unsettled Past: The Collision of DNA, Race, and History*, edited by Keith Wailoo, Alondra Nelson, and Catherine Lee, 143–163. New Brunswick, NJ: Rutgers University Press.

Ralushai, N. V. 1998. *Report of the Ralushai Commission of Inquiry into Traditional Leadership Disputes and Claims in the Northern Province of the Republic of South Africa.* Cape Town, SA: University of Cape Town.

Ramphele, Mamphela. 2008. *Laying Ghosts to Rest: Dilemmas of the Transformation in South Africa.* Cape Town, SA: Tafelberg.

Ramsay, Michèle, Jantina de Vries, Himla Soodyall, Shane A. Norris, and Osman Sankoh. 2014. "Ethical Issues in Genomic Research on the African Continent: Experiences and Challenges to Ethics Review Committees." *Human Genomics* 8 (15): 1–6.

Ramsay, M., and T. Jenkins. 1988. "Alpha-Globin Gene Cluster Haplotypes in the Kalahari San and Southern African Bantu-Speaking Blacks." *American Journal of Human Genetics* 43 (4): 527–533.

Ramutsindela, Maano F. 2015. "Transfrontier Conservation and Land Reform Policy." In *Land Divided, Land Restored: Land Reform in South Africa for the 21st Century*, edited by Ben Cousins and Cherryl Walker, 175–190. Johannesburg, SA: Jacana.

Rana, Junaid. 2011. *Terrifying Muslims: Race and Labor in the South Asian Diaspora.* Durham, NC: Duke University Press.

Rand Daily Mail. 1985. "Black Jews a Lost Biblical Tribe?" September 1.

Ranger, Terence. 1983. "The Invention of Tradition in Colonial Africa." In *The Invention of Tradition*, edited by Eric Hobsbawm and Terence Ranger, 211–262. Cambridge, UK: Cambridge University Press.

Ranger, Terence. 1993. "The Invention of Tradition Revisited: The Case of Colonial Africa." In *Legitimacy and the State in Twentieth-Century Africa*, edited by Terence Ranger and Olufemi Vaughan, 62–111. London: Palgrave Macmillan.

Rapp, Rayna. 1999. *Testing Women, Testing the Fetus: The Social Impact of Amniocentesis in America*. New York: Routledge.

Rassool, Ciraj. 2015. "Human Remains, the Disciplines of the Dead, and the South African Memorial Complex." In *The Politics of Heritage: Economies, Histories, and Infrastructures*, edited by Derek R. Peterson, Kodzo Gavua, and Ciraj Rassool, 133–156. Cambridge, UK: Cambridge University Press.

Reardon, Jenny. 2005. *Race to the Finish: Identity and Governance in an Age of Genomics*. Princeton, NJ: Princeton University Press.

Reardon, Jenny. 2006. "Creating Participatory Subjects: Race, Science, and Democracy in a Genomic Age." In *The New Political Sociology of Science: Institutions, Networks, and Power*, edited by Scott Frickel and Kelly Moore, 351–377. Madison: University of Wisconsin Press.

Reardon, Jenny. 2012. "The Democratic, Anti-Racist Genome? Technoscience at the Limits of Liberalism." *Science as Culture* 21 (1): 25–47.

Reiter, Rayna R., ed. 1975. *Toward an Anthropology of Women*. New York: Monthly Review Press.

Rich, Paul B. 1993. *Hope and Despair: English-Speaking Intellectuals and South African Politics, 1896–1976*. London: British Academic Press.

Robins, Steven. 2001. "NGOs, 'Bushmen' and Double Vision: The ≠khomani San Land Claim and the Cultural Politics of 'Community' and 'Development' in the Kalahari." *Journal of Southern African Studies* 27 (4): 833–853.

Robins, Steven, ed. 2005. *Limits to Liberation after Apartheid: Citizenship, Governance and Culture*. Athens: Ohio University Press.

Robins, Steven. 2008. "Rights." In *New South African Keywords*, edited by Nick Shepherd and Steven Robins, 182–194. Athens: Ohio University Press.

Rosaldo, Michelle Zimbalist, and Louise Lamphere. 1974. *Woman, Culture, and Society*. Stanford, CA: Stanford University Press.

Rose, Nikolas. 2006. *The Politics of Life Itself: Biomedicine, Power, and Subjectivity in the Twenty-First Century*. Princeton, NJ: Princeton University Press.

Royal, Charmaine D., John Novembre, Stephanie M. Fullerton, David B. Goldstein, Jeffrey C. Long, Michael J. Barnshad, and Andrew G. Clark. 2010. "Inferring Genetic Ancestry: Opportunities, Challenges, and Implications." *American Journal of Human Genetics* 86: 661–673.

Rubin, Gayle S. 1975. "The Traffic in Women: Notes on the 'Political Economy' of Sex." In *Toward an Anthropology of Women*, edited by Rayna Reiter, 157–210. New York: Monthly Review Press.

Rudnyckyj, Daromir. 2010. *Spiritual Economies: Islam, Globalization, and the Afterlife of Development*. Ithaca, NY: Cornell University Press.

Sanders, Edith R. 1969. "The Hamitic Hypothesis: Its Origin and Functions in Time Perspective." *The Journal of African History* 10 (4): 521–532.

Schapera, Isaac. 1929. "A Working Classification of the Bantu Peoples of Africa." *Man* 29:82–87.

Schlömann, Hr. Missionar. 1894. "Die Malepa in Transvaal." *Verhandlungen der Berliner Gesellschaft für Anthropologie, Ethnologie und Urgeschichte* 26:64–70.

Schneider, David M. 1984. *A Critique of the Study of Kinship*. Ann Arbor: University of Michigan Press.

Schramm, Katharina. 2014. "Claims of Descent: Race and Science in Contemporary South Africa." *Vienna Working Papers in Ethnography* 3:1–28.

Schramm, Katharina. 2015. "Enacting Differences, Articulating Critique: Recent Approaches to Race in the Social Analysis of Science and Technology." *Science as Culture* 24 (3): 340–350.

Schramm, Katharina. 2016. "Casts, Bones and DNA: Interrogating the Relationship between Science and Postcolonial Indigeneity in Contemporary South Africa." *Anthropology Southern Africa* 39 (2) 131–144.

Schramm, Katharina, Kristine Krause, and Greer Valley. 2018. "Introduction: Voice, Noise and Silence: Resonances of Political Subjectivities." *Critical African Studies* 10 (3): 245–256.

Schramm, Katharina, David Skinner, and Richard Rottenburg, eds. 2012. *Identity Politics and the New Genetics: Re/creating Categories of Difference and Belonging*. New York: Berghahn.

Schumaker, Lyn. 2001. *Africanizing Anthropology: Fieldwork, Networks, and the Making of Cultural Knowledge in Central Africa*. Durham, NC: Duke University Press.

Scott, Colin. 1996. "Science for the West, Myth for the Rest? The Case of James Bay Cree Knowledge Construction." In *Naked Science: Anthropological Inquiries into Boundaries, Power and Knowledge*, edited by Laura Nader, 69–86. London: Routledge.

Scott, Joan W. 1991. "The Evidence of Experience." *Critical Inquiry* 17 (4): 773–797.

Seeman, Don. 2009. *One People, One Blood: Ethiopian-Israelis and the Return to Judaism*. New Brunswick, NJ: Rutgers University Press.

Sharon, Jeremy. 2017. "'Who Is a Jew?' Can Now Be Answered by Genetic Testing." *Jerusalem Post*, October 3. https://www.jpost.com/Israel-News/Politics-And-Diplomacy/New-law-says-genetic-test-valid-for-determining-Jewish-status-in-some-cases-506584.

Shepherd, Nick, and Steven L. Robins, eds. 2008. *New South African Keywords*. Athens: Ohio University Press.

Shimoni, Gideon. 2003. *Community and Conscience: The Jews in Apartheid South Africa*. Cape Town, SA: Philip.

Shohat, Ella. 2006. *Taboo Memories, Diasporic Voices*. Durham, NC: Duke University Press.

Simpson, Audra. 2007. "On Ethnographic Refusal: Indigeneity, 'Voice' and Colonial Citizenship." *Junctures* 9 (1): 67–80.

Simpson, Audra. 2014. *Mohawk Interruptus: Political Life across the Borders of Settler States*. Durham, NC: Duke University Press.

Skorecki, K., S. Selig, S. Blazer, R. Bradman, N. Bradman, P. J. Waburton, M. Ismajlowicz, and M. F. Hammer. 1997. "Y Chromosomes of Jewish Priests." *Nature* 385 (6611): 32.

Slabbert, Melodie, and Michael S. Pepper. 2010. "'A Room of Our Own?': Legal Lacunae Regarding Genomic Sovereignty in South Africa." *Tydskrif vir Hedendaagse Romeins-Hollandse Reg (Journal of Contemporary Roman-Dutch Law)* 73:432–450.

Sommer, Marianne. 2010. "DNA and Cultures of Remembrance: Anthropological Genetics, Biohistories and Biosocialities." *BioSocieties* 5 (3): 366–390.

Soodyall, Himla. 2003. "Reflections and Prospects for Anthropological Genetics in South Africa." In *Genetic Nature/Culture: Anthropology and Science beyond the Two-Culture Divide*, edited by Alan H. Goodman, Deborah Heath, and M. Susan Lindee, 200–216. Berkeley: University of California Press.

Soodyall, Himla, Bharti Morar, and Trefor Jenkins. 2002. "The Human Genome as Archive: Some Illustrations from the South." In *Refiguring the Archive*, edited by Carolyn Hamilton, Verne Harris, Jane Taylor, Michele Pickover, Graeme Reid, and Razia Saleh, 179–192. Boston: Kluwer Academic.

South Africa, Department of Environmental Affairs. 2019. "Transfrontier Conservation Areas: Greater Mapungubwe Transfrontier Conservation Area." https://www.environment.gov.za/projectsprogrammes/transfrontier_conservation_areas#shashe.

South African National Government. n.d. "South African National Parks (SANParks) Overview." Accessed March 12, 2020. https://nationalgovernment.co.za/units/view/174/south-african-national-parks-sanparks.

South African San Institute. 2017. *San Code of Research Ethics*. March 6. http://trust-project.eu/wp-content/uploads/2017/03/San-Code-of-RESEARCH-Ethics-Booklet-final.pdf.

Spivak, Gayatri Chakravorty. 1993. *Outside in the Teaching Machine*. New York: Routledge.

Spurdle, Amanda B., and Trefor Jenkins. 1996. "The Origins of the Lemba 'Black Jews' of Southern Africa: Evidence From p12F2 and Other Y-Chromosome Markers." *American Journal of Human Genetics* 59 (5): 1126–1133.

Star, Susan Leigh, and James R. Griesemer. 1989. "Institutional Ecology, 'Translations' and Boundary Objects: Amateurs and Professionals in Berkeley's Museum of Vertebrate Zoology, 1907–39." *Social Studies of Science* 19 (3): 387–420.

Starn, Orin. 2004. *Ishi's Brain: In Search of America's Last "Wild" Indian*. New York: Norton.

Stayt, Hugh Arthur. 1931. "Notes on the Balemba." *Journal of the Royal Anthropological Institute of Great Britain and Ireland* 61:231–238.

Stewart, Kathleen. 2012. "Precarity's Forms." *Cultural Anthropology* 27 (3): 518–525.

Steyn, Maryna. 1994. "An Assessment of the Health Status and Physical Characteristics of the Prehistoric Population from Mapungubwe." PhD diss., University of the Witwatersrand.

Steyn, Maryna. 2011. "Mapungubwe and K2: Bones of Contention over 75 Years." In *Mapungubwe Remembered: Contributions to Mapungubwe by the University of Pretoria*, edited by Sian Tiley-Nel, 222–229. Pretoria, SA: University of Pretoria Press.

Strathern, Marilyn. 1988. *The Gender of the Gift: Problems with Women and Problems with Society in Melanesia*. Berkeley: University of California Press.

Strathern, Marilyn. 1991. *Partial Connections*. Savage, MD: Rowman and Littlefield.

Strathern, Marilyn. 1992a. *After Nature: English Kinship in the Late Twentieth Century*. Cambridge, UK: Cambridge University Press.

Strathern, Marilyn. 1992b. *Reproducing the Future: Essays on Anthropology, Kinship, and the New Reproductive Technologies*. New York: Routledge.

Sturm, Circe. 2002. *Blood Politics: Race, Culture, and Identity in the Cherokee Nation of Oklahoma*. Berkeley: University of California Press.

Sturm, Circe. 2011. *Becoming Indian: The Struggle over Cherokee Identity in the Twenty-First Century*. Santa Fe, NM: School for Advanced Research Press.

Sunder Rajan, Kaushik. 2006. *Biocapital: The Constitution of Postgenomic Life*. Durham, NC: Duke University Press.

Sylvain, Renée. 2005. "Disorderly Development: Globalization and the Idea of 'Culture' in the Kalahari." *American Ethnologist* 32 (3): 354–370.

TallBear, Kimberly. 2003. "DNA, Blood, and Racializing the Tribe." *Wicazo Sa Review* 18 (1): 81–107.

TallBear, Kimberly. 2013. *Native American DNA: Tribal Belonging and the False Promise of Genetic Science*. Minneapolis: University of Minnesota Press.

TallBear, Kim. 2018. "Making Love and Relations beyond Settler Sex and Family." In *Making Kin Not Population: Reconceiving Generations*, edited by Adele E. Clarke and Donna Haraway, 145–166. Chicago: Prickly Paradigm.

Tamarkin, Noah. 2011. "Religion as Race, Recognition as Democracy." *Annals of the American Academy of Political and Social Science* 637 (1): 148–164.

Tamarkin, Noah, and Rachel Giraudo. 2014. "African Indigenous Citizenship." In *The Routledge Handbook of Global Citizenship Studies*, edited by Engin F. Isin and Peter Nyers, 545–556. New York: Routledge.

Taussig, Karen-Sue. 2009. *Ordinary Genomes: Science, Citizenship, and Genetic Identities*. Durham, NC: Duke University Press.

Taussig, Michael T. 1986. *Shamanism, Colonialism, and the Wild Man: A Study in Terror and Healing*. Chicago: University of Chicago Press.

Templeton, Alan R. 2003. "Human Races in the Context of Recent Human Evolution: A Molecular Genetic Perspective." In *Genetic Nature/Culture: Anthropology and Science beyond the Two-Culture Divide*, edited by Alan H. Goodman, Deborah Heath, and M. Susan Lindee, 234–257. Berkeley: University of California Press.

Tenenbaum, Shelly, and Lynn Davidman. 2007. "It's in My Genes: Biological Discourse and Essentialist Views of Identity among Contemporary American Jews." *Sociological Quarterly* 48 (3): 435–450.

Thomas, David Hurst. 2000. *Skull Wars: Kennewick Man, Archaeology, and the Battle for Native American Identity*. New York: Basic Books.

Thomas, Deborah A. 2004. *Modern Blackness: Nationalism, Globalization, and the Politics of Culture in Jamaica*. Durham, NC: Duke University Press.

Thomas, Deborah A. 2009. "The Violence of Diaspora: Governmentality, Class Cultures, and Circulations." *Radical History Review* 103:83–104.

Thomas, Mark G., Tudor Parfitt, Deborah A. Weiss, Karl Skorecki, James F. Wilson, Magdel le Roux, Neil Bradman, and David B. Goldstein. 2000. "Y Chromosomes Traveling South: The Cohen Modal Haplotype and the Origins of the Lemba—The 'Black Jews of Southern Africa.'" *American Journal of Human Genetics* 66 (2): 674–686.

Thomas, M. G., K. Skorecki, H. Ben-Ami, T. Parfitt, N. Bradman, and D. B. Goldstein. 1998. "Origins of Old Testament Priests." *Nature* 394 (6689): 138–140.

Thompson, Charis. 2005. *Making Parents: The Ontological Choreography of Reproductive Technologies*. Cambridge, MA: MIT Press.

Thornberry, Elizabeth. 2011. "Defining Crime through Punishment: Sexual Assault in the Eastern Cape, c.1835–1900." *Journal of Southern African Studies* 37 (3): 415–430.

Thornberry, Elizabeth. 2019. *Colonizing Consent: Rape and Governance in South Africa's Eastern Cape.* New York: Cambridge University Press.

Tiley-Nel, Sian, ed. 2011. *Mapungubwe Remembered: Contributions to Mapungubwe by the University of Pretoria.* Pretoria, SA: University of Pretoria Press.

Tilley, Helen. 2010. "Africa, Imperialism, and Anthropology." In *Ordering Africa: Anthropology, European Imperialism, and the Politics of Knowledge,* edited by Helen Tilley and Robert J. Gordon, 1–45. Manchester, UK: Manchester University Press.

Trouillot, Michel-Rolph. [1995] 2015. *Silencing the Past: Power and the Production of History.* Boston: Beacon.

Trouillot, Michel-Rolph. 2003. *Global Transformations: Anthropology and the Modern World.* New York: Palgrave Macmillan.

Tsing, Anna Lowenhaupt. 1993. *In the Realm of the Diamond Queen: Marginality in an Out-of-the-Way Place.* Princeton, NJ: Princeton University Press.

Tsing, Anna Lowenhaupt. 2005. *Friction: An Ethnography of Global Connection.* Princeton, NJ: Princeton University Press.

Turner, Robin L. 2013. "Land Restitution, Traditional Leadership and Belonging: Defining Barokologadi Identity." *Journal of Modern African Studies* 51 (03): 507–531.

Turner, Robin L. 2016. "Lasting Legacies: Contemporary Struggles and Historical Dispossession in South Africa." *Comparative Studies of South Asia, Africa and the Middle East* 36 (2): 275–292.

UNESCO. n.d. "About World Heritage." Accessed October 8, 2019. http://whc.unesco.org/en/about/.

Vail, Leroy, ed. 1989. *The Creation of Tribalism in Southern Africa.* Berkeley: University of California Press.

Van Onselen, Charles. 1996. *The Seed Is Mine: The Life of Kas Maine, a South African Sharecropper, 1894–1985.* New York: Hill and Wang.

Van Warmelo, N. J. 1935. *A Preliminary Survey of the Bantu Tribes of South Africa.* Pretoria, SA: Government Printer.

Van Warmelo, N. J. 1937. "Grouping and Ethnic History." In *The Bantu-Speaking Tribes of South Africa,* edited by I. Schapera, 43–66. London: Routledge and Kegan Paul.

Van Warmelo, N. J., ed. 1940. *The Copper Miners of Musina and the Early History of the Zoutpansberg.* Pretoria, SA: Government Printer.

Van Warmelo, N. J. 1946. "Grouping and Ethnic History." In *The Bantu-Speaking Tribes of South Africa,* edited by I. Schapera, 43–66. London: Routledge and Kegan Paul.

Van Warmelo, N. J. 1950. "Grouping and Ethnic History." In *The Bantu-Speaking Tribes of South Africa,* edited by I. Schapera, 43–66. London: Routledge and Kegan Paul.

Van Warmelo, N.J. 1952. *Language Map of South Africa.* Pretoria, SA: Government Printer.

Van Warmelo, N. J. 1989. *Venda Dictionary: Tshivenda-English.* Pretoria, SA: van Schaik.

Van Warmelo, N. J., and W. M. D. Phophi. 1967. *Venda Law.* Pretoria, SA: Government Printer.

Vergès, Françoise. 2003. "Writing on Water: Peripheries, Flows, Capital, and Struggles in the Indian Ocean." *Positions: East Asia Cultures Critique* 11 (1): 241–257.

Vergès, Françoise. 2005. "One World, Many Maps." *Interventions: International Journal of Postcolonial Studies* 7 (3): 342–345.

Verslaggeefster. 1978. "Lemba's Glo Hul Redding Le in Apartheid." *Hoofstad* 11 (74): 2.

Vincent, Louise. 2008. "Cutting Tradition: The Political Regulation of Traditional Circumcision Rites in South Africa's Liberal Democratic Order." *Journal of Southern African Studies* 34 (1): 77–91.

Vora, Kalindi. 2015. *Life Support: Biocapital and the New History of Outsourced Labor.* Minneapolis: University of Minnesota Press.

Wade, Nicholas. 2014. *A Troublesome Inheritance: Genes, Race, and Human History.* New York: Penguin.

Wade, Peter. 2017. *Degrees of Mixture, Degrees of Freedom: Genomics, Multiculturalism, and Race in Latin America.* Durham, NC: Duke University Press.

Wade, Peter, Carlos López Beltrán, Eduardo Restrepo, and Ricardo Ventura Santos, eds. 2014. *Mestizo Genomics: Race Mixture, Nation, and Science in Latin America.* Durham, NC: Duke University Press.

Wagner, Sarah E. 2008. *To Know Where He Lies: DNA Technology and the Search for Srebrenica's Missing.* Berkeley: University of California Press.

Wailoo, Keith, Alondra Nelson, and Catherine Lee, eds. 2012. *Genetics and the Unsettled Past: The Collision of DNA, Race, and History.* New Brunswick, NJ: Rutgers University Press.

Wailoo, Keith, and Stephen Gregory Pemberton. 2006. *The Troubled Dream of Genetic Medicine: Ethnicity and Innovation in Tay-Sachs, Cystic Fibrosis, and Sickle Cell Disease.* Baltimore, MD: Johns Hopkins University Press.

Wainana, Binyavanga. 2005. "How to Write about Africa." *Granta* 92 (Winter): 92–94.

Walker, Cherryl. 2014. "Critical Reflections on South Africa's 1913 Natives Land Act and Its Legacies: Introduction." *Journal of Southern African Studies* 40 (4): 655–665.

Wasserstrom, Steven M. 1995. *Between Muslim and Jew: The Problem of Symbiosis under Early Islam.* Princeton, NJ: Princeton University Press.

Weitzman, Steven. 2017. *The Origin of the Jews: The Quest for Roots in a Rootless Age.* Princeton, NJ: Princeton University Press.

West, Martin. 1988. "Confusing Categories: Population Groups, National States and Citizenship." In *South African Keywords: The Uses and Abuses of Political Concepts*, edited by Emile Boonzaier and John Sharp, 100–110. Cape Town, SA: Philip.

Weston, Kath. 1991. *Families We Choose: Lesbians, Gays, Kinship.* New York: Columbia University Press.

White, Hylton. 2010. "Outside the Dwelling of Culture: Estrangement and Difference in Postcolonial Zululand." *Anthropological Quarterly* 83 (3): 497–518.

White, Hylton. 2015. "Custom, Normativity and Authority in South Africa." *Journal of Southern African Studies* 41 (5): 1005–1017.

White, Luise. 2000. *Speaking with Vampires: Rumor and History in Colonial Africa.* Berkeley: University of California Press.

Williams, Brackette F. 1989. "A Class Act: Anthropology and the Race to Nation across Ethnic Terrain." *Annual Review of Anthropology* 18:401–444.

Williams, J. Michael. 2010. *Chieftaincy, the State, and Democracy: Political Legitimacy in Post-Apartheid South Africa.* Bloomington: Indiana University Press.

Witz, Leslie, Gary Minkley, and Ciraj Rassool, eds. 2017. *Unsettled History: Making South African Public Pasts*. Ann Arbor: University of Michigan Press.

Worby, Eric. 1994. "Maps, Names, and Ethnic Games: The Epistemology and Iconography of Colonial Power in Northwestern Zimbabwe." *Journal of Southern African Studies* 20 (3) 371–392.

Wright, John. 2016. "Making Identities in the Thukela-Mzimvubu Region c.1770–c.1940." In *Tribing and Untribing the Archive: Identity and the Material Record in Southern KwaZulu-Natal in the Late Independent and Colonial Periods*, edited by Carolyn Hamilton and Nessa Leibhammer, 182–215. Pietermaritzburg, SA: University of KwaZulu-Natal Press.

Yanagisako, Sylvia Junko. 1985. *Transforming the Past: Tradition and Kinship among Japanese Americans*. Palo Alto, CA: Stanford University Press.

Yanagisako, Sylvia Junko. 2002. *Producing Culture and Capital: Family Firms in Italy*. Princeton, NJ: Princeton University Press.

Yanagisako, Sylvia Junko, and Jane Fishburne Collier. 1987. "Toward a Unified Analysis of Gender and Kinship." In *Gender and Kinship: Essays toward a Unified Analysis*, edited by Jane Fishburne Collier and Sylvia Junko Yanagisako, 14–50. Palo Alto, CA: Stanford University Press.

Yusoff, Kathryn. 2013. "Geologic Life: Prehistory, Climate, Futures in the Anthropocene." *Environment and Planning D: Society and Space* 31 (5): 779–795.

Yusoff, Kathryn. 2019. *A Billion Black Anthropocenes or None*. Minneapolis: University of Minnesota Press.

Zengin, Asli. 2019. "The Afterlife of Gender: Sovereignty, Intimacy, and Muslim Funerals of Transgender People in Turkey." *Cultural Anthropology* 34 (1): 78–102.

Zhan, Mei. 2009. *Other-Worldly: Making Chinese Medicine through Transnational Frames*. Durham, NC: Duke University Press.

Zhang, Sarah. 2018. "The First DNA Test as Political Stunt." *Atlantic*, October 15.

Zoloth, Laurie. 2003. "Yearning for the Long Lost Home: The Lemba and the Jewish Narrative of Genetic Return." *Developing World Bioethics* 3 (2): 127–132.

INDEX

Falashas, 1, 172

Fallahins, 94–95

Fassin, Didier, 24, 59, 203n67

feminism, Jewish, 70, 199n15

Fetakgomo, 120, 212n1

forced removals, 178

Freedom Charter (1955), 114–15

Fujimura, Joan, 11, 13

Fullwiley, Duana, 11, 62

funerals, 14–15, 65, 112, 120, 161, 168, 177, 218n23. *See also* rituals, burial

Ga-Maesela. *See* India/Indië (village); Mohlotl-wane (village)

Gencor Mining Company, 29, 41–44

gender: chieftaincy and, 209nn6–7; ethnic recognition and, 104; genetic ancestry research and, 9, 66, 198n8, 201n35, 208n10; kinship and, 122, 212n3; Lemba lineages and, 130–31, 142. *See also* Y chromosome studies

genealogies, Lemba, 148–52, 161, 172; chieftaincy and, 127–34, *131*, 140; endogamy and, 126, 142–44; politics of, 125, 130, 145. *See also* charts, genealogical

genealogy: genetic ancestry and, 122–23, 130, 134, 141, 144–45; Jewish identity and, 84, 208n9

genetic afterlives, 187, 194–95; and circulation of genetic data, 4–5, 23–24, 62, 200n28; citizenship and, 90, 122; definition, 4; diaspora and, 26, 59–60; and indigeneity, 156, 169–70, 172, 174; and other theorizations of afterlives, 23–24, 203n67; refusal as, 27; relatedness and, 144; research subjects as theorists, 4–5, 10–11, 22, 24–25

genetic ancestry, Lemba: interpretations of, 1–2, 10, 24–25, 62, 117, 134, 198n13; Jewish diaspora and, 70, 77; and the LCA, 30, 49, 188–90; Mapungubwe remains and, 156; moratorium on testing, 27, 187–92, 195; participation in research, 30–32, 51–52, 90, 98, 118, 191, 194–95; as puzzle, 17, 21; recognition and, 117, 134; South African politics and, 7, 61. *See also* Parfitt, Tudor; Parfitt Lemba ancestry study; Spurdle and Jenkins genetic ancestry study

genetic ancestry research, 101, 199n21, 200n28; critiques of, 11–14, 59, 207n3; di-

aspora and, 83–84; genealogy and, 122–23, 130, 134, 141, 144–45; human diversity and, 10; Jewish, 2, 6, 59, 70, 77; kinship and, 2, 13, 121, 144–45; Lemba oral histories and, 1, 3, 14, 49–52, 63, 188–89, 194–95, 197n6; Mapungubwe reburial and, 156; medicine and, 10, 199n23, 200n28, 207n1; migration histories and, 12–13, 188; and origins, 19, 21, 123, 145, 200n30; postcolonial, 204n68; public interpretations of, 11; race and, 2, 4, 10–11, 51–52, 198n10, 199n26, 202n55; relatedness and, 121, 144; religion and, 2, 4, 17; truth claims of, 4, 11, 13, 22, 27, 52, 188. *See also* diaspora, genetic; genetic afterlives

genetic ancestry testing: direct-to-consumer, 10, 12, 58–59, 123, 199n23, 203n62; kinship and, 145; politics of, 22–24, 200n28, 207n1

genetic citizenship, 26, 60, 85, 118

geneticists, 2, 4, 59, 184, 194; as knowledge producers, 10–14, 23–25, 30, 32, 118, 199n20; Lemba and, 17, 52, 61, 198n13; race and, 11, 62, 198n10, 204n68

genetic Jews, Lemba as, 2–3, 8, 10, 22, 55, 156, 190; alternatives to, 59; and cultural similarity, 74; and lost tribes of Israel narrative, 63

genetics, anthropological, 12, 199–200n26, 200n28

genomics, 10, 12, 52, 58, 86

geography: genetic, 13; racial, 23, 36, 123, 203n56. *See also* mapping, ethnic

Giraudo, Rachel, 215n8

God, 2, 29, 72, 221n44

Gordillo, Gastón, 24

graveyards, 112–13, 146, 212n32

Great Zimbabwe, 16, 218n26; Lemba and, 34–35, 46, 160, 164–65, 172, 197–98n6, 205n15; Mapungubwe kingdom and, 163

Grenn-Scott, Deborah, 70–73, 199n15

Group Areas Act, 7, 37. *See also* Bantustans

Hadji (clan), 16, 204n1, 213n4

Halkin, Hillel, 80

Hall, Stuart, 16, 202n47

Hamisi (clan), 15, 218n21

haplogroups, 13, 145

haplotype, 12–13, 21, 201n36

Haraway, Donna, 16, 22, 212n3

Hartman, Saidiya, 23–24

tradition: indigeneity and, 157; and Jewish identity, 63, 73–74, 76, 169; leaders and, 94, 104–5, 107–11, *108*, 116, 143, 170, 191, 212n30, 216n15; Lemba, 168–69; postapartheid, 88, 99. *See also* chieftaincy

traditional leadership, 94, 104, 109, 143, 191, 216n15; local municipalities and, 110–11, 212n30; unrecognized, 104–5, 107–9, *108*, 116, 170. *See also* chieftaincy

Traditional Leadership and Governance Framework Act (2003), 104

Transvaal, 7, 97, 136

travel, 37, 93. *See also* apartheid

Tregardt, Louis, 204n2

tribes: Jewish, 86; South African, 7, 32, 34–37, 92, 198n10, 205n14. *See also* lost tribes of Israel

Trichardt, Louis, 204n2

Trouillot, Michel-Rolph, 198n11

Tshivenda, 35, 64, 125–26, 197n1, 219n35

Tutsis, 1, 172

UNESCO, 153, 158, 160. *See also* heritage sites

United Independent Front (UIF), 138

University of Pretoria, 20, 162, 168, 170, 173–75, 183, 214n3, 220–21n42

University of the North, 1, 197n2

Van Warmelo, Nicolus J., 32–38, 205n6, 205n10, 205nn13–14

Venda, 15, 34–35, 72, 191, 213n9, 218n26; Lemba and, 8, 35–36, 39, 42, *44*, 45, 48, 75,

154, 166, 206n18; Mapungubwe remains and, 162–63, 185

Venda "homeland" (Bantustan), 8, 40, 42, 178, 210n12; Lemba lack of recognition in, 30, 37, 45, 48–49, 102

Vhalemba (term for Lemba), 35, 163

Vhangona, 162–63, 218n26

Vhangona Cultural Movement, 162, 175

Wade, Nicholas, 198n10

Wade, Richard, 153–54, 159, 165, 182, 198n10, 215n5, 217n19

Warren, Elizabeth, 200n33

White, Luise, 174

whiteness, 19, 46, 68–69, 75–76, 202n54, 206n22; white supremacy, 11

women, 70, 142

Worby, Eric, 203n56

xenophobia, 166, 219n33

yarmulkes, 78, 155, 208n17

Y chromosome studies, 3, 9, 13, 51, 62, 65–67, 89, 198n8, 208n10

Yemen, 15, 56, 94, 115, 172, 197–98n6

Yoruba, 71–72

Zimbabwe, 8, 16, 35, 77, 89, 136, 160, 194, 201n44, 208n16

Zion, 3

Zion Christ Church (ZCC), 78, 135, 150

Zionism, 6–7, 26, 61–62, 80–81, 85, 207n1, 208n9, 208n15